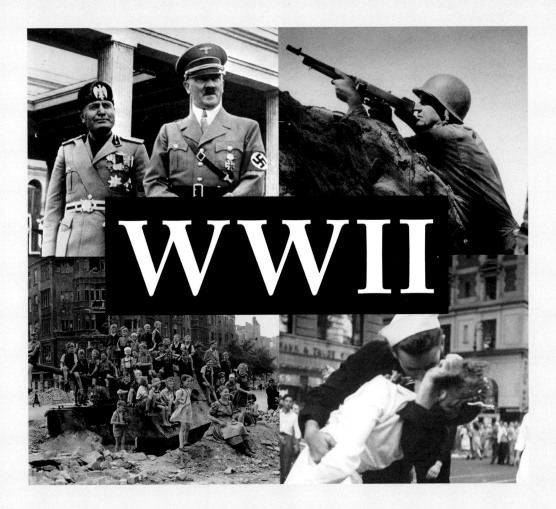

WWII

Publications International, Ltd.

ACKNOWLEDGEMENTS

Pages 4 and 6: Quotes from *Diary from the Years of Occupation (1939–1944)* by Zygmunt Klukowski and George Klukowski, Champaign: University of Illinois Press.

Page 143: *The Final Act.* Painting by John Meeks. Courtesy of www.subart.net. Used with permission.

Page 269: Quote from *Admiral Halsey's Story* by Admiral William F. Halsey and J. Bryan, III. Reprinted by permission.

PICTURE CREDITS

1000aircraftphotos.com; AKG, London; Alamy Images: Lebrecht Music and Arts Photo Library, popperfoto, Print Collector; **AP Images; Art Resource:** Bildarchiv Preussischer Kulturbesitz, HIP, Erich Lessing, Scala, SEF, Snark; **Australian War Memorial; Courtesy of Beaumont Estate; Between the Covers Rare Books; Bildarchiv PreuBischer Kulturbesitz:** Arthur Grimm, Hermann Hoeffke, Heinrich Hoffmann, Hanns Hubmann, Karl Paulmann, Karl Arthur Petraschk, SBB, Hedda Walther; **Courtesy of Doug Brooks; © Corbis:** Bettmann; **Department of Defense, www.Defenselink.mil; Deutschen Historischen Museum; Courtesy of Dustin Drase; Courtesy of John S.D. Eisenhower; Chris Fauver, artist; Franklin D. Roosevelt Library and Museum; Getty Images:** Stock Montage, Roger Viollet; **The Granger Collection, New York:** Rue des Archives, ullstein bild; **Harry S. Truman Library & Museum; David Hogan Collection; The Image Works:** Topham, Roger Viollet; **Imperial War Museum; Courtesy the office of Senator Daniel K. Inouye; KPA:** HIP/National Archives; **Courtesy of Lancastria Association of Scotland:** Frank Clements; **Library and Archives Canada; Library of Congress; Lockheed California Co.; Loyal Edmonton Regiment Museum, Edmonton, Alberta; Mary Evans Picture Library; © John Meeks 2004; National Archives, and Records Administration; National Geographic Society; National Security Administration; Naval Historical Center; NBCU Photo Bank; © Northstar Gallery 2007; Picture Alliance:** akg images, dpa, dpa/web, KPA/HIP/ National Archives, KPA/TopFoto; **PIL Collection; popperfoto.com; Public Domain; RIA Novosti; Robertstock.com; SGM Herb Friedman (Retired), Psywarrior.com; U.S. Patent and Trademark Office (USPTO); ullstein bild:** Archiv Gerstenberg, Tita Binz, Bunk, dpa, Voller Ernst, W. Frentz, The Granger Collection, Grimm, imagno, Kindermann, KPA/HIP Archive Collection, KPA/HIP/Jewish Chronicle Ltd., LEONE, Nowosti, pda, Stiftung, SVBilderdienst, Roger Viollet, Tele Winkler, Wittenstein, Wolff & Tritschler, Zitzow; **United Kingdom Government; United States Air Force; United States Army Center of Military History:** Army Art Collection; **United States Holocaust Memorial Museum Photo Archives:** Robert Abrams, Julien Bryan, Jerzy Ficowski, Anna Hassa Jarosky and Peter Hassa, Instytut Pamieci Narodowej, KZ Gedenkstaette Dachau, La Documentation Francaise, Muzej Revolucije Narodnosti Jugoslavije, National Archives and Records Administration, College Park, Jizchak Schwersenz, Der Stuermer-Verlag; **United States Marine Corps; University of Kent, British Cartoon Archive, Templeman Library; usmbooks.com; USS Arizona Memorial; Reproduced with the permission of West Dunbartonshire Council, Clydebank Central Library; www.calvin.edu/cas/gpa.**

ISBN: 978-1-68022-800-7

Manufactured in China.

8 7 6 5 4 3 2 1

CONTENTS

GERMANY MAKES ITS MOVE

SEPTEMBER 1939–MARCH 1940

"Kill without mercy all men, women, and children of Polish descent or language. Only in this way can we obtain the living space we need."

—Adolf Hitler, instructing subordinates on the conduct of Germany's Polish campaign

On September 1, 1939, Zygmunt Klukowski, a young Polish doctor, confided in his diary that everyone was talking about war. "Everybody," he continued, "is sure that we will win." The reality was startlingly different.

Germany's war with Poland was an uneven contest. Five German armies with 1.5 million men, 2,000 tanks, and 1,900 modern aircraft faced fewer than a million Polish troops with less than 500 aircraft and very few armored vehicles. In addition, German planning and technical support—and German understanding of the importance of modern tactical airpower—gave the aggressor great advantages.

Within five days, German forces occupied all of the frontier zones. By September 7, forward units were only 25 miles from Warsaw, the Polish capital. Polish air forces were eliminated, and the Polish army was split and encircled. By September 17, the war was virtually over. Ten days later, after a devastating air assault, Warsaw surrendered. "We were not yet ready," wrote Dr. Klukowski two weeks later, "to discuss the causes of our defeat.... This is a fact, but we just can't believe it."

This was the war Hitler had hoped for in 1939. But in addition to the localized conflict with Poland, the German invasion provoked a global conflict. Britain and France declared war on Germany on September 3 when it became clear that negotiating a German withdrawal was hopeless. In Britain and France, the populations had braced themselves for war in the closing weeks of the summer. There was little popular enthusiasm for war, but a strong wave of anti-German and anti-Fascist sentiment produced a resigned recognition that Hitler would only stop if he was faced by force.

Almost immediately, the British and French empires (except for Ireland) joined the contest, turning it into a worldwide war, fought not only in Europe but across the oceans. German invasion also triggered Soviet intervention. The terms of the German-Soviet pact, signed in August 1939, gave Stalin a sphere of influence in eastern Poland. On September 17, once it was clear that Poland was close to defeat, Red Army units moved into Poland and met up with victorious German troops along a prearranged frontier. On September 28, the two dictatorships signed another treaty, which divided Poland between them.

For the Western powers, this provoked fears of a totalitarian alliance against them. For Poland, dismemberment and harsh totalitarian rule were the reality. Britain and France did nothing to help their smaller ally. Their military staffs had drawn up a "war plan" during the summer of 1939 in which the loss of Poland was accepted as inevitable. The core of the plan was to blockade and contain Germany until the war of attrition forced the Germans to abandon the contest as they had done in 1918. Britain and France expected a war of at least three years. This explains why for the first six months of the war the Western states did very little. The lull was nicknamed the "Phony War"—a war with no fighting.

A small amount of naval activity did occur, which gave citizens on both sides something to cheer about. In December 1939, Britain's Royal Navy so damaged the German pocket battleship *Graf Spee* that it was scuttled in the South Atlantic. Conversely, German submarines began to sink Allied merchant ships. On October 14, 1939, a German submarine managed to penetrate the defenses of the main British naval base at Scapa Flow in the Orkney Islands, and there sank the battleship *Royal Oak*. The Germans bombed Polish citizens mercilessly, but for a while refrained from bombing cities in the West. The British only dropped leaflets on German cities.

The chief beneficiary of the war in Poland was the Soviet Union. Suffering almost no casualties, the Red Army took parts of Poland that had been seized by Russia and Austria back in the 18th century but returned to Poland after World War I. The region was integrated at once into the Soviet system. More than one million Poles, those regarded as a threat to the Communist order, were deported to labor camps in the Soviet Union. The three Baltic States— Latvia, Lithuania, and Estonia—had been assigned to the Soviet sphere by the August and September agreements. They were compelled by Soviet pressure to accept Soviet military garrisons and political advisers on their soil.

A political cartoon published in the London magazine *Punch* in 1939 vividly portrayed a widely held British view of Hitler and Stalin—of their duplicitous, avaricious, and evil natures. The cartoon also reveals the disastrous consequences of the German-Soviet nonaggression pact for the countries of Eastern Europe, including the division of Poland.

In the fall of 1939, the USSR demanded that the Finnish government cede some territory and allow bases on Finnish soil. Stalin had, in fact, already drawn up plans for a Communist Finland, and he expected the same response as the Baltic States had given. Instead, Finland rejected the Soviet demands, and on November 30 Soviet forces invaded along the entire Finnish frontier. Finland's army of 200,000 mounted a spirited defense. Only after the mobilization of

further Soviet forces in February 1940 did Finnish resistance wear down. Finland sought an armistice on March 6, and a week later it conceded all the territory and a base that had been originally demanded.

For Hitler, the Soviet advance in Eastern Europe and the spread of Communist influence were prices he had to pay for securing the German rear while Germany attacked Britain and France. But it was a dangerous situation. In October 1939, he hinted to his military staff that he would settle with the USSR as soon as he could. He hoped the West might seek terms, but when it became clear they were serious about war, he planned to attack the French front in November 1939. Poor weather prevented it, and Hitler reluctantly accepted a postponement until spring.

Urged forward by the German navy, Hitler decided to seize Norway and Denmark for the naval war against British trade supplies from America. What had begun as a war to extend German power in Eastern Europe had become an open and unpredictable conflict with the intervention of Britain and France. Only in Poland was the war really over. Dr. Klukowski watched in dismay as German troops looted shops and churches and forced Jews to give up their valuables and clean the streets. As he wrote late in 1939, "It is really hard to live in slavery."

German forces storm Poland At dawn on September 1, 1939, the *Wehrmacht*'s armored spearhead swept into Poland. Four light, six panzer, and four motorized divisions cut through the sizeable but thinly spread Polish forces. In a foretaste of *Blitzkriegs* to come, armor, infantry, and artillery fought as a closely coordinated team, while the *Luftwaffe* rained death from the skies. General von Bock's Army Group North struck into Poland from Pomerania and East Prussia. Simultaneously, General Rundstedt's Army Group South surged northeast from Slovakia and Silesia. Behind the German armored divisions, some 40 infantry divisions stood ready to exploit the panzers' successes. Everywhere, the woefully unprepared Polish forces were shocked by the speed, scale, and ferocity of the German onslaught.

1939

September 1: World War II begins as the Germans invade Poland with a three-front *Blitzkrieg*. They attack the Polish army with an overwhelming force of 1.5 million troops backed by tactical aircraft in the sky and mobile armor on the ground.

September 2: Poland pleads for assistance from sworn allies Britain and France. They respond the following day by demanding Germany's withdrawal and declaring war against the Nazi regime. India, Canada, Australia, and New Zealand (and soon South Africa) issue their own declarations of war.

September 3: Conservative parliamentarian Winston Churchill is named first lord of the admiralty. • Britain's Royal Air Force (RAF) carries out the first propaganda air raid of the war, salting northern Germany with six million pamphlets. • Without warning, a German U-boat torpedoes the *Athenia*, a British passenger ship carrying 1,400 civilians from England to Canada, killing 118.

September 4: The first RAF air assault is a disaster, with only eight of 29 bombers striking German naval bases. Ten of the RAF bombers get lost, seven are shot down, three attack one of Britain's own ships, and one attacks neutral Denmark. • Spain's General Franco offers his support to the Axis while publicly declaring neutrality.

September 5: The Nazis occupy the medieval Polish city of Kraków. • The United States officially declares its neutrality.

September 6: RAF Hurricanes and Spitfires that scramble during a false air raid alert end up shooting at each other, with the Spitfires downing the Hurricanes.

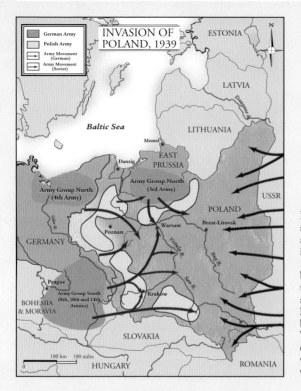

Poland succumbs The event that finally destroyed any residual hopes in London or Paris that appeasement might yet succeed was Hitler's invasion of Poland. At dawn on September 1, 1939, successive waves of bombers and fighter-bombers raided deep into Poland. Simultaneously, the tanks, artillery, and infantry of two German army groups, comprised of five separate armies, launched devastating attacks against the sizeable but outdated and poorly deployed Polish forces. Warsaw finally fell on September 27, the effectiveness of Germany's *Wehrmacht*, had been validated, and the *Blitzkrieg* concept of warfare was born.

The terrifying Stukas Close air support was a prerequisite for the success of the *Wehrmacht*'s *Blitzkrieg* operations. In 1939 and early 1940, the gull-winged, single-engine Junkers Ju-87 (Stuka)—with its three machine guns and a maximum bomb load of 1,540 pounds—was vital to such operations. The terror sirens of these diving aircraft struck fear into those on the ground below, while their bombs and guns amplified this terror with death and destruction. However, once opposed by more modern fighter aircraft—such as the British RAF's Spitfires and Hurricanes beginning in 1940—the Ju-87s proved vulnerable. They were subsquently utilized only occasionally in support of front-line offensive operations.

Poland's tanks The Polish army fielded some 500 tanks of various types. Their capabilities of firepower, mobility, and armored protection ranged from very good to patently obsolescent. The army's tactical doctrine emphasized the importance of maneuver, concentration of force, and economy of effort. In 1939, however, the lengthy process of converting the horse-mounted cavalry into armored units was still at an early stage. Also, despite the undoubted bravery, élan, and high training standards of many tank crewmen and junior commanders, some senior commanders held an outdated belief that tanks were merely fire support for the infantry, rather than the leading edge of aggressive advances.

1939

September 7: Wary of inflaming public sentiment and pulling the United States into the war, Hitler warns his military leaders against attacking passenger vessels.

September 8: President Roosevelt calls for a strengthening of the U.S. military and begins to use his constitutional power to call up the reserves, as the war in Europe has created a state of "limited national emergency."

September 13: Claiming that Polish civilians are attacking their troops, German military leadership vows to target Polish noncombatants, of whom thousands have already been murdered.

September 14: Germany loses its first ship of the war when a U-boat is depth-charged and sunk by British destroyers.

September 17: The Soviet Union invades Poland with 40 divisions, many waving white flags at a perplexed Polish population. Already beaten by the Nazis, Poland's army is unable to put up much of a fight, and the following day Russia will easily claim the territory it was promised by Germany when the two nations signed the Molotov-Ribbentrop Pact. • Five hundred die when the British Navy loses its first ship, the *Courageous*, which is sunk by a U-boat off Ireland.

September 18: Armed with inside knowledge of the German Enigma code, members of the Polish Cipher Bureau escape from Poland with two of the Enigma machines. They will arrive in Paris on October 1.

September 20: The *Luftwaffe* and the RAF clash for the first time, in the skies over the border between Germany and France, when German Me109s attack Fairey Battle bombers. The RAF loses two aircraft, while the Germans lose one.

London prepares for blackout In expectation of aerial assaults, the British mobilized civilians as well as the military. In 1940, after the defeat of France, other measures were needed. Air Raid Precautions organizations and air-raid wardens designated public shelters and advised citizens how to prepare their homes for possible bombardment. Here, workers paint a London curb to make it visible during a blackout.

British women join the fight Women gather at the recruitment office of Britain's Auxiliary Territorial Service (ATS), reformed in 1938 from the Women's Army Auxiliary Corps (WAACS) of World War I. By 1939 British women also could join the Women's Auxiliary Air Force (WAAF), the Women's Royal Naval Service (WRNS), and other military units. In December 1941, a British National Service Act began the conscription of childless widows and single women ages 20 to 30. British military women filled clerical, domestic, and medical positions; drove and maintained vehicles; manned antiaircraft guns, barrage balloons, and radar stations; ferried aircraft; deciphered coded messages; and served as spies.

Hitler Hears from Britain

When I entered the next room Hitler was sitting at his desk and Ribbentrop stood by the window. Both looked up expectantly as I came in. I stopped at some distance from Hitler's desk, and then slowly translated the British Government's ultimatum. When I finished, there was complete silence.

Hitler sat immobile, gazing before him. He was not at a loss, as was afterwards stated, nor did he rage as others allege. He sat completely silent and unmoving.

After an interval which seemed an age, he turned to Ribbentrop, who had remained standing by the window. "What now?" asked Hitler with a savage look, as though implying that his Foreign Minister had misled him about England's probable reaction.

—PAUL SCHMIDT, TRANSLATOR IN THE GERMAN FOREIGN MINISTRY, AFTER INFORMING HITLER THAT BRITAIN HAD JUST DECLARED WAR ON GERMANY, SEPTEMBER 3, 1939

"Please talk to me! What will become of me without you?"

Murder of the defenseless Kazimiera Mika, a 10-year-old Polish girl, stoops over the body of her older sister. The elder Mika girl and six other women, desperate for food, had been digging for potatoes in a field in besieged Warsaw when the *Luftwaffe* struck. Nazi fliers swooped down to within 200 feet of the ground and attacked the group with machine-gun fire. Two were killed. As the aircraft left, the 10-year-old Kazimiera ran to her fallen sibling. This was Kazimiera's first experience with the finality of death, and she was unable to understand why her sister could no longer speak to her.

1939

September 21: Pro-Nazi Iron Guardsmen assassinate Romanian prime minister Armand Calinescu, ostensibly because he was conspiring to blow up Romanian oil fields to keep them out of German hands.

September 22: Wartime shortages settle in as Britain begins rationing gas. Three days later, Germany will begin rationing bread and flour.

September 25: Warsaw is bombed into utter submission by the *Luftwaffe*. The city will surrender to the Nazis on the 27th.

October 5: The last of the Polish army lays down its guns. Of the more than half-million troops that faced the Nazis in the preceding month, most were taken prisoner while roughly 100,000 died in the fighting or fled the country.

October 6: While addressing the *Reichstag* in Berlin, Hitler accuses Poland of initiating hostilities. He insists that he has no territorial ambitions toward England, France, Belgium, Holland, and several others that he will attempt to occupy in the upcoming months and years.

October 7: Hitler moves forward with his plan to evict or kill Poles and annex their territory. He calls for the "elimination of the harmful influence of nationally alien populations, which constitute a danger to the Reich."

October 9: The U.S. Neutrality Act suffers a public relations setback when the German battleship *Deutschland* captures the *City of Flint*, an American cargo ship carrying farming supplies to England.

October 12: Rejecting Hitler's insincere peace proposals, British prime minister Neville Chamberlain asserts that "no reliance can be placed upon the promises of the present German government."

Displaced Poles Due mainly to the short duration of the Polish campaign, the numbers of civilians displaced as a direct result of the German bombing campaign were not particularly great—although this child's home lay in ruins. Meanwhile, an existing international perception that the *Luftwaffe* routinely used the terror bombing of civilians as a deliberate strategy was undoubtedly reinforced by the campaign.

Soviets take their half of Poland The notorious Nazi-Soviet nonaggression pact of August 1939 contained a secret protocol that called for Germany to take the western half of Poland and the USSR the eastern half. Hitler began his invasion of Poland on September 1. On the 17th, the Soviet government bluntly told the Polish ambassador in Moscow that Poland no longer existed as a nation. That very day, the Soviets began their effortless invasion of eastern Poland. Germany and the USSR completed their conquest of the country later that month. Here, a Soviet tank passes through the Polish town of Rakov.

The capital in ruins When the first assaults against the Polish capital proved unsuccessful, the Germans besieged Warsaw. They systematically bombed and shelled the city, causing extensive destruction and loss of life. The city's own air defenses were overwhelmed by the tempo of the *Luftwaffe* onslaught, while the outclassed Polish air force was effectively neutralized by September 17. Much of Warsaw's industrial and commercial heart—including its great complex of flour mills—was set ablaze, and its system of water-pumping stations and filtration plants was extensively damaged.

1939

October 12: The Nazis begin to consolidate the Jewish population in Germany's occupied territories. They send Austrian and Czechoslovakian Jews to Poland. • The Soviet Union sends Finland a list of territorial demands, which include a land exchange and the right to establish military bases. Finland will reply with its own acceptable terms on the 14th, but Russia will stand by its initial demands.

October 14: More than 800 sailors die when a German submarine torpedoes the *Royal Oak*, a British battleship.

October 26: Nazi Hans Frank is appointed governor general of a portion of German-occupied Poland, with his headquarters in Kraków.

October 28: A motion to amend the U.S. Neutrality Act to allow the sale of arms to besieged allies passes the Senate. It will clear the House and be signed by President Roosevelt on November 4. The change is contingent on the requirement that arms are not transported by American ships.

October 31: The SS imposes a series of arbitrary and highly restrictive laws on the Poles, including prohibitions against using phone booths and wearing felt hats. Violators can be given the death penalty.

November: In just one week, some 60,000 tons of supplies destined for the Allied cause are lost to German magnetic mines.

November 1: Western Poland officially becomes part of the Reich. Eastern Poland will become part of the Soviet Union two days later.

November 4: An anonymous person who signed himself "German scientist who wishes you well" leaves German weapons research secrets and a mine fuse on the windowsill of the British attaché in Oslo, Norway. • Warsaw's Jews are all herded into a ghetto.

Death tolls By the end of the four-week campaign in Poland, 50,000 German soldiers were dead, wounded, or missing. Polish losses amounted to some 70,000 soldiers killed and 130,000 wounded. Another 90,000 Polish soldiers escaped to Hungary, Lithuania, Romania, and Latvia; many of them later made their way to Allied lines. Initially, the *Wehrmacht*'s treatment of its 694,000 Polish prisoners was generally appropriate, although many civilians, a large proportion of them Jewish, were murdered. The SS and SD soon established themselves in German-occupied Poland, which was now regarded as a "nonexistent" state. Thereafter, the civilian population, especially Jews, suffered increasing oppression and persecution.

Germans, Soviets celebrate On September 17, 1939, after succumbing to invasions by Germany and the Soviet Union, the Polish government went into exile without surrendering. A remnant of Poland's army continued fighting into October, and guerrillas resisted into the winter. Nevertheless, on September 28 the nation was divided between the two conquering powers along the Bug River. Germany controlled about 73,000 square miles of Poland; the USSR about 78,000. Here, German and Soviet military forces hold a joint parade in Brest-Litovsk in October to celebrate Poland's destruction.

1939

November 8: Nine die when a concealed bomb detonates in a Munich beer hall 20 minutes after the departure of Hitler, the bomb's intended target.

November 13: Stalin orders the drafting of war plans against Finland following a breakdown in negotiations.

November 16: In Prague, Czechoslovakia, Nazi occupation forces violently suppress an uprising by students and dissidents.

November 23: Effective today, all Jews over age 10 living in Nazi-occupied Poland must wear the Star of David.

November 30: The Winter War begins with a Soviet invasion of Finland. In December, the Soviet Union will be expelled from the League of Nations for its aggression.

December: The upper age limit of British conscription is expanded twice this month. Initially, all men ages 19 to 41 are registered, and ultimately men as old as 60 and women ages 20 to 30 will be pressed into some level of service.

December 13–17: The Royal Navy engages the *Graf Spee*, a German warship, off the coast of Uruguay. After a protracted battle, the *Graf Spee* captain scuttles the ship near Montevideo.

December 17: Canada sends more than 7,000 troops to Britain to assist the Allies.

December 19: British scientists develop a technique, known as "degaussing," to suppress the trigger that trips Germany's magnetic mines.

December 20: The United States unveils a new policy in which it embargoes supplies to nations that target civilians and violate other rules of engagement in what will become known as a "moral embargo."

Joseph Stalin

By 1929 Joseph Stalin emerged as the undisputed leader of the Soviet Union. In the succeeding decade, he killed many millions of his compatriots, including all real and imagined potential rivals.

Decisions that Stalin made in the 1930s would have momentous wartime consequences. His policy of accelerating industrialization boosted the USSR's war-making potential enormously. However, his armed forces were initially stronger on paper than in reality, and his political purging of more than 35,000 military officers in 1937–38 left Soviet forces drastically weakened when the Germans invaded in June 1941.

As supreme commander and chairman of an all-powerful State Committee of Defense, Stalin oversaw the nation's complete and ruthless mobilization for war. He pushed his generals ruthlessly and used their subordinates as cannon fodder. Mere incompetence of a member of the general staff or government could bring anything from humiliating public censure to dismissal, torture, or years in prison. Stalin's limited personal experience of command in the Russian Civil War (1917–22) had included the defense of Tsaritsyn, which in 1942–43, as Stalingrad, became the site of an epic battle. Stalin felt qualified to pontificate on military affairs, and he made the final decision on every major wartime matter. He insisted on

the successful December 1941 counteroffensive, but also gave disastrous orders at Kiev in 1941 and Kharkov in 1942. He learned from these mistakes and, although his vanity extended to taking the titles marshal (1943) and generalissimo (1945), he increasingly gave his generals considerable initiative and even the right to put forward alternative strategies.

Once Stalin found able generals—such as Zhukov, Rokossovsky, and Konev—he stuck with them, although he refrained from personal attachment. He even refused a German offer to exchange his captured son, Yakov, who subsequently died in captivity. Stalin officially deemed as traitors all Soviet POWs as well as entire ethnic groups within the USSR. His Order 227, issued in July 1942 when the Germans advanced again, demanded that Soviets fight to the death and that cowards be severely punished.

From 1941 on, Stalin urged his allies to open a second front and relieve the pressure on the USSR. He proved a cunning diplomat at conferences with Roosevelt and Churchill. The British prime minister developed a relatively good relationship with Stalin, but American officials later were alarmed when "Uncle Joe" reneged on promises to democratize liberated Eastern Europe. Though Stalin enjoyed wartime popularity in the West, he would be demonized during the Cold War.

1940

January: Temperatures plunge throughout Europe during one of the coldest winters on record. • As many as 70 Jews succumb to starvation and other ills each day in the Warsaw Ghetto. • A study reveals that, in the four months since Britain instituted its policy of nighttime blackouts, traffic deaths have increased nearly sevenfold, with pedestrians comprising the majority of the fatalities. • China mines the Yangtze and Whangpoo rivers in a moderately successful effort to impede shipping by the occupying Japanese forces.

January 2: The Soviet army launches a major offensive against Finland on the Karelian Isthmus.

January 3: Despite the U.S. policy of neutrality, President Roosevelt's annual budget request to Congress includes $1.8 billion in defense spending.

January 4: Hitler hands control of all German means of war materiel production to his trusted aide, Hermann Göring.

January 5: Unable to agree with military generals on Britain's war strategy, Leslie Hore-Belisha resigns from government following his removal as war secretary by Prime Minister Neville Chamberlain.

January 8: In a dramatic turnaround, Finnish forces annihilate the Russian army's 44th Division. • Rationing is imposed in Britain on such dietary staples as bacon, sugar, and butter.

January 9: Richard Hildebrandt, the SS chief of Danzig and West Prussia, tells SS *Reichsführer* Heinrich Himmler that he had instructed his troops to execute more than 4,000 mentally ill Polish citizens. • More than 150 die when the massive British liner *Dunbar Castle* founders off the English coast after hitting a German mine.

Khrushchev rises through the ranks Nikita Khrushchev (*right, with Stalin*) became a Communist Party member in 1918 following wartime service in the army. His rapid political rise thereafter included membership in the Central Committee of the CPSU in 1934 and a place within the all-powerful *Politburo* in 1939. He was directly involved in the Soviet annexation of eastern Poland in autumn 1939, and later served in important military-political commissar positions in Kiev, Kursk, and Stalingrad. After Stalin's death in 1953 and Georgy Malenkov's six-month rule, Khrushchev vied for and achieved leadership of the Soviet Union.

BERLIN, den 1.Sept.1939.

Reichsleiter B o u h l e r und
Dr. med. B r a n d t

sind unter Verantwortung beauftragt, die Befug-
nisse namentlich zu bestimmender Ärzte so zu er-
weitern, dass nach menschlichem Ermessen unheilbar
Kranken bei kritischster Beurteilung ihres Krank-
heitszustandes der Gnadentod gewährt werden kann.

Nazis "euthanize" the handicapped In October 1939, Hitler signed this letter (backdated to September 1) authorizing Reichsleiter Philipp Bouhler and Dr. Karl Brandt to begin "euthanizing" physically and mentally handicapped people. Under the program Aktion T4, doctors could identify individuals as unsound and incurable, then put them to death. Neither patient nor family consent was required. Based on Nazi concepts of "racial hygiene" and supported by a desire to limit the costs of patient care, T4 systematically destroyed as many as 100,000 human beings. It was another demonstration of Nazi policies designed to eliminate those they considered unworthy of life.

1940

January 10: A German officer crashes his plane in Belgium, and proceeds to intentionally ignite a set of war plans in full view of Allied soldiers. The salvaged, partially charred papers reveal Hitler's plan for a January 14 invasion of Holland and Belgium.

January 13: As Germany continues its aggressive posturing against the lowland nations, Holland and Belgium begin the process of moving their respective armies to a war footing.

January 15: France and Britain are rebuffed in their efforts to gain permission to cross Belgian territory in their defense against German aggression.

January 16: Reports of Nazi crimes committed against the civilian population of occupied Poland reach France, where the Polish government-in-exile is established.

January 18: Five people die in a munitions plant explosion in Essex, England. Authorities suspect enemy sabotage.

January 20: In a speech admonishing neutral nations to support the Allied cause, Winston Churchill, Britain's first lord of the admiralty, claims, "Each one hopes that if he feeds the crocodile enough, the crocodile will eat him last." Churchill also denounces Russia's invasion of Finland.

January 21: Torpedoed by a German U-boat, the British destroyer *Exmouth* goes down with its 175-man crew.

January 22: The British government imposes a level of censorship on the media. It requires Ministry of Information approval of newsreels before release.

January 23: Allies France and Britain announce that they will no longer recognize the neutrality of the waters off the Americas, and that German ships operating in the area are subject to attack.

1940

January 24: Reinhard Heydrich, the chief of the Nazi Gestapo, is charged with overseeing the evacuation of all Jews from the Reich.

February 3: For the first time since the First World War, a German plane is shot down over England.

February 4: The Soviets attack Finland from the sky, killing 14 in the capital city of Helsinki.

February 5: France and England commit to providing the Finns with military aid to help them fend off the Soviets.

February 6: Britain launches a new poster campaign admonishing citizens not to discuss sensitive war information in public. The posters feature comical images of an eavesdropping Hitler and the slogan "Careless Talk Costs Lives."

February 9: U.S. undersecretary of state Sumner Welles leaves Washington on a futile mission to examine the possibility of a peace settlement in Europe.

February 10: The Soviet Union and Germany agree to strengthen their alliance through increased trading of war material. • President Roosevelt expresses American support for Finland in the face of Russian aggression. • Two British ships, *Salve* and *Servitor*, successfully sweep a German magnetic mine for the first time. • The occupying Nazis in Czechoslovakia place restraints on Jewish-owned businesses. They prohibit Jews from selling art, jewels, and precious metals, and force the closure of Jewish-owned textile and leather shops.

February 11: Some 140,000 Soviet troops attack Finnish defenses on the Karelian Isthmus in a bid to break Finnish resistance. This assault will prove successful for the Soviets, who will overwhelm the Finns with their sheer numbers.

Soviets battle ferocious Finns The Soviet Union's successful invasion of eastern Poland emboldened Stalin to attack Finland on November 30, 1939, beginning what was called the Winter War. But Stalin's purges of his officers and poor training had left his army largely ineffective. Moreover, Finland's outnumbered army fought back with surprising ferocity. Seen here are Finnish infantry on skis. Ill-equipped but innovative Finnish fighters also used "Molotov cocktails," glass jars filled with flammable fluid, to fight Stalin's troops. By March 1941, the Soviets had achieved a military victory, gaining considerable Finnish territory but at the cost of some 125,000 dead.

1940

February 12: With paper in short supply, Britain adds it to the growing list of commodities subject to rationing.

February 14: Not immune to the troubles in the rest of Europe, the Vatican institutes a rationing program.

February 15: One day after Britain declares it is outfitting its merchant vessels with guns, Germany announces that it will henceforth treat all British merchant ships as hostile combatants.

February 16: After an exhaustive search, the British Navy locates, detains, and boards the German ship *Altmark* in Norwegian waters. The Nazis had been using *Altmark* as a prison ship, and the boarding party quickly secures the release of 299 British prisoners taken by Germans from Allied ships.

February 17: Despite the danger of a defeat of Finland by the Soviets, the Finns' request for aid from their supposed ally Sweden is rebuffed.

February 18: The "moral embargo," America's refusal to deal with imperialist belligerents in Europe, is extended to the Soviet Union.

February 27: In an effort to boost morale, Winston Churchill wildly overstates Britain's success on the seas, claiming that half of Germany's feared U-boats have been sunk by the Allies.

February 28: Parts of the Enigma cipher machine are recovered from the wreckage of a German U-boat, adding to the Polish-supplied information on the Enigma puzzle in the hands of the Allies.

February 29: Food and gas rationing begins in France.

Romania's Iron Guard Led by Corneliu Codreanu, Romania's Fascist Iron Guard was the paramilitary arm of the Legion of the Archangel Michael, which had been formed in 1927. Drawing popular support from the peasants and workers during the Depression years, the Legion was the country's third largest political party by 1937. Fearing its growing power, King Carol suspended parliament in 1938 and imposed a right-wing dictatorship. Widespread violence ensued. Codreanu was murdered, the premier was assassinated, and many Legionaries were executed as traitors. Subsequently, however, the Guard enjoyed a brief political renaissance within General Ion Antonescu's pro-Axis dictatorship. Seen here, the Iron Guard forms a stolid line in front of the podium where Antonescu delivers a speech. The Guard's excesses provoked its final suppression in 1941.

The *Altmark* rescue The German supply ship *Altmark* supported the *Graf Spee's* cargo ship raids. After the *Graf Spee* was scuttled, the *Altmark* headed back for Germany, carrying some 300 British merchant sailors as prisoners. Pursued by the British destroyer *Cossack*, the *Altmark* steamed around the northern coast of Great Britain and into a Norwegian fjord in violation of Norway's neutrality. On February 16, 1940, the *Cossack* pulled alongside the *Altmark* and mounted a boarding party. Fighting hand-to-hand with bayonets and yelling "the navy's here," British sailors rescued the prisoners.

1940

March: According to the BBC, two out of three British citizens listen to "Lord Haw-Haw," the "omniscient," traitorous announcer of the German propaganda radio show *Germany Calling*.

March 1: Facing shortages of darker dyes for servicemen's uniforms, British women are asked to wear only light-colored clothing. • Hitler orders his generals to create a plan for the invasion of Norway and Denmark.

March 2: The Allies ask Sweden and Norway for the right to cross their territory for the purpose of sending troops to reinforce a flagging Finnish force, but are refused.

March 6: A delegation leaves Helsinki for Moscow to negotiate the terms of Finland's surrender to the Soviets.

March 7: The *Queen Elizabeth*, the new flagship of Cunard's luxury liner fleet, arrives in New York at the end of a daring high-speed crossing of the German U-boat-infested Atlantic.

March 9: A belated offer of troops and material support from the Allies is relayed to Helsinki.

March 11: The United States has relaxed its arms embargo for its once and future allies, selling several P-40 fighters to Britain and France.

March 12: Marched for some 18 hours in a blizzard, 72 of 1,000 German Jewish deportees succumb to the elements in Lublin, Poland. • The Soviet Union and Finland sign a peace treaty in which Finland surrenders substantial strategic territory, including the city of Viipuri and the port of Hangö. The new order comes at a cost of some 25,000 Finnish lives and the deaths of nearly 70,000 Soviets.

March 14: Some half-million Finns pour out of the Soviet-occupied territory shortly after the cessation of hostilities.

Sweden's "Neutrality"

When war broke out in September 1939, Sweden declared its neutrality as it had in every European conflict since 1814. Swedes opened their doors to those at risk of capture and imprisonment by Nazis. They sheltered almost 8,000 Jewish refugees in 1943, protected 44,000 Norwegians fleeing from German occupation, and sent one of the true heroes of the war, Raoul Wallenberg, to Hungary to save the lives of thousands of Jews. While Swedish citizens took pride in their humanitarian efforts, most of them did not know that their government was also providing important resources to the Nazis.

Crew members of a Swedish ship

Sweden remained neutral when the Germans invaded Denmark and Norway in April 1940, and the nation resisted Germany's request to allow its troops to travel along the Swedish railroad. However, this resolve weakened as the war progressed and when it looked like no nation could stop the Nazi conquest. The Swedish government permitted German troops to travel its railroads to Norway in June 1940, and to transport a whole division from Norway to Finland for its invasion of the Soviet Union.

Swedish cooperation with the Nazis did not end with transportation. The Swedes supplied Germany with about 30 percent of the iron ore the Germans used to manufacture weapons. Sweden also provided credit to the Germans, who repaid their debt with gold, including 13 tons of gold that the Nazis had stolen from Belgium and the Netherlands. Sweden's support continued until it became apparent that an Allied victory was inevitable.

1940

March 14: The Polish government, operating in exile in France, reveals that Hitler attempted to persuade Poland to join him in an invasion of the Ukraine. • Nazi *Reichsmarschall* Hermann Göring orders all German citizens to surrender any metal that may be recycled into war materiel. • Japan's new Zero fighter planes prove formidable when 12 return from an encounter with Chinese fighters over Chengtu, having destroyed 27 of 30 Chinese planes with no casualties of their own.

March 16: James Isbister, of the Scottish village Bridge of Waithe, becomes the first United Kingdom civilian killed in an air raid since the First World War.

March 18: Hitler meets with Italian dictator Benito Mussolini to discuss Italy's entry into the war. It is determined that Mussolini's troops will attack France.

March 19: Avenging Germany's March 16 attack on Scapa Flow, 50 RAF bombers attack a seaplane base at Sylt, a German island in the North Sea.

March 20: Finance Minister Paul Reynaud succeeds Édouard Daladier as prime minister of France. • Having failed in his bid to convince Europe's belligerents to lay down their weapons, U.S. undersecretary of state Sumner Welles departs Genoa, Italy, for his return voyage to the United States.

March 27: As diplomatic relations between the Allies and Russia become difficult because of Soviet aid to Germany, Paris requests the removal of the Soviet ambassador.

March 28: Britain and France agree to not act independently in establishing treaties with any third nation.

March 30: Japan establishes a Chinese puppet government in Nanking, which the United States refuses to recognize.

Heavy-duty British bomber The twin-engine Wellington was one of the most famous bombers of the war—carrying up to 4,500 pounds of bombs, including the massive 4,000-pound "Blockbuster." The Wellington first entered squadron service with the RAF Bomber Command in 1938, and some 11,460 were eventually built. The aircraft was the RAF's principal night bomber from September 1939 until 1942. The amount of battle damage that Wellingtons could safely absorb was particularly appreciated by its five-man crews.

THE WAR AGAINST THE WEST

APRIL 1940–JUNE 1941

The "Phony War" began and ended with the German invasion of neighboring states—Poland first, in September 1939, and then Denmark and Norway in April 1940. Here, the similarity ended. Germany invaded Scandinavia in 1940 due to Germany's naval war against the British and their American suppliers, and to protect the winter route for iron from Sweden. And unlike the invasion of Poland, the attacks on Denmark and Norway launched a permanent state of fighting in Europe that lasted right down to German defeat in May 1945.

The brief northern campaign was one of the most successful of Hitler's gambles. On April 9, German forces entered Denmark and occupied the peninsula without serious resistance. A seaborne and airborne force, covered by a German air screen, then invaded Norway. Despite stubborn Norwegian resistance, and the landing of British and French troops in support in northern Norway, the Norwegian government agreed to an armistice on June 9. However, many German warships were sunk or damaged in this operation.

On May 10, Hitler had his forces in the West—after months of patient preparation—launch the attack on France through the Low Countries and the Ardennes Forest farther to the south, which the Allies had thought impassable by a modern army. A few hours after German troops crossed the Dutch border, an act of long-term significance took place in London when Winston Churchill succeeded Neville Chamberlain as British prime minister. At that moment, Churchill later wrote, "I felt as if I was walking with destiny."

The first weeks of Churchill's premiership proved disastrous for the Allies. German plans to push heavily armored divisions along forested terrain, supported by waves of aircraft, succeeded well beyond the expectations of many German generals. The French defensive line was pierced, and within days a gap burst open in the Allied front that could not be closed. The British Expeditionary Force was pushed back toward the sea around the port of Dunkirk, France, and faced annihilation—until General Rundstedt and Hitler ordered German forces to stop on May 24 to refit and prepare to break the new French defense line further south. By the time the attacks began again on May 26, the British had planned a hasty marine retreat. By June 4, 338,000 troops, one-third of them French, had been evacuated.

Though the "miracle of Dunkirk" has long been celebrated in Britain, it represented an ignominious defeat. The surviving French resistance slowly crumbled. On June 14, German forces entered Paris; on June 22, the French sued for an armistice, and German victory was complete. While a similar campaign during World War I had lasted four years and cost the lives of 1.5 million Germans, this campaign was over in six weeks. This time, Germany lost 30,000 men.

The reasons for the rapid German victory have been debated often. The Allies, including Dutch and Belgian forces, had a clear advantage in number of army divisions, tanks, and armored vehicles. Airpower favored the Germans, but only because German air forces were concentrated in an aerial spearhead that pushed forward in coordination with the armored divisions on the ground. Military competence and strategic daring counted for something on the German side. The central problem for the Allies was the dispersal of their troops. Because French commander Maurice Gamelin had sent his reserve army

northward, it could not plug the Ardennes gap. Aircraft were stationed all over France and Britain, but were not concentrated at the front; and the system of communications on the western side worked poorly. The argument that French soldiers lacked stomach for the fight because French society was in some sense "decadent" is difficult to prove. Their morale was poor because they sensed that they were poorly led.

German victory in June 1940 had profound consequences. For the British and French, it was the worst possible outcome. France was defeated, its northern half as well as its Atlantic coast occupied by German forces. Britain was isolated from Continental Europe and had no prospect of reentering it to dislodge Hitler without the help of powerful allies (i.e., the United States and Soviet Union). France was now ruled by the authoritarian Marshal Philippe Pétain, who set up a new government center at Vichy, where his regime pursued policies that mimicked those of other Fascist states.

On June 10, 1940, Mussolini's Italy declared war on Britain and France. Thus, a powerful enemy lay across Britain's main route in the Mediterranean to its eastern empire. Hitler was faced with the pleasing but unexpected prospect of German domination of Europe. On July 19, he announced before the *Reichstag* proposals for a European peace if Britain would accept the reality of German dominance and end hostilities. Churchill's government rejected it. British society braced itself for a possible invasion.

Hitler faced a critical dilemma in the summer of 1940. Successful beyond his expectations, he wanted to subordinate Britain in order to prepare for conflicts with the Soviet Union and the United States. When Britain refused to accept a German peace, Hitler ordered his forces to prepare to invade. The *Luftwaffe* (air force) was given the task of softening British resistance.

On July 31, a few days before the air attacks began in earnest, Hitler called his commanders together and told them that he had abandoned his and their hopes of invading the Soviet Union in the fall of 1940, and instead would begin that operation in the spring of 1941. German troops were sent into Romania and military arrangements were made with Finland since these two countries were to join Germany in invading the Soviet Union.

While the invasion of Britain (Operation Sealion) was being prepared, the *Luftwaffe* began its assault. This was the start of what would become known as the Battle of Britain. Waves of bombers, strongly supported by fighter aircraft, first attacked British air fields and sources of air supply. In September, they attacked the whole military and urban infrastructure within range of German fighters. The Germans' goal was to create conditions for landing an invasion force on the coast of southern England. The air battle was regarded as decisive only because the failure to eliminate the RAF would force the postponement of what the Germans considered a risky operation.

The defending British fighter force had difficulty preventing German bombing, but it was able to inflict high levels of attrition on the attacking force thanks to the first successful use of radar detection. From July to the end of October, the RAF lost 915 aircraft while the Germans lost 1,733. The number of fighter pilots and fighter aircraft on the British side remained at roughly the same level as at the start of the battle, but German numbers declined. By mid-September, it was evident that the *Luftwaffe* was making little headway, and the first phase of the Battle of Britain was over.

The second phase was more deadly and more prolonged. On September 17, Hitler postponed Sealion, and the *Luftwaffe* was given the task of knocking Britain out of the war by bombing alone. Heavy raids were directed at military and economic targets as well as urban areas, and civilian casualties were heavy. More than 40,000 British citizens were killed during the course of the "Blitz," which came to be directed at all major ports and industrial and commercial centers.

By December 1940, the German leadership expected Britain to surrender. "When will Churchill capitulate?" Joseph Goebbels wrote in his diary. Bombing did produce widespread disruption and local panic, but at no point did the British government consider surrender. Gold and foreign exchange reserves were moved to Canada, and preparations were made for guerrilla activities in any portion of the country occupied by the Germans. The public was heartened by news of British victories in East Africa and Libya against Italian-led forces, and the knowledge that British bombers were regularly attacking German cities in return.

Hitler gambled on forcing a British surrender, but his thoughts turned increasingly to the prospect of the invasion of the Soviet Union. His fanatical anticommunism was certainly one reason. He was also attracted by the oil and raw-material resources of the Soviet area—as well as the region's vast wheat lands, which had long been regarded in Germany as a potential area for colonization, or "living space." Strategic calculation also pushed him toward war. On the one hand, defeat of the Soviet Union, he believed, would eliminate the last prospect that Britain had for creating an anti-German alliance, and thus would hasten British surrender. Defeat of the Soviet Union would also free Japan to move in the Pacific. Thus, there was not one cause but many for Hitler's directive to "crush Soviet Russia in a rapid campaign."

While Germany was fighting in the West, the Soviet Union took advantage of the situation. In June 1940, the three Baltic States were incorporated formally into the Soviet Union, just as eastern Poland had been. In addition, the Soviets forced Romania to hand over the territories of Bessarabia and northern Bukovina. In all of these areas, social and political opponents of the Soviet Union were rounded up and deported or murdered. In the Katyn Forest and two other sites, thousands of captured Polish officers were liquidated, their bodies buried in huge mass graves, each with a bullet hole in the back of the neck.

Stalin's ambitions continued to expand. The Soviets pressured Bulgaria to concede Soviet bases, and they urged Turkey to concede rights over the straits that separated the Black Sea from the Mediterranean. In October 1940, Mussolini launched a war against Greece. On September 27, Germany, Italy, and Japan signed the Tripartite Pact, dividing the world into spheres in which they could each establish a "new order."

In November, Soviet foreign minister Vyacheslav Molotov was invited to Berlin to discuss prospects for a further German-Soviet agreement. Molotov laid down terms for Soviet influence in Bulgaria and Turkey. Joachim von Ribbentrop, the German foreign

With Germany's victory in the West apparently assured, Hitler and his senior military commanders turned their eyes to Soviet Russia. Much of the strategic planning for Operation Barbarossa was carried out at Hitler's Alpine retreat—the Berghof—during high-level conferences such as this one, pictured in July 1940.

minister, agreed to nothing and urged the Soviet Union to turn toward India as a sphere of expansion. Three weeks later, Hitler approved the operational plans for invasion of the Soviet Union, and on December 18 he signed War Directive 21 for Operation Barbarossa.

The plan called for launching the attack in May 1941, but transportation and supply problems forced postponement into June. Using bases in Hungary, Bulgaria, and Romania—all states that had now come into the German orbit—Hitler planned to rescue his Italian ally, whose troops were bogged down in the conflict with Greece. When Hitler demanded transit rights through Yugoslavia, anti-German elements launched a coup in Belgrade. German forces attacked Yugoslavia on April 6, and by April 30 the whole of the Balkan peninsula was in German hands.

The Germans maintained utmost secrecy regarding their preparations, but intelligence sources alerted Moscow. Stalin, anxious that nothing should provoke war, refused to accept the warnings and made every effort to appease the Germans. Though some Soviet reserves were moved to the frontier in May and June, nothing could stop the massive assault by more than three million German, Romanian, Finnish, and other forces along the whole Soviet line in the West. In the early hours of June 22, 1941, they launched the largest invasion in world history.

The Maginot Line Soon after World War I, under the direction of Minister of War André Maginot, France constructed formidable concrete obstacles, machine gun posts, and forts along its borders with Germany, Italy, and later Belgium. In 1939–40, France hurried to improve the secret fortifications. Underground bunkers that could house thousands of men included such amenities as a wine cellar, morgue, chapel, hospital, and dental clinic. These preparations gave the French military a false sense of security. Invading German forces simply maneuvered around the Maginot Line.

1940

April 2: Chinese Nationalists score a victory when they reoccupy the city of Wuyuan after successfully ambushing some 3,000 Japanese troops.

April 5: In what will become known as the Katyn Forest Massacre, Soviet secret police murder more than 4,000 Polish prisoners of war. The Soviet government will deny culpability until 1989. Around the same time as Katyn, more than 15,000 other Polish POWs are killed at other locations.

April 8: Despite Norway's neutrality, the Allies mine coastal waters in the region in an effort to impede German activity.

April 9: Germany attacks Norway and Denmark on the pretext that occupation is necessary to preserve their neutrality. Norwegian Fascist leader Vidkun Quisling quickly moves to create a pro-Nazi government. As a result, his surname will become synonymous with traitor.

April 10: Denmark surrenders to Germany. • Wary of abandoning its neutrality, Belgium declines the Allies' offer of "preventative aid." • The German cruiser *Königsberg* is sunk by British warplanes, marking the first time in history that a large warship is sunk by an aerial assault.

April 14: Allied troops arrive in Norway to counter the German invasion force.

April 15: MI6, Britain's secret intelligence service, unravels the Enigma code used by the *Wehrmacht* during the Norwegian campaign.

April 18: The Allies occupy Norway's Faeroe Islands to prevent the strategically important region from falling into Nazi hands.

1940

April 27: SS *Reichsführer* Heinrich Himmler orders the construction of a concentration camp in Oświęcim, Poland. Known as Auschwitz in German, the facility will play a central role in the Nazi plan to exterminate Europe's Jews. • The Reich issues an official declaration of war against neutral Norway.

April 29: President Roosevelt sends a personal message to Mussolini in which he beseeches him to work for peace.

April 30: Carnegie Institute president Samuel Harden Church publishes a letter in *The New York Times* offering a $1 million reward to whomever can capture Hitler alive. • The Allies make a hasty retreat from Norway under the pressure of an intense German aerial assault. • The Nazis establish a Jewish ghetto in Łódź, Poland. • Hitler warns his generals to be prepared to invade Western Europe within 24 hours of receiving his orders on any date after May 5.

May 2: Mussolini contacts Roosevelt. He suggests that Italy's continued recognition of the Monroe Doctrine is contingent on America's continued neutrality in the European war.

May 7: President Roosevelt directs the Navy's Pacific Fleet to remain at the ready off the coast of Hawaii.

May 10: Asserting that the Allies are planning to use neutral nations Belgium, Luxembourg, and the Netherlands as a staging area for an attack on Germany, Hitler invades the Low Countries. • Winston Churchill becomes Britain's prime minister when Neville Chamberlain, who was losing support in Parliament, resigns. • Communication centers are targeted in the first RAF bombing raid over Germany.

Britain's flying boat The British Short Sunderland flying boat saw wide service during World War II, proving especially valuable in antisubmarine operations. Crewed by seven to 11 men and carrying machine guns, bombs, or depth charges, the Sunderland could remain in the air for as long as 11 hours searching for U-boats with its radar. The patrol bomber became such an effective sub killer that German admiral Karl Dönitz suspected that spies were tipping off the Allies about U-boat movements. The Sunderlands also proved useful for reconnaissance and water rescue missions. Total production was 749 aircraft.

Francisco Franco

Following Hitler's one and only meeting with Fascist Spanish dictator Francisco Franco, in October 1940, he told his aides that he would just "as soon have three or four teeth pulled out" than have to bargain with Franco again. Hitler met with the Spanish dictator for nine hours with the hope that he could gain Franco's permission to march the German army through Spain to support an assault on Gibraltar. Capture of this British-controlled peninsula would give Hitler a stepping stone to North Africa.

The German leader found Franco's price too high, however. Franco demanded military and financial assistance as well as control of portions of France's holdings in northwest Africa. Hitler was agreeable to the colonial demands, but insisted on German ownership of bases on the coast and islands off Northwest Africa. Over this issue, Franco withdrew his offer to join Germany in war against Britain.

After the Spanish monarchy fell in 1931, conservative and radical parties alternately assumed power in Spain. During this time, Franco's military fortunes rose and fell. Following a bloody civil war, Franco assumed absolute power on April 1, 1939.

Both Hitler and Italian dictator Benito Mussolini sent aid to Franco during the civil war due to his Fascist leanings. When Hitler was rebuffed by the Spanish dictator, he did not take retaliatory action against Spain. Throughout the remainder of the war, however, Franco provided men, support for German U-boats, and valuable resources to the Germans while declaring Spain's neutrality.

British dive-bombers prove effective Fires rage unchecked on the German light cruiser *Königsberg* after the first successful British air attack on a warship. On April 10, 1940, Blackburn Skua dive-bombers located the *Königsberg*—already damaged by Norwegian shore artillery—in Bergen Harbor, Norway. The Skuas dove out of the rising sun and dropped their 500-pound bombs from heights ranging from 3,000 feet to as low as 200 feet, proving the effectiveness of dive-bombing to a skeptical RAF establishment. The *Königsberg* lost electrical power and, unable to control the fires, sank within three hours.

1940

May 11: The Allies land in the Dutch West Indies to guard the oil resources of Aruba and Curaçao against German saboteurs. • Luxembourg falls to German troops.

May 11–12: In what is regarded as the Allies' first significant air raid against a civilian population, the RAF attacks Mönchengladbach, Germany, losing three planes in the process.

May 12: England and Scotland begin the practice of detaining German and Austrian men ages 16 to 60 in internment camps.

May 13: In his first speech before the House of Commons as prime minister, Winston Churchill delivers the famous line: "I have nothing to offer but blood, toil, tears, and sweat." • Northeast France is under heavy assault as several panzer divisions cross the Meuse River near the town of Sedan.

May 14: Rotterdam, Netherlands, capitulates after a heavy German bombing campaign devastates the city, claiming 980 lives and more than 20,000 buildings. • The Netherlands government flees The Hague. It will establish itself in exile in London. • The Royal Air Force suffers its greatest defeat to date in this conflict, losing 45 of 109 airplanes while attacking German troop positions in France.

May 15: The Nazi campaign in the Netherlands ends when the Dutch army surrenders to the *Wehrmacht*. • Concerned about Japan's activity in the Pacific Theater, Churchill asks Roosevelt for ships, planes, ammunition, and an American naval presence in Singapore and Ireland.

May 16: President Roosevelt asks Congress for a $1.2 billion increase in defense spending to mobilize the Army and Navy and procure an additional 50,000 planes a year.

Nazi paratroopers succeed in Belgium German paratroopers who have just taken the "impregnable" Fort Eben-Emael in Belgium relax after their success. In history's first glider-borne assault, nine silent, engineless aircraft landed on the Eben-Emael roof on May 10, 1940. The gliders discharged 77 paratroopers, who quickly sealed in the fort's 650 defenders. Resistance was over in 30 minutes, and the entire garrison surrendered in 30 hours. These German special forces had practiced their attack on a similar fort. Additional troops from 10 other German gliders seized key bridges in the area.

Germans storm France, Low Countries On May 10, 1940, German tanks, troops, and bombers smashed into France and the Low Countries in a *Blitzkrieg*—a swift attack with combined air and mobile land forces— that was totally unexpected by the Allies. Belgium, Luxembourg, and the Netherlands fell quickly. Hitler's tanks charged through the Ardennes forests, bypassed the static French defenses, and drove westward across northern France to the English Channel. By May 21, the Germans had split the Allied forces in two. Here, a French tank crewman surrenders to German forces.

Belgians face death, forced labor Belgian civilians hide from German soldiers. During the May 1940 *Blitzkrieg*, planes strafed and bombed Belgian military personnel and nonmilitary citizens alike, killing some 30,000 civilians. After Belgium surrendered, many of the nation's highly skilled workers were forced into German industrial jobs—including positions at arms factories. These Westarbeiter (workers from the West) in the Arbeitseinsatz (labor deployment) program faced severe penalties if they refused to work in Germany.

1940

May 17: A Nazi occupying force marches into Brussels, Belgium. Antwerp, Belgium, will capitulate the next day.

May 21: According to reports out of Berlin, the French Ninth Army has been completely destroyed.

May 22: The Emergency Powers Act passes in Britain. It grants Churchill total control of the resources needed to run the nation's war machine.

May 24: London decides to pull its troops out of a defeated Norway.

May 26: The Allies launch Operation Dynamo, a massive rescue operation to save troops surrounded by the Axis in Dunkirk, France. In just one week, nearly 350,000 British, French, and Belgian soldiers will be evacuated while *Luftwaffe* planes try to hinder the operation.

May 27: Germany takes the port city of Calais, France—a mere 26 miles across the Channel from Dover, England.

May 28: King Leopold III orders the surrender of the 500,000-man Belgian Army, an order that will lead to his deposition at the hands of the Belgian government, which is in exile in France.

June 3: More than 250 Parisians lose their lives when the city endures an air assault by some 200 *Luftwaffe* planes.

June 4: Churchill delivers the memorable "fight on the beaches" speech before the House of Commons, claiming, "We shall never surrender."

June 5: The French capture *Luftwaffe* pilot Werner Mölders. He will be liberated at the armistice near the end of the month, resume flying, and ultimately be credited with more than 100 victories before being killed in an accident.

Bad strategy dooms the Dutch The Netherlands was woefully unprepared for Germany's ground and air *Blitzkrieg* in May 1940. Dutch strategic planning had been shaped by an underestimation of Germany, strong pacifist influences, appeasement policies, refusal to coordinate with Britain and France, and a dependence upon defensive strong-points (such as this steel-gated bridge over the Maas River) and obstacles— including flooding large areas of Holland. Consequently, the Germans quickly overwhelmed the sizable but outdated, ill-equipped, and largely immobile Dutch army. While some Dutch citizens formed an effective resistance movement beginning in 1942, anti-Semitism and pro-German collaboration were also in evidence.

Calm before the storm First Lord of the Admiralty Winston Churchill congratulates sailors of HMS *Hardy* on April 19, 1940, for distinguishing themselves during the fighting in Norway. With the British Expeditionary Force in France and the German onslaught seemingly checked for the moment, Churchill had cause for guarded optimism. But the respite was brief. Within a few weeks, Norway, Denmark, and France would fall to the Germans. Elevated to prime minister in May after the resignation of Neville Chamberlain, Churchill faced a possible German invasion with a drastically weakened military and a Home Guard of boys and old men armed with everything from old rifles to pitchforks.

1940

June 5: Marshal Philippe Pétain becomes prime minister of France, replacing Paul Reynaud.

June 7: Norwegian leadership flees the country and establishes a government-in-exile in London. • Berlin suffers its first bombing raid of the war when it is attacked by a single French aircraft, a four-engine Farman 223.

June 8: More than 1,500 British sailors perish when German ships sink the aircraft carrier *Glorious* and its escort of two destroyers.

June 9: A German panzer division crosses the Somme River and surrounds the French 10th Army.

June 10: After a lengthy delay, Italy enters the war with an invasion of a weakened France, already wounded by the German army. • With German troops only 50 miles from Paris, the French government relocates to Tours, France. • Mussolini declares war against both Britain and France, while Canada reciprocates by declaring war on Italy. South Africa, Australia, and New Zealand will join Canada the following day.

June 11–12: The RAF bombs Italy, losing one plane while scoring 10 hits on Turin and two on Genoa.

June 12: Italy launches its air war, dropping bombs on civilian targets on the British protectorate Island of Malta. • With Italy's entry into the war, President Roosevelt declares that the United States will offer material support to the Allies.

June 14: France asks the United States to intervene as the Nazis occupy Paris.

Winston Churchill

Winston Spencer Churchill did more than any other leader to attain Allied victory in World War II. On May 10, 1940, on the very day that Hitler unleashed his *Blitzkrieg* against the Low Countries, Churchill succeeded Neville Chamberlain as prime minister. As Britain endured the fall of France, the Battle of Britain, and the Blitz, Churchill rallied the nation. It was his as well as Britain's "Finest Hour."

The son of a British aristocrat and an American heiress, Churchill grew up in Blenheim Palace. A low achiever in school, he became a cavalry officer in wars in India and Africa, finding adventure while discovering a knack for writing. During the Boer War, his escape from Boer captivity catapulted him into a parliamentary seat. The ambitious young politician rose swiftly, opportunistically switching from the Conservatives to the Liberals and back.

By 1914 the 39-year-old had become first lord of the admiralty, running the world's most powerful fleet. Churchill conceived the imaginative but inept invasion of Turkey on Gallipoli during World War I, which cost him power with its defeat and saddled him with a reputation as a dangerous strategic visionary. After serving as a battalion commander on the Western Front, Churchill returned to office as minister of munitions. Following the war, he helped to shape the modern Middle East.

Churchill led a coalition government through defeats in the Mediterranean and a never-ending battle in the Atlantic. Though he was a determined conservative, in June 1941 he welcomed the Soviets as allies, knowing that Russian resistance weakened Germany.

With the American entry into the war, Britain's role as the mainstay of Allied power weakened. Churchill took part in a succession of conferences with Stalin and Roosevelt, helping to reshape Allied strategy worldwide.

Churchill's strategic vision was inspired but often flawed, and his military advisers worked to dissuade him from his wilder flights. Thinking that Italy represented a "soft underbelly" was perhaps his most startling mistake. He also has been damned in Canada for the bloody repulse at Dieppe and in Australia for the loss of Singapore.

Despite his flaws, Churchill's decisive leadership and ability to inspire helped Britain achieve victory. In July 1945, Churchill's Conservatives lost office in the election. His *History of the Second World War*, a racy mixture of memoir and on-the-spot history, still powerfully, and often mistakenly, shapes how we understand World War II.

1940

June 15: Despite pleas from both France and Britain, the U.S. Congress continues to refuse to intervene in Europe, with some legislators going so far as to suggest that England and France surrender to Hitler.

June 16: In an 11th hour rescue attempt, Britain offers to unite its empire with that of France. The following day, France will ask Germany for an armistice, requesting "peace with honor." • Italy sinks the British submarines *Grampus* and *Orpheus* in the first Mediterranean naval conflict of the war. • Prime Minister Eamon de Valera mobilizes the Irish military in preparation for an Axis invasion of nearby England.

June 17: About 2,500 British troops perish when five *Luftwaffe* bombers attack the *Lancastria*, a Cunard luxury liner being used to transport troops. • With most naval forces focused on the Pacific Fleet, the U.S. Navy asks Congress for $4 billion to build an equally strong Atlantic fleet.

June 18: The RAF pulls out of France, and the French military hastily retreats from the *Wehrmacht*. French general Charles de Gaulle, speaking from London, pleads with his countrymen to continue to resist Germany, claiming "France has lost a battle, but France has not lost the war." • In a meeting with Hitler in Munich, Mussolini is bitterly disappointed to find that he will not be granted large tracts of French territory. Hitler hopes that by offering France easy surrender terms, the French will be less likely to continue fighting from North Africa.

June 19: With the German conquest of France complete, the exiled governments of Poland and Belgium move to London.

The evacuation of Dunkirk Dunkirk evacuees escape by ship. In late May 1940, Hitler agreed with General Rundstedt to order a temporary halt. The reprieve lasted 48 hours and gave the British time to set up defenses and begin evacuation of 338,000 Allied troops. Hermann Göring promised that the *Luftwaffe* could destroy the Allied troops, but Dunkirk was too close to British air bases. The British evacuees included many highly experienced soldiers who were eager to return to the fight, but they had lost all of their equipment.

The *Luftwaffe*

Through the early years of World War II, Nazi Germany's enemies feared the *Luftwaffe*, the most advanced and powerful air force in the world. This mighty force began (with Soviet assistance) as a clandestine program in the 1920s. After 1933 the *Luftwaffe* expanded to include 20,000 personnel and 1,888 aircraft. In 1936 the second generation of aircraft—including the Messerschmitt Bf 109 fighter, the Junkers 87 (Stuka) dive-bomber, and the Heinkel 111 bomber—were released. Most were trialed in 1937 during the Spanish Civil War.

The *Luftwaffe* was integral to the *Blitzkrieg* that swept away nearly all before it from 1939 to '41. Crucial was its tactical ground support, through dive-bombing, strafing, level bombing, and parachute operations. Its aircraft also sank 750,000 tons of Allied shipping in 1939 and more than four million tons in 1940. During the Battle of Britain, the Germans attempted to use the *Luftwaffe* to win a campaign on its own, as a strategic force. In failing, many of its best pilots were killed.

A *Luftwaffe* demonstration over Nuremberg, Germany

The *Luftwaffe* contributed substantially to victories in the Mediterranean and the USSR in 1941, but an agonizing decline followed. While the *Luftwaffe* responded effectively initially to the Anglo-American Combined Bomber Offensive of 1943, Hitler's preoccupation with retaliatory bombing hampered Germany's defense. Moreover, from late 1943, the Allies concentrated on destroying the *Luftwaffe*, targeting German fighters over the Reich, aircraft factories, and oil plants. The *Luftwaffe* was finished as an effective force by D-Day late in 1944, when only 170 aircraft faced 12,000 Allied planes in northern France.

From then until war's end, *Luftwaffe* fighters offered negligible aerial resistance. While Soviet armies were most responsible for the German army's defeat, Western air forces played a major role in crushing its aerial counterpart. The innovative last generation of German aircraft included jet and rocket fighters, but the quantity, fuel, and trained pilots needed to alter the war's course were simply not available.

FALL OF FRANCE
1940

- - - German Offensives
- - - Allied Forces Movement
Maginot Line
(44) Number of Divisions

The invasion of France On May 10, 1940, German general Bock's Army Group B struck into Belgium and the Low Countries. This was only a diversionary attack, as the main assault by General Rundstedt's Army Group A was launched from the Ardennes forests, while General Leeb's Army Group C secured the southern flank and pinned down some 30 French divisions. By June 25, France had fallen.

Hundreds killed, wounded in Paris A Parisian victim of German bombing raids lies in a hospital bed. The German bombardment of Paris inflicted some 900 casualties, including 254 dead. Most of the victims were civilians and many were schoolchildren. Designed to produce terror, the air attack had the desired effect. Fleeing civilians clogged all roads around Paris, where some were strafed by German planes.

France's formal surrender The railway car in which French marshal Ferdinand Foch had dictated terms to Germany in 1918 was dragged out of its storage shed and returned to the same forest clearing near Rethondes. CBS war correspondent William Shirer noted in Hitler's expression "a sort of scornful, inner joy at being present at this great reversal of fate—a reversal he himself had wrought." On June 22, 1940, the Germans dictated armistice terms that left most of France occupied and set up Vichy France in the area that remained (roughly the southern third of the country).

1940

June 20: Japan coerces defeated France to allow landings of Japanese naval vessels in French Indochina. Japan also admonishes authorities in French Indochina to stop assisting the Nationalist Chinese.

June 21: Churchill calls for the outfitting and training of 5,000 paratroopers.

June 22: France surrenders to Germany, and will surrender to Italy on the 24th. A formal cease-fire will take hold on the 25th. • Britain uncovers the German Knickebein system when it locates a radio beam targeting the Rolls-Royce airplane engine factory and leading back to a transmitter in Germany. The system has been helping to guide *Luftwaffe* bombers to their targets.

June 23: Charles de Gaulle forms the French National Committee while exiled in London. Britain's government will recognize him as the French leader in exile on the 28th. • Hitler takes a brief, triumphant tour of Paris.

July 1: Churchill sends a letter to Moscow in which he requests a meeting to discuss German imperialism. Pleased with his agreement with Germany, Stalin maintains that Russia will avoid conflict with Hitler. • The French government moves to Vichy, France.

July 2: Hitler orders his generals to draft plans for Operation Sealion—the invasion of Britain.

July 3: With the Vichy regime running France, Britain takes measures to prevent the occupying Nazis from controlling the French navy. The British sink parts of France's fleet in Algeria and commandeer French ships in British ports.

Germans sink the *Lancastria* The Cunard liner *Lancastria*, refitted for military transport, helped evacuate British troops and civilians from France. On June 17, 1940, the loaded ship was struck by German Junker 88 airplanes near the port of St. Nazaire. The bombs—one of which is said to have gone down the ship's funnel—were fatal. The *Lancastria* rolled over and sank in minutes. Many who went into the water choked on spilled fuel oil or died when the oil slick caught fire. Of the estimated 4,000 to 9,000 on board, fewer than 2,500 survived.

1940

July 4: Great Britain and France break off diplomatic relations.

July 5: Sweden allows the Nazis transit rights as Germany tries to get supplies and troops to and from Norway. • Romania announces its alliance with Germany and Italy, one day after King Carol oversees the installation of a pro-Axis government. • Vichy France attacks British Gibraltar with planes from its bases in French Morocco. • President Roosevelt launches a limited embargo against Japan, banning the shipment of materials that could be used to feed the Japanese war machine.

July 10: Berlin's Jewish Affairs Office proposes an emigration plan that would move as many as four million European Jews to Madagascar. • Roosevelt details his plans for an army of up to two million men, and asks Congress for the funds to make this plan a reality.

July 11: Germany installs Philippe Pétain as leader of unoccupied France.

July 13: Hitler orders the annihilation of the RAF, which he sees as a necessary first step to any invasion of the British mainland.

July 16: More than 20,000 French citizens are driven from Alsace-Lorraine when the Nazis annex the region. • Naturalized Jews are stripped of their French citizenship by France's Vichy government.

July 18: Britain acquiesces to Japan's demand that the Burma Road be closed to shipments of war materiel for three months, cutting off China's link to outside aid. • Germany begins propaganda broadcasts in the United Kingdom, agitating for Scottish separatism.

Bush launches atomic project In 1940 American research scientist Vannevar Bush proposed a National Defense Research Committee (NDRC) to coordinate the nation's scientific and military activities. Appointed NDRC chairman, Bush soon became convinced that an atomic bomb was feasible and started a research and development program. In March 1942, Bush wrote to President Roosevelt that an atomic bomb "might be determining in the war effort." With FDR's approval, Bush established the Military Policy Committee, which was granted oversight of the Manhattan Project.

British attack French ships The French battleship *Bretagne* burns in an Algerian port after being hit by British fire on July 3, 1940. Following the defeat of France, Britain moved to prevent French warships from falling into Nazi hands. A British ultimatum to the French commander in Algeria (where the substantial French fleet was of particular concern) demanded that the French ships either join with the British, sail under control to a British port, sail to a French port in the West Indies and be demilitarized, or be entrusted to the U.S. When no response came in six hours, Churchill gave the order to attack. In the ensuing Battle of Oran, the British damaged and destroyed several French warships, killing more than 1,200 French sailors.

Hitler contemplates British invasion Hitler, Heinrich Himmler (*to Hitler's immediate left*), and staff officers view the English coastline from the cliff top at Calais while contemplating their plans for Operation Sealion. Hitler had assumed that Britain would submit once France had collapsed, but when it became clear that Britain would fight on he ordered the invasion plans to be finalized. Prerequisites for success were air supremacy, the clearance of mine-free channels, and the neutralization of the Royal Navy. However, the RAF's defeat of the *Luftwaffe* in September 1940 and the continuing British naval presence in the Channel resulted in the plan being postponed—and eventually abandoned.

British submarines The HMS *Taku* (*pictured*) was one of the oceangoing T-class boats that formed the mainstay of the British submarine fleet. Royal Navy submarines operated in shallow waters that were heavily mined and well defended by antisubmarine forces. Of more than 50 deployed, nearly one out of three was destroyed, usually going down with all hands. Nevertheless, Royal Navy subs took a heavy toll on German ships in Norwegian waters. In the dangerously shallow and clear Mediterranean, British subs successfully interrupted German and Italian supply routes to Africa. British submarines also landed and picked up clandestine agents in various areas, and supported Allied efforts in the Malacca Straits and seas near Indonesia.

1940

July 21: Estonia, Latvia, and Lithuania join the Soviet Union under duress.

July 22: Hitler's strings-attached "peace offer" is rejected by London. • The Special Operations Executive is created by Britain's War Cabinet to carry out acts of sabotage against Nazi Germany in occupied countries.

July 24: Nearly 50 civilians are killed in an Italian air raid of Jerusalem.

August 1: Hitler orders increased bombing of strategic British targets in preparation for Operation Sealion, which he intends to launch on September 15.

August 3: East Africa's British Somaliland is overrun by a large contingent of Italian troops.

August 5: Hitler and Mussolini confer in Rome, with Mussolini assuring Hitler he will soon open the North African front with an assault into Egypt toward the Suez Canal.

August 8: In an effort to persuade India to take a more active role in promoting British interests in Southeast Asia, Britain promises its colony a new postwar constitution.

August 9: Due to greater needs on other fronts, British troops abandon Shanghai.

August 11: The U.S. Army announces plans to send 4,000 tanks to Britain.

August 15: Germany is dealt a major blow during the Battle of Britain. Intending to knock out the RAF, the *Luftwaffe* actually loses more than twice as many aircraft—75 compared to Britain's 32.

August 17: Germany blockades Britain, heavily mining its waters and vowing to attack all approaching ships, whether belligerent or neutral.

Japan and French Indochina

The fall of France and creation of the Vichy regime in 1940 benefited the Japanese in their war in China and their anticipated advance into Southeast Asia. The Japanese estimated that 41 percent of supplies reaching Chiang Kai-shek's Nationalist Chinese forces came through the port of Haiphong in French Indochina—which was comprised of the French colony of Cochinchina and the French protectorates of Cambodia, Laos, Annam, and Tonkin.

Evacuation of French colonial forces in French Indochina

Using diplomacy and threats, as well as a "mistaken" incursion that killed more than 800 French troops, the Japanese forced the Vichy French regime to close the Yunnan railway in September 1940 and then to allow Japanese troops to occupy northern Indochina. There they consolidated their blockade of China and prepared for southward expansion. In July 1941, Japanese forces occupied southern Indochina, where they met no opposition. Vichy's accommodating responses to the Japanese demands of September 1940 and July 1941 contrasted sharply to its resistance to simultaneous demands from the British and Free French in Dakar and Syria.

When the American government tried to avert war in late 1941, one of its key demands was that the Japanese evacuate French Indochina. Japan would have left the southern portion if the U.S. made concessions on the oil issue. That could not and did not happen. So, after Japan took Malaya in January 1942, Indochina sprouted Japanese air and naval bases, and became a valuable staging post for troops.

The Blitz

"The bomber," British prime minister Stanley Baldwin had told a somber Parliament in 1932, "will always get through." The examples of Guernica in Spain, as well as Japanese attacks in China, suggested that Baldwin had been correct. After Britain's declaration of war in September 1939, its citizens prepared for the anticipated German bombing Blitz (a contraction of *Blitzkrieg*). The British launched barrage balloons to force bombers to high altitudes, while antiaircraft batteries ringed industrial targets.

Since only a few bombs fell until mid-1940, Britain did have ample time to prepare. The government raised a dramatically resourceful civilian Auxiliary Fire Service. Moreover, it organized medical services and evacuated some three million women and children to the country. (Middle-class families hosting them learned appalling truths about the lives of the urban working class.) An efficient and dedicated Air Raid Precautions organization enforced civil defense measures, including a strict blackout, while many families built air raid shelters. In London especially, thousands sought protection in public shelters and famously in Underground stations, a sign of official unpreparedness as much as popular stoicism.

When the air strikes came in August 1940, German bombers attacked London by day and night. What happened in London was the defining experience of the Blitz, but most large English cities were attacked as well. The notorious raid on Coventry, for instance, destroyed the city's center and killed more than 500 people.

The psychological basis of the attacks, that bombing would destroy a population's resolve, proved spectacularly wrong. "Britain Can Take It" became a popular motto, and though some cities approached panic at times, most people grew defiant rather than demoralized.

By mid-1941, when Germany's *Luftwaffe* joined the war against Russia, the sustained attacks against Britain largely ended. However, just days after the D-Day landing in June 1944, the first V-1 pilotless planes fell on London. In the fall of that year, V-2 ballistic missiles followed. Civilians wearied by five years of war were forced to endure a particularly terrifying weapon.

Some 70,000 British civilians died during the attacks of 1940–41 and 1944. But to this day, citizens still celebrate and romanticize the "spirit of the Blitz."

Antiaircraft guns defend London On September 7, 1940, only 92 antiaircraft (AA) guns were deployed about London, and the fire-control arrangements failed almost at once. Thus, the *Luftwaffe* enjoyed three nights with virtually no AA fire directed against it. However, by September 11, some 200 AA guns were put in place, together with supporting searchlights, so that a blaze of light and a curtain of fire (*pictured*) greeted the bombers that night. Few hits were claimed, but the guns and barrage balloons did force the bombers to fly much higher. In addition, this display of firepower boosted the morale of many Londoners.

Blitz bombing kills 43,000 From September to mid-November 1940, an average of 200 Axis aircraft bombed London on every night but one. Meanwhile, *Luftwaffe* fighter bombers and single bombers on precision bombing missions also attacked the capital by day. Regular air raids then continued until May. Destruction was widespread and severe. This massive crater was possibly caused by one of the *Luftwaffe's* huge 2,500-kilogram "Max" *Sprengbombe Cylindrisch* bombs. Countrywide, from September 1940 to May 1941, the Blitz caused 43,000 civilian deaths and 139,000 serious injuries, as well as laying waste to many residential areas and industrial, dockland, and infrastructure facilities.

1940

August 20: Churchill offers Roosevelt the use of military bases in the West Indies and Newfoundland.

August 23–24: The *Luftwaffe* bombs London. Though oil facilities east of the city are targeted, London proper sustains most of the damage. The RAF will retaliate two nights later, attacking Berlin for the first time.

August 28: Liverpool, England, suffers its first bomb raid.

August 31: In the greatest one-day loss for the RAF to date, the *Luftwaffe* takes out 38 planes and critical airfields in southern Britain.

September 5: France's Vichy government severs diplomatic ties with Holland, Luxembourg, Belgium, and Norway. • As many as 4,000 German troops perish when the transport ship *Marion* founders after taking a direct hit from a British torpedo. • German authorities seize Jewish-owned businesses following Luxembourg's annexation by Germany and adoption of the Nuremberg Laws.

September 6: Fascist general Ion Antonescu and his Iron Guards take control of the Romanian government. Romania's King Carol is forced to abdicate after ceding much of Transylvania. • The U.S. Navy transfers the first eight of 50 destroyers promised to the Royal Navy in exchange for U.S. bases at Bermuda and other British possessions.

September 7: The *Luftwaffe* turns its attention from British military to civilian targets. This is part of what will be called the Blitz.

September 10: Italian troops stage themselves in Albania prior to their planned assault on Greece.

September 11: The *Luftwaffe* bombs London, inflicting heavy damage on St. Paul's Cathedral and Buckingham Palace.

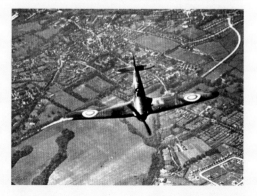

Hurricanes, Spitfires defend Britain In 1937 the RAF's first monoplane fighter—the Hurricane Mark I (*pictured*)—entered squadron service. It boasted a top speed of more than 300 mph, eight machine guns (replaced with cannons in late 1940), and an operating radius of up to 600 miles. This formidable aircraft, together with the Spitfire (introduced in 1938), proved to be the mainstay of RAF Fighter Command during the crucial Battle of Britain. Using radar to track the approaching German bombers, RAF headquarters sent these Hurricanes and Spitfires to intercept. They inflicted crippling losses upon the *Luftwaffe*, which helped prevent a German invasion.

1940

September 13: An anemic British force is pushed back when Italy embarks on its first significant assault on the North African front, marching five army divisions into Egypt from Libya. • The African war continues with a 20-mile incursion by Italian troops from occupied Ethiopia into British Kenya. • King George VI and Queen Elizabeth remain in London, despite narrowly missing being struck by bombs that tore through the roof of Buckingham Palace.

September 15: Canada conscripts its single men, ages 21 to 24. • Hitler postpones Operation Sealion after another botched air battle leaves the *Luftwaffe* with 60 planes lost while the RAF loses 26.

September 16: The U.S. Congress passes the Selective Training and Service Act, which will enable the registration and conscription of American males ages 21 to 35.

September 17: Seventy-seven British children, en route to Canada to escape the destruction of war, die when a U-boat sinks their ship, *City of Benares*.

September 21: Officials in London permit Londoners who do not have access to bomb shelters to use the Underground for that purpose. At one point, more than 170,000 people will be sleeping in the "Tube."

September 23: In a sign of horrors to come, SS chief Heinrich Himmler decrees that gold teeth should be removed from the mouths of dead concentration camp inmates.

September 25: American intelligence agents crack Japan's diplomatic code, known as "Purple." Along with Britain's deciphering of the German Enigma machine, this is a significant victory for Allied intelligence.

Fighting fires during the Blitz In 1940 and '41, Britain's fire services included full-time and part-time regular firefighters as well as part-time auxiliaries. The full-time firefighters worked shifts of 48 hours on duty followed by 24 hours off, and they were joined during the particularly busy night hours by the part-time auxiliaries. Here, firefighters battle a blaze in London. Initially, the firefighting response to major fires that involved operations across local authority boundaries was hampered by the fire service's localized and excessively parochial system of command and control. However, after the Blitz ended in May 1941, all of these semiautonomous forces were brought together to form the National Fire Service.

The Importance of Radar

During the war, combatants used radar to detect ships and planes far beyond the range of the human eye. In simple terms, radar (radio detecting and ranging) utilizes transmitters to bounce radio waves off distant objects, revealing the objects' location, speed, and distance.

The use of radio waves to detect distant or unseen metallic objects was first demonstrated by German scientist Christian Hulsmeyer in 1904. However, it was the British who first used radar for a military advantage, as they built a series of radar stations along the English coast in 1938 to detect approaching aircraft. Known as the Chain Home, this system subsequently played a crucial role in the victory over the *Luftwaffe* during the Battle of Britain.

1940

September 27: France's Vichy government orders all Jews to carry cards identifying them as such. • The Axis is sealed with the signing of the Tripartite Pact, an economic and military alliance among Germany, Italy, and Japan.

September 29: Luxembourg is formally incorporated into the Reich.

October 3: Warsaw's Jews are herded into the city's Jewish ghetto.

October 4: With Operation Sealion temporarily delayed, Hitler meets with Mussolini in an effort to enlist Italy to take on Britain on alternate fronts. • Fearing Japanese aggression in the Pacific, Churchill requests naval reinforcements from Roosevelt to defend Britain's colony of Singapore.

October 7: With Ion Antonescu's assent in Romania, Germany occupies that country on the pretext of protecting its oil fields from British saboteurs. • Japan formally voices its objection to the American ban on sales of fuel, scrap metal, and machine tools to Asia.

October 9: London's Cathedral of St. Paul sustains serious damage to the roof and altar when it is struck by a German bomb.

October 12: Hitler reschedules his invasion of Britain for April 4, 1941, leading Churchill to joke that Britain is "waiting for the long-promised invasion. So are the fishes." • In a speech that implies that the U.S. may be ready for a greater role in the war, Roosevelt claims that Americans "reject the doctrine of appeasement," calling it "a major weapon of the aggressor nations."

Nazis ghettoize Warsaw's Jews Polish and Jewish laborers contribute to the construction of a 10-foot-high wall that will enclose the Jewish ghetto of Warsaw. After the 1939 German takeover of Poland, Gestapo chief Reinhard Heydrich ordered Jews into segregated living areas. In the fall of 1940, Heydrich used the pretext of a typhus outbreak in Jewish neighborhoods to force the city's Jews into a 3.5-square-mile section of town. Non-Jewish Poles were moved out of the area. That November, the ghetto wall's 22 gates were closed, sealing off 360,000 Jews (one-third of Warsaw's entire population) from the rest of the Polish capital.

U-boats feast on Allied ships In 1940 Germany had a small but effective fleet of submarines, such as the U-boat *Krieg* seen here. In addition to

successful attacks on British warships, German U-boats proved especially deadly against Allied merchant shipping. The fall of France provided a 2,500-mile coast from which to unleash U-boat "wolf packs" against still-unescorted transatlantic merchant convoys. That fall, U-boats sank some 200 Allied ships. However, these early successes led Hitler to conclude that he had enough submarines and could shift to building surface ships for war with the U.S. He did not increase production until mid-1941, by which time Britain had acquired more destroyers and developed better defenses.

1940

October 13: More than 150 people die when a London bomb shelter sustains a direct hit during an air raid. Another 64 will be killed on the 15th when bombs strike the Balham Underground Station. • Stalin sends Foreign Minister Molotov to Berlin to negotiate Soviet adherence to the Tripartite Pact.

October 15: London's primary water source, a pipeline that carries some 46 million gallons every day, is severely damaged in a bombing raid.

October 17: More than 1,500 British civilians have been killed in German bombing raids in the past week alone.

October 18: In defiance of Japan, Britain restores China's trade route to the West by reopening the Burma Road.

October 18–19: German U-boats attack two British convoys, sinking more than 30 ships.

October 22: The Nazis begin to deport Jews from parts of Germany to southern France.

October 23: Francisco Franco, Spain's Fascist leader, is unmoved by a nine-hour meeting with Hitler, and refuses to ally Spain with the Axis.

October 26: With more than 150,000 Italian troops at the ready, Mussolini attempts to justify his inevitable invasion of Greece by claiming that Greece has attacked Albania.

October 28: Mussolini sends Italian troops into Greece in an invasion attempt that will end in total disaster for the Italians.

November 3: British troops and RAF units land in Greece to help repel the invading Italian army.

1940

November 5: The tremendously popular Franklin Roosevelt is elected to a third term, a break from the presidency's traditional, though not mandated, two-term limit.

November 7: The RAF bombs the Krupp munitions factory in Essen, Germany. • Irish prime minister Eamon de Valera denies Britain the use of Irish naval bases.

November 8: Hitler's annual observance of his 1923 coup attempt is interrupted by an RAF air raid on Munich.

November 9: Germany begins the process of expelling some 180,000 French citizens from Alsace-Lorraine, the partially ethnically German region in southern France.

November 11: In the first successful attack by carrier-based warplanes, a flight of 20 RAF biplanes bombs Taranto, destroying or damaging half the Italian fleet. • Fifty-five Polish intellectuals are murdered in the first of many mass executions at Dachau, the concentration camp outside of Munich.

November 12–14: Soviet foreign minister Molotov meets with Hitler to discuss possible Soviet adherence to the Tripartite Pact.

November 14: Much of the British city of Coventry, including its stunning medieval cathedral, is destroyed in a *Luftwaffe* raid in which 449 bombers attack the region. • In an embarrassing defeat for the Italian military, the Greek army pushes the Italians out of Greece and follows their retreat into Albania.

November 16: Hamburg, Germany, is blasted by RAF bombers.

French colonial troops Members of the First Battalion AEF (Afrique Equatoriale Française) charge across the desert. The French military had a long history of filling its ranks with colonial troops. Before the fall of France in 1940, more than 100,000 men had been recruited from West Africa alone. Following the armistice, the four territories of French Equatorial Africa—Gabon, Chad, and present-day Republic of the Congo and Central African Republic—sided with the Free French. About 100,000 Africans served with the Free French from 1943 to '45, participating in the fighting in North Africa, Italy, and southern France.

_U-48_ sinks more than 50 ships On September 11, 1940, Herbert Schultze, commander of the German submarine _U-48_ (_pictured_), sent a terse radio message to Winston Churchill, announcing that he had sunk the British steamer _Firby_. After giving the wreck's coordinates, Schultze added, "Save the crew, if you please." Fast, agile, and far-ranging, the _U-48_ was commissioned on April 22, 1939, and proved herself the most successful German U-boat of the war, sinking more than 50 ships and damaging others during its 12 patrols. By June 1941, the _U-48_, already becoming obsolete, was relegated to training exercises.

1940

November 20: Hungary signs the Tripartite Pact, joining Germany, Italy, and Japan in the Axis. • In what will become known as the "100th Regiment Offensive," Chinese Communists stage guerrilla raids against Japanese forces.

November 22: The Greeks overwhelm Italy's Ninth Army and occupy Korçë, an Albanian town strategically important to the Italians.

November 23: Romania follows Hungary's lead and signs the Tripartite Pact, joining the Axis. Slovakia will join the following day.

November 25: A wood-bodied De Havilland Mosquito prototype—a fast, light, and agile British fighter that will become known as the "Timber Terror"—takes to the air for its first flight. • Bulgaria postpones signing the Tripartite Pact.

November 26: Pierre Ryckmans, the governor general of the Belgian Congo, declares war on Italy. Italy will declare war on Belgium the following day. • Workers begin the construction of a 10-foot-high wall around the Jewish ghetto in Warsaw, Poland.

November 27: In an effort to bolster his power, Romanian dictator Ion Antonescu orders his Iron Guard to execute 64 officials who are loyal to the government of King Carol.

November 29: Plans for the Nazi invasion of the Soviet Union, dubbed Operation Barbarossa, are finalized.

December 1: Italy begins rationing its key staple: pasta.

December 6: A major upheaval in the Italian military command follows the disastrous invasion of Greece, as the army's chief of staff resigns. The chief of the Italian navy will resign on December 8.

Bombs pummel Liverpool Citizens inspect a demolished school and damaged houses after a 1940 German bombing raid on Liverpool, England. That year, Liverpool was hit with more than 300 air attacks. In addition to the well-known London Blitz, German bombers struck at industrial cities and ports all over England, Scotland, and Wales. *Luftwaffe* planes flew from Scandinavia to targets in northeastern Great Britain. The fall of France provided the Germans with new bases, putting even the shipyards and aircraft factories of Belfast, Northern Ireland, within range.

1940

December 8: Desperately outmatched, Italy pleads with Germany for assistance with its campaign against Greece.

December 10: Hitler is forced to cancel a planned invasion of Gibraltar when Spain's General Francisco Franco refuses to assist. • In London, British officials hang Jose Waldberg and Carl Meier. Both are convicted spies for Nazi Germany.

December 11: Britain recaptures the Egyptian city of Sidi Barrani from Italy following a surprise offensive of 30,000 British soldiers against a larger Italian contingent.

December 18: Hitler approves the outline for plans for a massive German invasion of the Soviet Union.

December 20: The small Dutch navy escapes in its entirety across the English Channel to safety in Britain.

December 23: Jacques Bonsergent becomes the first French citizen executed by the Nazis in Paris, following an altercation with a German officer.

December 25: With Italian bombers threatening, the town of Bethlehem is blacked out on Christmas for the first time in memory.

December 27: The *Luftwaffe* begins its firebombing of London. Over the next several days, some 20,000 British firemen will struggle to extinguish the flames.

December 28: Resource-pinched Japan begins an alternate-fuel program by which private automobiles will be powered by charcoal.

December 29: Finally abandoning America's isolationist stance, Roosevelt publicly recommends a program of direct arms aid to Great Britain.

Benito Mussolini

Italy's Benito Mussolini was a Socialist journalist until the Great War made him an ardent nationalist. In Milan, Italy, in 1919, he founded the *Fasci di combattimento* (Combat Groups), the basis of the Fascist Party. By 1922 it controlled the government, and in 1925 Mussolini assumed dictatorial powers.

In foreign policy, Mussolini sought to create a new Roman empire by employing the violence and threats that were central to his domestic program. However, he did not develop armed forces capable of fulfilling this fantasy, although in 1935–36 Italian troops conquered the African country of Abyssinia. This aggressive action brought domestic acclaim and ineffective sanctions by the League of Nations. The fateful Rome-Berlin Axis followed. Mussolini consolidated his alliance with Hitler by participating in the Spanish Civil War, accepting the *Anschluss*, and facilitating the Munich Conference. Regardless, in September 1939 he declared Italy's neutrality. Only when Germany's conquest of France was imminent did he join Germany.

The war proved disastrous for Mussolini. Though Hitler accepted "*Il Duce*" as an ally,

he never consulted him. Mussolini's invasion of Egypt in September 1940 ended in a costly retreat before smaller British forces. Only German general Rommel's arrival saved the Italian colony of Libya. Mussolini's botched invasion of Greece was similarly salvaged with German help, but Abyssinia was soon lost. Mussolini's forces contributed substantially to Rommel's successes in North Africa, but his renewed imperial hopes evaporated at El Alamein in Egypt.

In addition, Mussolini's fleet was decimated at Taranto, Italy, and his army in Russia was virtually destroyed after the Battle of Stalingrad. Defeat in Tunisia was followed by the invasion of Sicily in July 1943, which led Italy's Fascist Grand Council to dismiss him.

Mussolini was arrested by order of King Vittorio Emanuele III, but German paratroops rescued him in September 1943. Because Italy had just surrendered to Germany and was under Nazi occupation, Mussolini was installed as puppet ruler of the Italian Socialist Republic. With defeat inevitable, he sought to flee Italy in 1945, but partisans found and executed him and his mistress on April 28.

1941

January 1: A portion of Bremen, Germany, burns out of control when nearly 100 RAF planes hit the city with firebombs.

January 2: In an early indication of the dark days to come, all Jews in the Netherlands are required to register with the authorities.

January 3: After two straight days of air assaults by the RAF, Australian ground forces capture Libya's Italian-occupied town of Bardia. • The *Luftwaffe* arrives in Albania to aid Italy's counteroffensive against Greek forces. • In an effort to encourage Irish prime minister de Valera to continue to resist Allied requests to use neutral Ireland's military bases, Germany bombs Northern Ireland three times over the course of 24 hours.

January 6: In a congressional speech that features his principle of four freedoms—of speech, of religion, from want, and from fear—President Roosevelt promotes his lend-lease plan to "act as an arsenal" and provide material support to European allies.

January 7: Japanese admiral Yamamoto puts on paper Operation Z, a scheme to attack U.S. and British military positions in Hawaii, the Philippines, Java, the central Pacific islands, and elsewhere.

January 8: In his annual budget request to Congress, Roosevelt asks for an increase in defense spending to a total of $10.8 billion for 1942.

January 9: A prototype of the British-built Avro Lancaster long-range heavy bomber makes its maiden voyage.

January 10: Britain loses control of shipping in the central Mediterranean when the *Luftwaffe* cripples the carrier *Illustrious*, which had been escorting supply convoys to Malta. Shipping routes to North Africa are now laid open for the Germans.

The Sheffield Blitz Sheffield was a key British armaments center that produced everything from bayonets to armor, including crucial components of the Spitfire aircraft. Inevitably, the "Steel City" became a target of German bombing, though not at the sustained level expected. The Sheffield Blitz occurred on the nights of December 12 and 15, 1940, when more than 660 people were killed and nearly 80,000 buildings damaged. The bombs fell on the city center (*pictured*) rather than the steelworks, which remained largely untouched. Though many civilians took cover in Anderson shelters, some were killed while sheltering in basements, most tragically in the Marples Hotel.

Half-tracked vehicles Engineers of half-tracked vehicles achieved mobility and agility by combining a conventional front-wheel steering system with the tracked rear drive. These vehicles were used in many roles by the Allies and the Axis, including weapon carriers, antiaircraft gun platforms, artillery prime-movers, armored personnel carriers, and recovery vehicles. The U.S. and Germany led the way in half-track development. Pictured is a U.S. M2A1 White carrier, many of which were supplied to America's allies through Lend-Lease. Meanwhile, Germany developed an extensive range of half-tracks, from the Kettenkraftrad motorcycle tractor to heavy-duty utility and fighting vehicles.

1941

January 10: The Soviets spend about $7.5 million worth of gold for a small area of southern Lithuania that had been promised to Germany but was occupied by the Red Army. • After advancing over the Albanian border in pursuit of the retreating Italian army, Greece captures the town of Klisura, near the Greek-Albanian frontier.

January 13: Hitler demands that King Boris of Bulgaria sign the Tripartite Pact, fight alongside the other members of the Axis, and allow the Germans to attack Greece from Bulgarian soil. The unstated yet obvious result of a Bulgarian denial is invasion.

January 14: Germany puts Romania on notice that the time has come for it to begin fighting alongside the other members of the Axis.

January 15: Emperor Haile Selassie returns to Ethiopia five years after he was sent into exile by an Italian occupation force.

January 19: Italy retreats in the face of a British attack on forces in Eritrea and Ethiopia on the same day that Hitler and Mussolini discuss the ongoing difficulties on the North African and Albanian fronts. Hitler agrees to send German troop support to Libya.

January 19–21: Forces controlled by Romanian dictator Ion Antonescu brutally suppress a coup attempt by the leadership of the Iron Guard.

January 21: The United States suspends its "moral embargo" on exports destined for the Soviet Union.

January 22: The Allies occupy Tobruk, Libya, in a remarkably unbalanced battle that leaves the Italians short 25,000 soldiers at the expense of 400 Australian and British casualties.

January 24: The United States denies a Vichy French request to welcome German Jewish refugees to America.

The *Bismarck* sinks the *Hood* The German battleship *Bismarck* fires toward the British battle cruiser *Hood* on May 24, 1941. According to Lieutenant Esmond Knight, who witnessed the attack while on the British *Prince of Wales,* "a great spouting explosion issued from the centre of the *Hood*, enormous reaching tongues of pale-red flame shot into the air, while dense clouds of whitish-yellow smoke burst upwards, gigantic pieces of brightly burning debris being hurled hundreds of feet in the air....*Hood* had literally been blown to pieces." Of the *Hood's* crew of more than 1,400 men, only three survived.

1941

January 26: Japan's imperialist plans are evident when Foreign Minister Yosuke Matsuoka calls for a "new order" in Asia.

January 27: Joseph Grew, the American ambassador in Tokyo, passes on to Washington a rumor that Japan is planning a surprise attack on the U.S. naval base at Pearl Harbor, Hawaii.

January 29: Representatives from the United States and Britain secretly meet in Washington to discuss joint military strategy if the U.S. is forced into war.

January 30: In an effort to cut the British supply chain, Germany threatens to torpedo any neutral ship carrying supplies to Allied troops.

January 31: The government of Turkey denies Churchill's request to station 10 squadrons of RAF planes and pilots on Turkish soil.

February 1: Recognizing a need to protect merchant ships in the Atlantic, the U.S. Navy creates the Atlantic Fleet, with Rear Admiral Ernest J. King commanding.

February 8: The Lend-Lease Bill, designed to provide a framework through which the United States can assist the Allies while maintaining neutrality, passes the House of Representatives. It will pass the Senate on March 8.

February 14: Roosevelt cautions Yugoslavia's Prince Paul against aligning with Germany on the same day that Hitler sends an ultimatum demanding cooperation.

February 15: The Nazi administration in Austria inaugurates its plan to deport Austrian Jews to Polish ghettos.

1941

February 19: Nomura Kichisaburo, the Japanese ambassador to the U.S., asserts that any war between Japan and the United States would occur only at America's discretion.

February 20: El Agheila, Libya, is the site of the first desert battle between the British and German armies.

February 22: Some 400 Jews a week perish of starvation in the Warsaw Ghetto, a grim figure that will not improve with the enforcement of the new daily bread ration of three ounces per adult.

February 24: Hitler reports great success in the Battle of the Atlantic, claiming that in the past 48 hours alone, Germany has sunk British cargo weighing more than 200,000 tons. • Despite British pleas, the United States will not be sending any ships to protect the territory of Singapore against Japanese aggression in the East.

February 25: Advocates for the Netherlands's Jews are silenced by the SS, which puts an end to public demonstrations objecting to Jewish persecution.

February 26: The Nazi occupation government in northern Holland declares martial law in the wake of a series of attacks on Germans—attacks that the Nazis claim were perpetrated by Jews.

February-March: British troops take a heavy toll on Italian forces at Cyrenaica, Ethiopia, and elsewhere in Africa.

March 1: Auschwitz commandant Rudolf Höss is informed that he will receive 130,000 prisoners for his new camp, 10,000 of whom will be forced into slave labor at the IG Farben company's synthetic rubber plant.

March 2: One day after Bulgaria's King Boris III is coerced into accepting Hitler's terms and joins the Axis, the German army marches into Bulgaria.

Germans score victories in Libya German general Rommel's preemptive strike into Cyrenaica, the eastern coastal region of Libya, in March 1941 was a strategic masterstroke. Although parts of his *Afrika Korps* were still forming, he had judged correctly that the British and Commonwealth forces were exhausted after their successful campaign against the Italians, and that they believed no German offensive was possible before May. Accordingly, within a week of arriving in North Africa in February, German troops (*pictured*) were reconnoitering their opponents' positions. The Libyan towns of El Agheila and Mersa Brega fell on March 24 and April 1, respectively, and Tobruk, Libya, was besieged. Meanwhile, Italian morale was restored and all the British successes of 1940–41 reversed.

1941

March 5: Britain breaks all diplomatic ties with Bulgaria.

March 6: In his Battle of the Atlantic Directive, Churchill underscores the importance of neutralizing U-boats and aerial assaults on British shipping. • British shipping in the Mediterranean faces a new obstacle, as Germany begins to pepper the Suez Canal with aircraft-delivered acoustic magnetic mines.

March 12: Roosevelt asks Congress for $7 billion in military credits to Britain under the new Lend-Lease law.

March 13: Realizing that success in Greece is dependent on an ability to move troops through Yugoslavia, Hitler steps up pressure on the Yugoslav government to join the Axis. • Glasgow, Scotland, is hit by its first significant air raid of the war. More than 230 *Luftwaffe* planes hit the Scottish city with hundreds of tons of explosives and tens of thousands of incendiary devices.

March 20: U.S. undersecretary of state Sumner Welles informs the Soviet ambassador of an intelligence report with the plan for the German attack on the Soviet Union.

March 23: German U-boats are dominating the Battle of the Atlantic, sinking more than 59,000 tons of British shipping in the past week alone.

March 25: In advance of any action in the Baltic States, some 60,000 ethnically German people from Latvia, Estonia, and Lithuania have been resettled on German territory. • Facing German occupation, Yugoslavia formally joins the Axis and agrees to the provisions of the Tripartite Pact.

March 27: Yugoslavia throws a wrench into Hitler's plans when military officers, demanding a neutral Yugoslavia, overthrow the government that capitulated to the Axis, and place a teenaged King Peter II on the throne.

Battle of Cape Matapan A Royal Navy Fairey Fulmar flies air cover over the British fleet at the Battle of Cape Matapan off Crete on March 27–29, 1941. The combined force of British Royal Navy and Australian Navy ships protecting convoys bound for Greece engaged an Italian naval force. The heaviest fighting occurred after dark on March 28. Aided by radar, which the Italian ships lacked, British warships sent three enemy heavy cruisers and two destroyers to the bottom with heavy loss of life. Britain lost only a single torpedo bomber. After the battle, the Italians temporarily conceded the eastern Mediterranean to the British, who could now concentrate more on the fighting in North Africa.

British unwelcome in Iraq Indian troops guard an Iraqi oil refinery in 1941. Iraq had been independent since 1932, but Britain retained privileges there. The British maintained air bases at Habbaniya and Basra, had the right to pass troops through Iraq, and held commercial interest in oil refineries. The wartime government was initially pro-British, but on April 3, 1941, pro-Axis Rashid Ali El-Ghailani became prime minister following a coup. Britain dispatched a brigade to Basra, but Rashid Ali refused entry to further brigades until it left. Iraqi troops surrounded Habbaniya, but British aircraft and the garrison defeated them by early May. British reinforcements arrived, and Rashid Ali fled to Germany.

1941

March 28: The Italian fleet is decimated and nearly 2,500 sailors die when the British sink three of its cruisers and two destroyers at the Battle of Cape Matapan. • The Eagle Squadron, comprised of American pilots operating under the British flag, is ready for battle. • Plutonium-239, a uranium isotope that will prove critical in the development of nuclear weapons, is discovered by a team of American physicists.

March 29: The Royal Navy traps Italian warships in waters between Greece and Crete. Three Italian cruisers are sunk and an important Italian battleship, *Vittorio Veneto*, is badly damaged.

March 30: The U.S. Navy commandeers ships flying the flags of Axis nations stationed in ports across the United States.

April 2–3: Count Teleki, the prime minister of Hungary, takes his own life because Hungary is joining Germany in an invasion of Yugoslavia, with which he had signed a non-aggression treaty.

April 3: Stafford Cripps, the British ambassador to Moscow, delivers a warning to Stalin from Churchill that an attack on the Soviet Union by Nazi Germany could happen any day.

April 4: Under pressure from the advancing Allies, the Italians abandon the Ethiopian capital of Addis Ababa. South African troops will occupy the city for the Allies on the 6th. • Hitler assures Japanese leaders that Germany will fight the United States if Japan attacks the U.S. in the Pacific.

April 5: The Soviet air force test-flies its new MiG-3 fighter for the first time. • The gulf between Hitler and Stalin grows when Yugoslavia signs a nonaggression treaty with the Soviets, drawing the ire of the Germans.

British Colonial Soldiers

Colonial soldiers defended and extended the British Empire as early as the 18th century, with the volunteer, professional Indian Army proving its worth during the Great War. From the beginning to end of World War II, this combined force expanded from 200,000 men to 2.5 million.

Colonial troops from India and Africa

Indian divisions served in the Middle East, North Africa, Italy, Malaya, and Singapore, and constituted the bulk of British forces in Burma. Increasingly mechanized and led by Indians at battalion level, they formed the basis of what would be the regular post-independence armies of India and Pakistan. Large numbers of Gurkhas (brave warriors from Nepal) and the traditional "martial races" volunteered, but the British Indian Army also recruited across India's ethnic spectrum.

Colonial troops generally remained loyal. However, the Burma Rifles proved unreliable, while gunners of the Ceylon Garrison Artillery mutinied on the Cocos Islands in 1942. Moreover, the Indian Army's rapid expansion in 1940–41 led to demoralization and disasters in Malaya. It also led to the loss of about 40,000 men who surrendered in Singapore to the Japanese, who subsequently assigned them to the Japanese-controlled Indian National Army. However, the Indian Army remained "loyal to its salt" despite defeats as well as famine and nationalist unrest in India itself.

African soldiers from British colonial possessions served against the Italians in East Africa. From 1943, East and West African divisions fought the Japanese in Burma. Led by British officers, they gained a reputation for toughness. Military service gave African soldiers wider horizons, transforming the political expectations of Britain's African colonies. Within two decades, these colonies would gain independence.

1941

April 5: General Rommel's *Afrika Korps* and Italian forces drive eastward against Libya, forcing a British retreat.

April 6: A four-front attack overwhelms Yugoslavia, as the German army storms the country from Bulgaria, Romania, Hungary, and Austria. Belgrade, the capital, is destroyed and thousands are killed when the Germans initiate their invasion with a Sunday attack. • Germany attacks Greece by way of Bulgaria.

April 7: London severs all ties to Budapest, as Hungary is now wholly under the influence of Nazi Germany. • Britain's plans to help defend Greece are complicated when *Luftwaffe* bombers blow up a ship packed with explosives in the port of Piraeus, damaging critical port infrastructure in the process.

April 9: Concerned that Berlin has designs on bases in Greenland, the United States obtains the rights to provide military protection to the remote but strategically located island. • In Croatia, a pro-German region of Yugoslavia, Germany and Italy create a puppet state as German troops approach the Croatian capital of Zagreb.

April 9–10: Berlin is badly damaged and the State Opera House is gutted during a large RAF attack on the city.

April 10: Rommel begins a siege of Allied positions at Tobruk, Libya. • The USS *Niblack*, a destroyer on a rescue mission off the coast of Iceland, drops depth charges near a German submarine. The incident is the first case of American hostile fire directed at a German ship.

April 12: A German panzer corps takes the Serbian capital of Belgrade, Yugoslavia, while the Croatian people of Zagreb welcome the German army invasion.

German troops storm Greece Hitler had no desire to conquer Greece in 1941. However, after Mussolini's imprudent invasion of the eastern Mediterranean nation failed early in 1941, the *Führer* had no choice but to come to his partner's rescue. On April 6, 1941, the Germans launched their invasion of Greece from Bulgaria, which had recently joined the Axis. Pictured here are German troops crossing the Pineios River in the Greek region of Thessaly, using boats and a makeshift bridge. By May 11, mainland Greece and all of its surrounding islands except Crete were fully under Axis occupation. Some 50,000 British troops were forced to hastily evacuate Greece.

Hess crashes in Scotland On May 10, 1941, German official Rudolf Hess made an unauthorized visit to Britain. He was arrested after he broke his ankle in a parachute jump from his Messerschmitt, which crashed just south of Glasgow, Scotland. Hess, whose German title of deputy *Führer* put him in charge of the Nazi Party apparatus, was on a solo mission. He said he wanted to negotiate a peace in which Britain would be safe from attack if it gave Germany a free hand in Europe. Dismissed as insane by the British and Hitler, Hess remained in Allied imprisonment until his death in 1987.

1941

April 13: Confident that there will be no German invasion, Stalin shores up his eastern frontier with the signing of a Japanese-Soviet neutrality pact.

April 14: With supply lines stretched to the limit, Rommel's *Afrika Korps* is forced to halt its stunning advance across Libya, just beyond Tobruk. • Egypt's King Farouk secretly tells Hitler that he would welcome a German invasion force and expulsion of the British.

April 16: Representatives of the United States and Japan meet in Washington to resolve their differences. Roosevelt opens the talks by laying out what he sees as four critical points in international relations: territorial integrity, noninterference, equal opportunity for commerce, and stability in the Pacific.

April 20: Greece surrenders to the Axis the day after Prime Minister Alexander Korizis commits suicide in despair.

April 22: Germany's newly formed *Afrika Korps*, comprised of two army divisions, arrives in Tripoli, Libya, to aid the foundering Italian army in North Africa.

April 26: Rommel's *Afrika Korps* advances, forcing the British to back out of Libya and into Egypt.

April 30: The Nazi Party bans the display of the crucifix in schools across Bavaria, inciting anger through this deeply Catholic region of southern Germany. The crucifixes will be restored.

May 1941: SS *Reichsführer* Heinrich Himmler decrees that writing one's name, simple arithmetic, and obedience to Germans is all the education needed for the non-German, eastern population of the conquered territories.

Bombs destroy House of Commons Winston Churchill examines the remains of the House of Commons, destroyed by bombs dropped on the night of May 10, 1941. The raid was architecturally the most damaging to London. The Westminster Abbey and Lambeth Palace were also harmed. Westminster Palace, of which the Commons was part, was hit many times during the war, but remained in use throughout. The House of Commons continued to meet in the chamber of the House of Lords, while the lords met elsewhere.

Germany forced to ration food Even after war began in 1939, Hitler did not want to enforce rationing. He believed that shortages of food and other goods had contributed to the so-called "stab in the back," which he felt had caused Germany's loss of World War I. After invading Poland and other European countries, Germany ruthlessly exploited them to keep Germany well supplied. But after Germany began to experience military failures, especially the catastrophic 1941 invasion of the USSR, rationing became a necessity. Rationing cards such as these—which entitled bearers to meat, eggs, and bread—were complicated. Rationing efforts were far more successful in Britain than in Germany.

Britain takes control in Iraq In May 1941, British forces rolled into Baghdad to bring about regime change. For the rest of the war, Iraqi officials cooperated with the British. However, many historians believe that the easy British victory heightened both Arab nationalism and Islamic fundamentalism. Especially troubling to the British were the intrigues of Grand Mufti Muhammed Amin al-Husseini—a man of deceptively gentle manners and soothing voice. The grand mufti was a favorite of Hitler, for whom he recruited Muslim soldiers.

1941

May 2: The pro-Axis government of Iraq calls for German assistance as Britain occupies Basra and its surrounding oil fields.

May 5: Though apprised by Tokyo of the fact that Japan's secret Purple code is most likely compromised, the Japanese ambassador to the United States determines that is not the case, and makes no changes to the code.

May 7: Stalin is named Soviet premier by the *Politburo.* • The German vessel *München* is captured in the North Atlantic, with a complete cipher book on board. Two days later, Royal Navy divers will access a sunken German U-boat that includes an Enigma machine complete with rotor settings and another cipher book. These discoveries will lead the Allies to break the Enigma code and change the course of the Battle of the Atlantic for several months.

May 10: In a bizarre incident, third-ranking Nazi Rudolf Hess flies to Scotland solo and parachutes into British custody, claiming that he is there to negotiate peace with Britain. Hitler suggests that Hess has taken leave of his senses.

May 10–11: London is hit with its most intense *Luftwaffe* bombing raid of the war. Nearly 1,500 lives are lost, and landmarks such as the British Museum, House of Commons, and Westminster Abbey are badly damaged.

May 12: The British Army in North Africa, desperately short on materiel, is given a new lease on life when a British convoy reaches Alexandria, Egypt, with some 240 tanks and 40 Hurricanes.

May 14: Some 3,600 Jews are arrested and detained in Paris by the occupying Nazi Gestapo.

U.S. funds Soviet war effort Harry Hopkins, who was instrumental in developing the U.S. Lend-Lease program, was one of President Roosevelt's most trusted diplomatic advisers. In June 1941, Hopkins met with Winston Churchill, then went on a mission to Moscow. He carried a letter in which Roosevelt asked how the U.S. could most effectively "make available the assistance which the United States can render to your country in its magnificent resistance to the treacherous aggression by Hitlerite Germany...." Following negotiations, FDR extended up to $1 billion lend-lease credit to the Soviet Union.

U.S. arms the British Large quantities of U.S.-made Thompsons were purchased for the British Army in 1940–41, quickly filling the serious capability gap revealed during the *Blitzkrieg* of 1940. The Thompson M1 submachine gun—with a 20-round box magazine and a rate of fire of 700 rounds per minute—provided a useful short-range assault weapon for many combat and specialist troops. The M1 would be superseded by much lighter and cheaper submachine guns, including the American M3 "Grease Gun" and the British Sten Gun.

1941

May 15: Sigmund Rascher, a doctor, *Luftwaffe* captain, and associate of Himmler, requests permission to use Dachau prisoners as test subjects for his medical experiments. He will become known especially for his hypothermia experiments, which will take 300 lives.

May 15: Roosevelt places 11 French ships in U.S. ports under U.S. jurisdiction due to Vichy France's compliance with the Nazis.

May 19: In gratitude, and as an incentive to continue its cooperation and collaboration, Germany releases 100,000 French prisoners and reduces the reparations payments it has demanded from the Vichy government.

May 20: In a spectacular but costly air assault on Crete, Germans drop nearly 23,000 paratroopers and glider soldiers onto its northwest coast. While succeeding in taking the island, the German death toll will be unacceptably high. • The Nazi central office of immigration forbids any future emigration of French Jews.

May 22: Fearing that Germany will attempt to seize the strategically critical Azores, Roosevelt calls for U.S. military occupation of these Atlantic islands.

May 24: The British battleship *Prince of Wales* and the cruiser *Hood* encounter the German battleship *Bismarck* and cruiser *Prinz Eugen* in the Denmark Strait. A ferocious, 20-minute gun battle ensues, ending with the sinking of the *Hood* and the deaths of 1,416 crewmen.

May 27: President Roosevelt, noting that the struggle in Europe has become a "war for world domination," suggests that any German occupation of either the Cape Verde Islands or the Azores would threaten U.S. security and draw a commensurate response.

U.S. breaks Japan's Purple code This machine, constructed in 1940 by U.S. cryptanalysts, was used to read "Purple," the Japanese diplomatic code (not, it should be noted, the Japanese naval code). Purple offered millions of cipher combinations. The Japanese considered the system unbreakable, but they made the mistake of phasing it in gradually while still employing the previous "Red" code, which U.S. intelligence had been reading for some time. The overlap helped U.S. cryptanalysts break the Purple code and reproduce the machine, which employed telephone stepping switches rather than the more traditional rotor system. The cryptanalysts were hailed as "magicians," and the intelligence derived from reading Purple was known as "Magic."

Japanese barbarity Japanese troops execute Chinese civilians in a scene repeated countless times during the war. Japanese barbarity toward the Chinese stemmed from a sense of racial superiority, as well as frustration with persistent Chinese resistance to the occupation. Japanese soldiers commonly used live civilians, and Chinese and British prisoners of war, for bayonet practice. Officers decapitated prisoners for sport, even holding contests. One Japanese officer recalled that "if more than two weeks went by without my taking a head, I didn't feel right." An estimated 10 million Chinese civilians died at Japanese hands during the war.

American code-breaker Colonel William F. Friedman was the U.S. War Department's chief cryptanalyst, heading the team that broke the Japanese diplomatic ("Purple") code. Friedman was born in Russia, but his father immigrated to the United States to escape growing anti-Semitism when Friedman was still a child. A graduate of Cornell University, Friedman went to work for a Chicago research laboratory, where he became interested in codes and ciphers. He entered the Army in 1918 and is credited with introducing mathematical and scientific methodology to cryptology. His wife, Elizabeth, was also a gifted code-breaker and is buried next to him at Arlington National Cemetery.

1941

May 27: The battleship *Bismarck*, pride of the Nazi fleet, is sunk by British warships with most of its 2,000-man crew aboard.

May 31: Britain once again assumes control of Iraq following the implosion of its pro-Axis government.

June 1941: A series of attacks by Croatians against their Serbian countrymen in the newly created pro-Axis state of Croatia leaves hundreds dead.

June 1: Britain completes the evacuation of Crete.

June 2: Perhaps reevaluating his alliance with the inept Mussolini, Hitler declines to alert Mussolini of his plans to attack Russia when the two Fascist leaders meet at the Brenner Pass.

June 3: Hundreds of Jews are murdered, and their shops looted, in a series of riots in the streets of Baghdad.

June 6: Hitler issues his "Guidelines for the Conduct of the Troops in Russia." One provision, known as the *Kommissarbefehl*, calls for the execution of any captured Soviet commissars.

June 8–9: Free French and British forces drive deep into Syria.

June 11: Roosevelt agrees to send U.S. troops to man a British garrison in Iceland. The move will free a British division to be reassigned to a more critical war zone, without exposing U.S. troops to a combat situation.

June 12: In an agreement designed to strengthen the alliance, 14 Allied nations make a pact in which they agree to neither make nor honor separate treaties with any of the Axis nations.

June 14: Soviet foreign minister Molotov shrugs off intelligence indicating that Germany has Russia in its crosshairs, famously claiming that "only a fool would attack Russia."

German soldiers ready for action "The world will hold its breath and make no comment," declared Adolf Hitler as he ordered Operation Barbarossa. On June 22, 1941, German troops such as these—in top condition and high spirits—marched and rolled into Russia. Many Russian soldiers were killed or captured before they knew a war had started. Some, eager to escape Stalin's oppressive regime, actually welcomed capture. The jubilant Germans expected to capture Moscow, Leningrad, and the Caucasus very quickly and to destroy the Red Army within four months.

Timoshenko can't prevent onslaught Soviet Marshal Semyon Timoshenko was one of the few capable military commanders to survive Stalin's purges of the 1930s. When the Germans launched Operation Barbarossa, Stalin went into seclusion—some historians say into emotional collapse—for more than a week. In July 1941, Stalin appointed Timoshenko to replace Western Front commander D. G. Pavlov (who had been dismissed and executed). Although Timoshenko slowed the German offensive, he was unable to stop it. Stuck with the blame for the unpreparedness of Russian troops, Timoshenko was demoted from front-line command.

The fortitude of Soviet soldiers When Germany attacked, the Soviet army infantry was badly equipped, poorly trained, and demoralized by purges of its leadership. Russian troops were so severely battered by a string of military disasters that many Western military experts expected them to last only a few weeks. On July 3, 1941, Stalin made an emotional radio broadcast imploring his people to defend the mother country. German victory seemed so inevitable that Hitler made plans for reducing his forces. However, Russian resistance actually increased as equipment and territory were lost, and as large numbers of their soldiers were taken prisoner or killed. In August, a Red Army counteroffensive took Yelnya. The Germans also suffered heavy losses. That winter, the Russians gained heart from their stand before Moscow, and became convinced that they could stop the German juggernaut.

Stukas knock out Soviet tanks Puffs of smoke rise from Soviet tanks that were hit by German Stukas. Russia's large, well-equipped tank units were poorly maintained and usually operated by untrained crews. Since the Red Army artillery often lacked both ammunition and transportation to move their guns, ground air defenses were nearly nonexistent. In the early days of Germany's invasion, the *Luftwaffe* took a heavy toll on Russia's mechanized divisions. On the opening day of Operation Barbarossa, German planes also destroyed 2,000 Soviet aircraft, most of which were lined up on the ground in peacetime fashion, meaning neat, unprotected rows.

Lithuanians see Germans as liberators In late June 1941, Lithuanian women greet German troops with flowers. In the Baltic nations, as in other areas under Soviet rule, most people were eager to escape Stalinist oppression. Local citizens welcomed the Germans as liberators until they discovered that "Germanization" was even more brutal than "Sovietization." Some historians contend that if Hitler had understood the potential value of the initially enthusiastic civilian welcome, and encouraged it, he might have fomented rebellion against Stalin, and undercut Russia's ability to resist invasion.

1941

June 15: German high command instructs its warships to destroy submarines belonging to Russia. If caught, the Germans are told to claim to have mistaken the Soviets for Brits.

June 16: Rudolf Hess, still in British custody after his solo parachute trip to Scotland, breaks his leg attempting suicide on a flight of stairs. • The U.S. announces the expulsion of all Italian and German tourist and consular personnel, effective July 10.

June 17: Operation Battleaxe, a major Allied push to relieve besieged troops at Tobruk, Libya, fails.

June 19: Germany and Italy shutter U.S. consulates and expel diplomats.

June 22: German sentries murder their counterparts at the Russian border at Brest-Litovsk, touching off Operation Barbarossa, the largest army attack in world history. Three million German troops march into Russia along the entire 1,800-mile frontier. Though outnumbered by the Soviets, the Germans have the element of surprise.

June 23: The commander of the Russian bomber group takes his own life when the Soviets come out on the losing end of a wildly unbalanced dogfight, losing 500 planes while downing about 10 *Luftwaffe* aircraft. By the end of the week, the Soviet air force, the world's largest, will be down 2,000 planes and all but destroyed.

June 25: Roosevelt authorizes arms shipments to the Soviet eastern port of Vladivostok.

June 26–28: Finland, Hungary, Croatia, and Slovakia declare war on the Soviet Union.

June 30: After a series of catastrophic failures, Stalin orders the execution of the military leadership on the Soviet Union's western front.

AXIS ON THE ATTACK

JULY 1941–DECEMBER 1941

On July 3, 1941, a little more than a week after the German invasion of the Soviet Union, Joseph Stalin spoke for the first time to the Soviet people about the progress of the war. He called the citizens of his nation "brothers and sisters," a term he had never used before. It was an intimacy born of the terrible crisis they shared. Stalin admitted that the enemy had succeeded in breaking through, and he urged his compatriots to annihilate the intruders with every means possible. Many Soviet memoirs attest to the power of his words, which reached out to millions of citizens clustered around primitive radios or streetside loudspeakers. The Soviet people were urged to rouse themselves for what was to become the largest military contest of all time.

The Axis assault on June 22, 1941, had caught Soviet forces almost entirely unprepared. Finnish armies in the north, Romanian armies in the south, and a three-million strong German force between them drove forward at a relentless pace, encircling whole Soviet armies. On June 28, German forces reached the Belorussian capital of Minsk. Riga was captured three days later, and by the first week of July German armies were approaching the Ukrainian capital of Kiev. By late July, German bombers came within range of Moscow. By August 19, Leningrad—the Soviet Union's second largest city—was cut off by German and Finnish forces, though it could not be captured outright.

Soviet officers pushed their soldiers to make suicidal attacks on German positions, as Stalin insisted that death was better than surrender. Nonetheless, by September Axis troops had rounded up more than two million Soviet prisoners and destroyed much of the Red Army's tank and aircraft strength. By October 3, when Hitler flew back to Berlin to address the German people, he was confident that the Soviet dragon was killed "and would never rise again." German production plans for weapons were changed: Large numbers of aircraft and additional naval power were added for the coming confrontation with Britain and the United States. New models of tanks had, however, been ordered, as the Germans discovered that

Soviet tanks were superior to their own.

Hitler's changing strategic vision was a reaction to the increasing collaboration between the two Anglo-Saxon powers. Though President Roosevelt was constrained by a public opinion that was not yet prepared for full-scale belligerency, the United States had begun to give the British Empire extensive assistance. In December 1940, Roosevelt had introduced a program of aid for Britain. It was called Lend-Lease to give the impression that something eventually would be given back. In March 1941, the plan passed through Congress. So relieved was Churchill that he described Lend-Lease as "tantamount to a declaration of war."

At the same time, the U.S. Navy entered the great naval conflict in the Atlantic, where German submarines threatened the vital trade lifeline from North America to Britain. This conflict cost the Allies 5.6 million tons of shipping from September 1939 to March 1941. In April 1941, the U.S. Navy began to cover part of the western Atlantic Ocean, and in July it began anti-submarine air patrols from Newfoundland. Consequently, convoy shipping across the Atlantic became more successful.

The Anglo-American relationship was sealed in August 1941 when Churchill and Roosevelt met aboard the American cruiser *Augusta* at Placentia Bay off the coast of Newfoundland. There, Churchill sketched out a document, which would become known as the Atlantic Charter, for the two statesmen to sign. It was not an alliance, as Roosevelt neither wanted nor could make a formal commitment to American belligerency. Instead, it was a statement of common political intent made in the name of liberal democracy for the restoration of a world based on political freedoms, open trade, and the self-determination of peoples. In private, the two men also agreed to give all possible help to the Soviet Union, to warn Japan against further encroachments in the Far East, and to involve American forces more fully in the Atlantic battle.

The summer of 1941 marked the beginning of the mass murder of Europe's Jews. Between the outbreak of war and June 1941, Jewish populations under German control in Eastern Europe had been herded into ghettos, their valuables seized and their livelihoods destroyed. In occupied Western Europe, Jews were compelled to wear the distinctive yellow star, and their property was seized or handed over on unfavorable terms. But only with the invasion of the Soviet Union were Jews systematically murdered. Pre-1941 instructions to German security units, the *Einsatzgruppen*—and to units of the regular police—made it clear that they should kill all Jews. On the assumption that most partisan activity was Jewish-inspired, whole villages were destroyed and their inhabitants murdered by the German army as well as by the police and security units.

From June 1941, Nazi security forces in Russia did not spare Jewish women and children. At Babi Yar outside Kiev, more than 34,000 Jews were slaughtered. In Serbia and in western Poland, Jews were killed systematically. Hitler at last approved deportation for German Jews as well, and the first trainloads arrived in the East in October 1941. At some point, a decision was made to augment the continuing murder by police and security men with mass murder at extermination camps in occupied Poland.

The precise moment of this decision is unclear, but the camps were under construction beginning in autumn 1941 and the first gassing began at Chelmno in January 1942. In December 1941, Hitler told an assembly of party leaders in a closed session that global war signaled a final war to the death against the Jewish enemy. The mass killing that began in 1941 ended in 1945 with the estimated death of approximately six million European Jews. They were killed not only by German security forces, but by the *Wehrmacht*, locally recruited anti-Semitic militia, and the troops of Germany's allies.

Only some of this race war was evident to the West in 1941. The United States was much more concerned with the threat to security posed in East Asia and the west Pacific by the continued belligerence of

Japan. This was a crisis brought on by the German victories in Europe. Japan had used the opportunity presented by the defeat of France and the Netherlands, and the German threat to Britain, to pressure western colonial possessions in Southeast Asia. Japan coveted this area because it contained large reserves of vital raw materials—oil, rubber, and tin in particular—which were essential for the Japanese war effort.

The American reaction to continued Japanese aggression in China had been to impose a partial trade embargo in September 1940, but that only heightened Japanese determination to seize further economic resources. Japanese leaders began to argue that war with the United States was almost inevitable. The driving force behind Japan's strategy of southward expansion was its huge navy, which relied heavily on oil. To secure the northern perimeter of the Japanese empire, Japan signed a nonaggression pact with the Soviet Union in April 1941. In July, Japanese forces moved into southern Indochina. When the United States. responded to this threat by tightening the embargo, the Japanese army and navy agreed that unless diplomatic pressure could undo the economic stranglehold that Tokyo had anticipated, they would attack the United States, the Dutch, and the British Empire.

The Japanese war was not inevitable. However, once Germany had invaded the

Soviet Union and apparently removed the threat from Japan's northern frontier, the southward advance became an attractive option for the Japanese leadership. During all of 1941, the Germans viewed the idea that Japan would occupy the United States in the Pacific as a strategic bonus. The Germans, in fact, urged Japan to do so, promising the Japanese that they would join in war against the United States.

In September 1941, the Japanese armed forces presented Emperor Hirohito with a plan for war if the United States did not end the embargo through diplomatic agreement. The emperor favored a solution short of war, and for two more months negotiations continued between Japanese and American officials to find a formula for peace. American intelligence could read the Japanese diplomatic (but not naval) codes, and knew that war was a very strong possibility. When General Tojo Hideki became Japan's prime minister in October, he set a deadline of November 30 for negotiations. This deadline was intercepted and decoded by the Americans.

Meanwhile, the Japanese navy developed detailed operational plans to secure a Pacific perimeter to protect seizure of Malaya, the Philippines, and the Dutch East Indies. On November 26, U.S. secretary of state Cordell Hull sent a set

On August 14, 1941, U.S. president Franklin Roosevelt is welcomed aboard the *Prince of Wales* by British prime minister Winston Churchill at Placentia Bay, Newfoundland. There, the two leaders developed an Anglo-U.S. war strategy underlined by the principles of the Atlantic Charter, which eventually would become the United Nations Declaration.

of proposals to the Japanese negotiators that included the withdrawal of all Japanese forces from China and Indochina. Subsequently, it was suggested that if the Japanese would withdraw from southern French Indochina, they could buy all the oil they needed, but Japan insisted on war. A task force of six fleet aircraft carriers and accompanying warships approached the Hawaiian Islands. Undetected on the early morning of December 7, they attacked the U.S. Pacific Fleet stationed in Pearl Harbor, destroying or damaging more than 300 planes and eight battleships, and

In China, the long-running and ruthless Japanese campaign of conquest continued unabated. Here, Japanese troops assault Yichang on July 22, 1941. Japan's strategic successes in China subsequently enabled its forces to strike southwest into Indochina and south into the Pacific region.

killing more than 2,000 men. Roosevelt summoned Congress, which voted to declare war that same day.

The opening of a second major theater of war meant that even more of the world was engulfed in the conflict. Japan fought to achieve an Asian and Pacific new order, as Germany and Italy fought for domination in Europe and the Mediterranean. On December 11, Hitler declared war on the United States. Having planned for war with the U.S. since the 1920s, but not yet having built the warships for that conflict, he now had a navy on his side. War meant that German submarines could attack U.S. shipping without restriction. It also meant

that Germany—now aided by a powerfully armed Japan—could begin the contest for a world in which, in Hitler's warped mind, only German or Jew would triumph.

Hitler's ongoing war with the Soviet Union, however, was no sure thing. In December, Red Army divisions began a major offensive around Moscow to force back German armies that had been prevented from capturing the capital. Against German soldiers who were at the end of tired supply lines in cold weather—for which the Germans had not prepared—the Soviets made substantial progress. The German army had already been driven back at the southern end of the front in late November. Soon after the German defeat before Moscow, they also suffered a defeat at the northern part of the front.

This news thrilled Churchill, as did America's entry into the war. After Pearl Harbor, he telephoned Roosevelt, who told Churchill that Britain and America were "in the same boat now." His words were hauntingly ironic. A few days later, the British battleship *Prince of Wales*—which had transported Churchill to negotiate the Atlantic Charter—was sunk by Japanese naval bombers in the South China Sea.

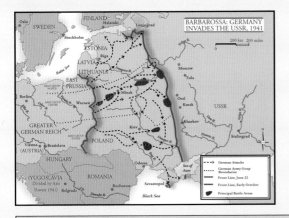

Map labels: Oslo, SWEDEN, FINLAND, Helsinki, Stockholm, Leningrad, ESTONIA, Baltic Sea, LATVIA, Riga, Moscow, LITHUANIA, Tula, EAST PRUSSIA, Berlin, ARMY GROUP NORTH, Minsk, Orel, ARMY GROUP CENTER, Warsaw, Kursk, USSR, Kharkov, GREATER GERMAN REICH, Kiev, ARMY GROUP SOUTH, Stalingrad, Vienna, Bratislava, POLAND, HUNGARY, (AUSTRIA), Odessa, Sea of Azov, (YUGOSLAVIA), ROMANIA, Divided by Axis Powers 1941, Bucharest, Sevastopol, Belgrade, Danube R., Black Sea

BARBAROSSA: GERMANY INVADES THE USSR, 1941
200 km   200 miles
0

German Attacks
German Army Group Boundaries
Front Line, June 22
Front Line, Early October
Principal Battle Areas

Operation Barbarossa At dawn on June 22, 1941, more than four million Axis soldiers (of whom at least three million were German), 3,360 tanks, and 7,000 artillery pieces—supported by 2,000 aircraft—stormed across the German-Soviet border. What Russia called the Great Patriotic War had begun. Initially, three German army groups—comprised of some 120 divisions—swiftly overwhelmed the Red Army's front-line defenses and struck deep into Soviet territory. However, despite the *Wehrmacht*'s early successes, Operation Barbarossa eventually proved to be Hitler's greatest strategic mistake, for he had badly underestimated the Soviet Union's military-industrial capability, its geography, and its environment.

1941

July 1: Riga, the capital of Latvia, is overwhelmed by a German occupation force.

July 2: The first member of the RAF's American Eagle Squadron to be killed in action dies in a midair collision over France. • The Japanese military bolsters its strength with a million-man draft.

July 2–3: German *Einsatzgruppen* (Special Action Groups), charged with the execution of Hitler's plan to exterminate Jews, murder 7,000 Jews in the Polish city of Lvov.

July 3: Stalin calls for a "scorched earth" defense, in which both the Red Army and ordinary Russian citizens would lay waste to the land as they retreat from the advancing Germans, leaving nothing to support the enemy troops.

July 5: Josip Broz Tito, Yugoslavia's Communist Party leader, calls for armed resistance against the German occupation.

July 6: Churchill sends a message to Stalin expressing the hope that the great powers can join forces to fight the German menace. • The occupying Nazis order the murder of 2,500 Jews in Kovno, Lithuania.

July 7: In relief of British troops, U.S. forces arrive in Iceland to defend the strategically located island.

July 7–8: More than 100 RAF Vickers Wellington bombers attack Cologne, Germany, causing widespread damage.

July 8: The RAF raids the German naval base of Wilhelmshaven. • The occupying Nazis decree that all Baltic Jews must wear identifying yellow Stars of David.

July 9: George Johnson Armstrong, a British naval engineer who offered his services as a spy to the Nazis while stationed in the United States, is executed for treason.

"Even the wives of the frontier guards were in the firing line, carrying water and ammunition, and taking care of the wounded. Some of the women were firing at the advancing Nazis...."

—Soviet general I. I. Fedyuninsky, on the early weeks of the German invasion of the Soviet Union

The fate of Soviet POWs The Belorussian city of Minsk fell to the encircling advances of the Second and Third Panzer Groups on June 28, 1941, just six days after the start of Operation Barbarossa. During that week, panzer units captured more than 200,000 Soviets. Here, large numbers of those prisoners are transported in railway coal trucks from Minsk to Poland, where they would be interned or possibly moved on to camps further west. Thereafter, they probably would be used as slave labor while routinely experiencing deliberate maltreatment and appalling living conditions. Two-thirds of all Soviet POWs would be worked, starved, or shot to death.

Fighting in the Ukraine In the Ukraine during the summer of 1941, Field Marshal Rundstedt's Army Group South had more difficulties than in the middle and north. The panzer groups fought their way across the sun-baked and seemingly endless Russian steppe. Soviet resistance held up the German advance. The Germans then struck behind the Red Army defending Kiev and surrounded them, capturing huge numbers of prisoners and equipment. Close-quarter fighting was typically carried out by the German infantry divisions. Assault engineer units that followed some days behind dealt with the many pockets of resistance that had been bypassed by the armored forces. German soldiers used flamethrowers (including this *Flammenwerfer* 35) extensively, particularly on bunkers and trench systems.

Japan's Need for Oil

Japan's desire for economic independence and the establishment of a commanding presence in East Asia required access to resources, particularly oil. On July 24, 1941, the quest to conquer these resources prompted Japanese forces to enter southern Indochina.

President Roosevelt reacted harshly, freezing Japanese assets and placing oil exports to Japan under restrictive licensing. From the Japanese perspective, the situation was untenable. At least 65 percent of Japan's petroleum products came from American firms. The embargo would paralyze the country economically and leave the military with only 18 months of oil from reserve oil stocks. Japan's military demanded that the government either obtain a diplomatic settlement that would preserve Japanese interests or step down so a new government could prepare for war. Time was critical. Under the American restrictions, Japan would grow weaker as the Allies grew stronger. If diplomacy failed, Japan must fight. Of course in the end, diplomacy did fail. Japan attacked Pearl Harbor on December 7, 1941, and the U.S. declared war on Japan the next day.

1941

July 10: Stalin demotes Marshal Timoshenko, the Red Army commander-in-chief, and assumes the position himself.

July 12: Representatives from Britain and the Soviet Union meet in Moscow to sign a mutual aid treaty.

July 16: About 600,000 Russians are trapped when the German army encircles the Soviet city of Smolensk.

July 22: With their supply lines stretched to the breaking point, German troops are forced to stop their progress through Russia for the first time in the campaign.

July 24: Nearly 4,500 Jews are murdered by Nazi *Einsatzgruppen* in the town of Lachowicze, Poland. • The Vichy French government hands southern Indochina over to the Japanese.

July 26: General Douglas MacArthur is called out of retirement by President Roosevelt to assume command of United States forces in the Far East.

July 31: In a memo to SS chief Reinhard Heydrich, Nazi *Reichsmarschall* Hermann Göring authorizes the "Final Solution" (complete annihilation) for Europe's Jews.

1941

August 5: German forces destroy Russia's 16th and 20th armies in the "Smolensk pocket." Germans capture more than 300,000 soldiers. • Romania kicks off the 73-day Siege of Odessa, which will end in October with the Romanian occupation of the Ukrainian city.

August 8: The Soviets suffer a crushing defeat at Roslavl, near Smolensk, as the Germans capture some 38,000 Russian prisoners of war.

August 10: Both Britain and the Soviet Union promise military aid to Turkey in the event that Germany pursues a policy of aggression against the Eurasian nation.

August 12: Roosevelt and Churchill announce the Atlantic Charter. • The Nazi occupation force in Romania requires all Jews to make themselves available for forced labor assignments.

August 13: Chungking, China, is largely in ruins after a week of bombing at the hands of the Japanese air force.

August 14: Josef Jakobs, a German spy, becomes the last person executed in Britain's legendary Tower of London.

August 16: Stalin accepts a joint proposal by the United States and Britain to meet in Moscow and develop a comprehensive plan on the aid that Britain and the U.S. will try to deliver to the Soviet Union.

August 17: Syracuse, Sicily, suffers an RAF bombing raid.

August 18: Hitler orders the remaining 76,000 Berlin Jews (out of an original 110,000) deported to Poland's ghettos.

August 24: In the Ukraine, Soviet forces mount an intense defense against German invaders.

Germans encircle Smolensk On July 15, 1941, a double breakthrough by Army Group Center's panzers cut off thousands of Soviet troops to the west of Smolensk and enabled the city's encirclement. Smolensk fell to an attack on July 16. Strong Soviet resistance continued in the pocket until August 5, by which time the Germans had captured some 310,000 prisoners, 3,205 tanks, and 3,120 guns. The fighting had been particularly intense, as evidenced in this photo by the weariness of the *Waffen-SS* "*Totenkopf*" (Death's Head) troops. Following their victory, the Germans paused for two weeks for reinforcement, regrouping, and maintenance.

1941

August 24: In response to domestic discontent, Hitler orders a stop to his policy of exterminating the mentally ill. Since the beginning of the war, more than 70,000 such people have died at the hands of the Nazis. The policy will be continued in a decentralized manner, with another 100,000 dying by May 1945. Thousands also will be killed in German-occupied areas.

August 25: Spitsbergen, a remote Norwegian island best known as a historical whaling center, becomes a strategic war base with the arrival of British commandos. • The Allies occupy Iran on two fronts, with the British marching in from the south and the Red Army from the north.

August 26: In a stunning execution of the "scorched earth" war strategy, the Soviets will blow up their Dnieper Dam, the largest in the world. • The U.S. unveils plans to send a delegation to meet with Chiang Kai-shek's Nationalist Chinese government to determine what assistance they need to battle Japanese imperialism.

August 27: German submarine *U-570* is improbably captured by an RAF Hudson plane that drops four depth charges, which prompt the submarine's crew to surrender.

August 28: Vichy France's antiterrorist laws lead to the execution by guillotine of three members of the French Resistance. • The Japanese government sends a memo to Roosevelt offering disingenuous assurances that Japan has no imperialist designs on any foreign nation.

August 30: The last rail supply route to Leningrad is blocked when German troops occupy Mga, Russian.

September: "Potato Pete," a British food ministry creation, launches a campaign that urges citizens to eat plenty of unrationed potatoes.

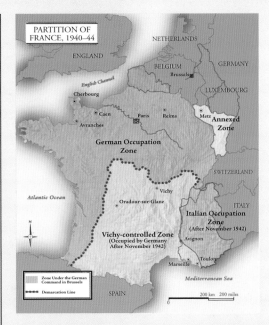

The divisions of France After France capitulated to the Germans on June 22, 1940, France was divided. The elderly Marshal Philippe Pétain headed an authoritarian, nationalistic, anti-Semitic, and non-Republican Vichy regime that over time collaborated extensively with the Germans. The remaining French armed forces were divided between Vichy and Charles de Gaulle's Free French, with the latter exiled and commanded from England. Eventually, on November 11, 1942, the Germans and Italians violated the terms of the 1940 armistice by occupying the whole of France.

Massacre at Babi Yar

On September 24, 1941, shortly after the Germans' successful 45-day battle for Kiev, Red Army engineers exploded a number of land mines that had been pre-positioned in key buildings in the city center. One of these was the Hotel Continental, in which the Germans had just established their headquarters. The devastation was enormous, with hundreds of German troops killed or severely injured and 25,000 Kiev residents left homeless.

Execution of Jews at Babi Yar

Even though the attack had been carried out by Russian soldiers, the German high command blamed the city's Jewish community, and ordered it to assemble for "resettlement" on September 29. These Jews, together with a number of Gypsies, were then marched away in groups into the nearby forests by troops of *Sonderkommando 4a* of SS *Einsatzgruppe* C along with Ukrainian militiamen. Over a two-day period, the groups arrived at Babi Yar, a ravine. There they were summarily shot and then buried in a huge pit. In total, some 34,000 Jews died at Babi Yar. Subsequently, the Germans stated that they had solved Kiev's housing problem by evacuating an "adequate number of apartments."

Far from condemning the atrocity, several non-SS senior officers applauded such actions. Among them was Field Marshal von Reichenau, commander of the German Sixth Army, who issued a directive emphasizing the need for his soldiers to "fully understand the need for severe but just atonement of the Jewish subhumans." While *Einsatzgruppen* would go on to execute hundreds of thousands of Jews during the war, Babi Yar was the largest individual massacre.

1941

September 1: The U.S. Navy's Atlantic Fleet assumes convoy protection in the North Atlantic from Iceland to Newfoundland. • Tokyo spars with Moscow over the inadvertent mining of a Japanese fishing boat off the coast of Vladivostok. The Japanese are enraged when Russia refuses to pay for the boat, insisting it would not have happened had the boat not been unacceptably close to Russia's shore.

September 3: Russian prisoners of war and Jews become the first victims of the poison gas Zyklon B, the newly preferred Nazi execution method, at Auschwitz.

September 5: The Soviet Union evacuates all children under age 12 from the capital of Moscow as German troops move toward the city.

September 7: French Resistance fighter Pierre Roche is executed by the Nazi occupation force.

September 7–8: Some 200 RAF planes mount the biggest air raid to date on Germany's capital of Berlin. The British will bomb the city for four solid hours overnight.

September 8: The German army places Leningrad in a state of siege. A desperate Stalin will ask Churchill for immediate military aid. The siege will last for 900 days. • Concerned that Russia may be harboring a homegrown population of Nazi sympathizers, Stalin exiles 600,000 Volga-area ethnic Germans to Siberia.

September 9: Iran surrenders to the Allies, agreeing, among other things, to deport Axis spies posing as diplomatic and tourist staff. Iran will order the "diplomats" and others out on the 13th.

Soviet partisans Soviet partisan groups were initially offshoots of the many Red Army units cut off by the German advance in 1941. However, being untrained in guerrilla warfare, they were very vulnerable. Moreover, their relentless suppression—often led by special SS counter-partisan units—was invariably brutal, usually culminating in collective reprisals and summary executions. However, such excesses actually boosted partisan recruitment. Beginning in 1942, the Soviet high command exerted better-coordinated political and military control over the partisans, whose operational significance increased from 1943. Although totalling as many as 700,000 and causing some 35,000 Axis casualties, their main impact was in the rear areas, where they disrupted communications, carried out raids and sabotage, gathered intelligence, and told the local population that the Soviet regime was coming back.

Hitler insists on autumn offensive
On September 30, 1941, Field Marshal Rundstedt's Army Group South advanced to seize Kharkov, cross the lower Don, and reach the Caucasus oil fields. In agreement with army chief of staff general Franz Halder, Hitler ordered Army Group Center and Army Group North to launch coordinated thrusts against Moscow and Leningrad. Although the German offensive in the South initially made some progress (pictured is the 37mm Pak 35/36 L/45 anti-tank gun in Kharkov), it was driven back at the end of November. In December, due to a disagreement with Hitler about the retreat in the South, Rundstedt was relieved of command.

Zhukov leads Soviet offensives In 1941 Stalin appointed Georgi Konstantinovich Zhukov chief of the general staff. In September, Zhukov assumed command of the Leningrad Front—just as the German advance halted. Then, as commander of the Western Front defending Moscow, he won a less ambiguous victory against Army Group Center, forcing a German withdrawal. He continued his offensive through the winter. Later, as deputy supreme commander to Stalin, Zhukov helped to oversee the Soviet battle for Stalingrad (1942–43), seized the strategic initiative at Kursk (1943), and directed part of the 1944–45 offensives into Poland and Germany—including the hard-fought capture of Berlin.

Britain dominates in Mediterranean
Upon becoming Britain's prime minister in 1940, Winston Churchill defied his admirals and wielded his considerable naval expertise against the Axis powers in the eastern Mediterranean. Under his leadership, British aircraft destroyed Axis U-boats as they surfaced to recharge their batteries. British warships, such as the tiny corvette HMS *Daisy* (*pictured*), were also remarkably successful at destroying submarines. Commissioned in October 1941, the *Daisy*'s service was distinguished but short. The ship foundered on January 2, 1942, while en route from Alexandra to Tobruk.

1941

September 11: A shoot-on-sight order is handed down to U.S. Navy ships running convoy protection operations on the seas. • Aviator and isolationist Charles Lindbergh delivers a speech in Des Moines, Iowa, in which he blames the deepening U.S. involvement in the European war on Britain, Roosevelt, and Jews.

September 16: The Russian front at Kiev collapses in the face of intense German pressure, and some 500,000 Soviets surrender. Kiev will officially fall to the Germans in two days. • Mohammed Reza Pahlevi takes the Shah's throne of British-occupied Iran when his father, Reza Khan, abdicates. • In an effort to quell partisan violence in the Soviet Union, German field marshal Wilhelm Keitel orders his troops to randomly execute 100 Russian civilians every time a civilian kills a German soldier.

September 17: At least one day too late, the Red Army high command orders its men to retreat from the city of Kiev.

September 18: Already suffering high casualties, the captured Russian troops in the surrounded region of Kiev begin to be summarily executed by the Germans. The Soviet death toll in defense of Kiev will top 350,000. • Japanese military leaders are instructed to prepare their troops for operations in the Pacific.

September 20: The Soviet Union receives advance notice of a German attack on Moscow, thanks to Britain's success in capturing and decoding Enigma encryptions.

September 22: A Ukrainian militia squad does the Nazis' dirty work, murdering 28,000 Soviet Jews near the town of Vinnitsa.

Americans help out in Iceland American soldiers stationed in Iceland needed heavy protective clothing against the freezing weather. In July 1941—months before the U.S. would officially enter the war—President Roosevelt sent troops to relieve British forces in Iceland. Soon after the Nazi occupation of Denmark in 1940, the British had moved into Iceland in order to keep northern sea lanes open. When British forces were badly needed elsewhere, U.S. troops took over the defense of the small country.

"Rats of Tobruk" In 1941, during the longest siege in British history, predominantly Australian troops defended the strategic Libyan seaport of Tobruk from forces led by German commander Erwin Rommel. William ("Lord Haw-Haw") Joyce, the British radio announcer who broadcast Nazi propaganda from Berlin, derisively described Tobruk's defenders as rats. Desperate but valiant Allied troops embraced the name, calling themselves the "Rats of Tobruk" as they tunneled to escape Axis bombing, launched daring and ruthless raids, and commandeered enemy weaponry, such as the antiaircraft gun pictured here.

The many uses of the M3 tank The M3 was the most important American light tank of the war, with more than 13,000 produced. First built in March 1941, it underwent numerous improvements. For example, the first model was riveted and the final was entirely welded. A gyrostabilizer was incorporated in 1941 to enable it to fire accurately while moving. The M3 was fast and mechanically reliable but lightly armored and armed. Allied armies employed it—thanks to Lend-Lease—in conditions ranging from the North African desert to Soviet snow and Pacific jungles. The tank was called the M3 or, unofficially, the Honey. Mine-exploder and flame-thrower versions were also made.

1941

September 23: Nazis murder the residents of the village of Krasnaya Gora in retaliation for the killing of three German soldiers by Russian resistance fighters.

September 24: German U-boats enter the Mediterranean for the first time, via the Strait of Gibraltar.

September 27: The United States launches the *Patrick Henry*, the first of more than 2,700 so-called Liberty ships. These are relatively inexpensive, quickly constructed merchant ships used to ferry war materiel from the United States to Europe. • About 100,000 Japanese troops are trapped when 11 Chinese divisions cut their escape route, turning the tide in the battle for Changsha, China.

September 28–30: In the largest German mass murder of the war, 34,000 Russian Jews are ordered to the outskirts of Kiev by a resettlement order, corralled, marched to the edge of the Babi Yar ravine, and shot.

September 29: Hitler issues a directive ordering Leningrad razed to the ground. He claims that the welfare of the city's three million residents is a problem that cannot be solved.

October 1: More than 3,000 Jewish residents of Vilna, Lithuania, are murdered by Nazi occupation forces.

October 2: Hitler launches Operation Typhoon, a plan to send the *Wehrmacht* into the Soviet capital of Moscow. • With most of the Jews of Paris either dead or deported, the Nazi Gestapo turns its eye toward the destruction of synagogues.

October 3: In a brash and, it will soon become apparent, premature speech delivered at the Berlin *Sportpalast*, Hitler claims that Russia is "broken and will never rise again."

Soviet citizens, industry relocate Operation Barbarossa gave the Germans control of 60 percent of the existing Soviet armaments industry, and up to 74 percent of its strategic resources and energy output. The Soviets needed to relocate much of their population and industry into the hinterland. More than 10 million people were evacuated or fled as refugees. In addition, 2,000-plus industrial plants were eventually reestablished in the Urals, Siberia, Kazakhstan, and other portions of Central Asia. Pictured is an electrochemical plant under construction at Chirchik, Uzbekistan. By late 1944, Soviet armaments production had more than doubled.

Children fight for Russia Although surprised by Germany's invasion in June 1941, Soviet Russia speedily mobilized to fight what was generally recognized to be a war of survival—Russia's "Great Patriotic War." Men, women, and children were soon fully committed to the war effort. Here, children train with replica weapons with adult military instructors. In Moscow, children conducted street patrols and enforced air raid precautions. In the occupied areas, they gathered intelligence, carried messages, and fought alongside the partisans. Their actions prompted a German order that any child found on a railway line was to be shot.

1941

October 3: Indian spiritual leader Mohandas Gandhi suggests that Indians should employ his passive resistance techniques to stymie the British war effort.

October 4: The United States and Great Britain agree to a regular monthly shipment of tanks and planes to the Soviet Union.

October 7: Some 17,000 Polish Jews from the town of Rovno are tortured and executed at the hands of the Nazi SS.

October 9: Claiming that adherence to the Neutrality Act is not possible when faced with the "unscrupulous ambitions of madmen," Roosevelt asks for congressional permission to arm the U.S. merchant fleet.

October 10: The vast majority of voters in the Grand Duchy of Luxembourg boycott a referendum calling for Germany's annexation of their small nation. • In a remarkable effort to maintain production during wartime, the Soviets continue a mass relocation of Moscow-area factories to locations in the East.

October 12–13: Nuremberg, Germany, withstands a large-scale, overnight assault by the RAF.

October 16: While Stalin remains, most Soviet officials flee Moscow, taking the body of a dead but well-preserved Lenin with them. The government relocates to the eastern city of Kuibyshev. • A massive defense perimeter, including more than 5,000 miles of trenches, is constructed around Moscow by a half-million Muscovites—mostly women, children, and old men. • Prince Konoe, prime minister of Japan, resigns. General Tojo Hideki will succeed him the following day.

The craft of sniping Sniping represented the ultimate professional challenge for an infantryman, as it required marksmanship and field-craft skills as well as initiative, judgment, and intelligent awareness. A single sniper—who targeted officers, other commanders, radio operators, and weapons specialists—could have a significantly detrimental impact upon an enemy's morale and operations. Here, a Soviet sniper steadies a Mosin 1891 rifle fitted with a telescopic sight. The Red Army also used female snipers. Although sniping was carried out by all sides, snipers risked being shot if caught, as the nature of their task often provoked exceptional anger among their opponents.

Grand mufti meets Hitler Grand Mufti Muhammed Amin al-Husseini (*left*)—an Islamic scholar, religious leader, and member of a powerful Palestinian clan—fought against Jewish immigration and the establishment of a Jewish state in the British Mandate of Palestine. In 1941 al-Husseini fled to Germany. Meeting with Hitler on November 28 (*seen here*) and other Nazi leaders, al-Husseini pushed to extend Germany's Jewish extermination program. Hitler promised him that all Jews in Palestine and elsewhere in the Middle East would be killed. Since Hitler intended to turn the area over to Mussolini, he would not announce support for Arab independence.

1941

October 17: The United States suffers its first military casualties when 11 sailors die aboard the torpedoed destroyer *Kearny*.

October 21: The Nazis retaliate for a series of attacks against Reich soldiers by Serbian partisans by massacring thousands of residents of Kragujevac.

October 23: Charles de Gaulle warns French partisans to stop attacking Germans, hoping that German reprisals will stop.

October 26–27: Some 115 bombers with the RAF attack Hamburg, Germany, during the overnight hours.

October 27: The Nazis test-drive a van designed to dispatch its occupants with engine exhaust. They will kill nearly 300 Polish Jews from Kalisz with this technique. • German *Einsatzkommandos* murder some 9,000 Lithuanian Jews, nearly half of whom are children.

October 30: Roosevelt extends a $1 billion loan to the Soviets under the provisions of the Lend-Lease Act. • After a month in which it rained incessantly, the Germans are forced to postpone their Moscow campaign while the ground dries out.

October 31: The Nazi SS commander in Estonia reports the successful extermination of essentially all Estonian Jews. • In a series of 45 strikes, the *Luftwaffe* "softens" the defenses of Moscow prior to a ground attack. • The United States loses its first ship in combat when the destroyer *Reuben James* sinks off the Icelandic coast, claiming the lives of 115 sailors.

November: Over the next month, some 11,000 Soviet civilians will starve to death during the Siege of Leningrad.

The tide turns at Rostov Despite the onset of October's mud and November's snow, panzers of Germany's Army Group South reached Russia's Don River on November 21, when Rostov fell. However, on November 30, Soviet Marshal Timoshenko's newly constituted Southwest Front counterattacked. Rostov was recaptured by Soviet troops (*pictured*), and the Germans were pushed back about 60 miles. Although not a catastrophic reversal, this was nevertheless Germany's first such enforced large withdrawal. It accompanied mounting German casualties, increasing logistic and maintenance problems, escalating partisan activity, and the full onset of Russia's winter. The Germans had not prepared for winter weather because they had assumed victory would be theirs within a few months.

Across the sea, corpses soaking in the water,
Across the mountains, corpses heaped upon the grass.
We shall die by the side of our lord.
We shall never come back.

—Verse from the Japanese Man'yōshū anthology of poetry, which was popular with Japanese servicemen

Japanese prepare for attack Crew members on a Japanese aircraft carrier cheer as their planes take off for Pearl Harbor on December 7, 1941. "As boys," one Zero fighter pilot later recalled, "we were told we should join the military when we grew up because that was the best way to bring honor to Japan." The plan to open war with the U.S. by attacking Pearl had been approved in mid-October. To train for the attack, mock-ups of U.S. warships were used by air squadrons to simulate level and dive-bombing on moving and fixed targets. All was ready by mid-November 1941.

Japanese strike Ewa station first U.S. Marines armed with Springfield 03 rifles look skyward for Japanese planes at Ewa Marine Corps Air Station southwest of Pearl Harbor on December 7, 1941. Ewa came under air attack about two minutes before the main enemy raid struck Pearl Harbor. Eighteen to 24 enemy fighters descended to within 25 feet of the ground to strafe the base. They destroyed 33 out of 49 U.S. aircraft on the ground and damaged the remainder.

Attack on Pearl Harbor

At 8.00 a.m. on Sunday, December 7, 1941, nearly 200 Japanese carrier-borne aircraft attacked Pearl Harbor in Hawaii. Although the possibility of an air attack on Pearl Harbor had been discussed for years, the defenders were indeed surprised. U.S. Pacific Fleet Admiral Husband Kimmel and Lieutenant General Walter Short (Hawaii's army commander) had considered an attack strategically pointless. Nevertheless, radar had detected the approaching enemy aircraft, and a Japanese submarine had been attacked outside the harbor, but these warnings went unheeded.

The first wave of the attack inflicted terrible damage to the airfields and to a half-dozen ships—most notably the *Arizona*, *Oklahoma*, and *California*—before departing at about 8:30 a.m. Thirty minutes later, another 170 aircraft attacked, concentrating on previously undamaged ships. This wave lost 20 planes to antiaircraft fire before its departure at 10 a.m. signaled the end of the raid. American casualties included 21 ships damaged or sunk (all but three would be salvaged) and 3,600 men killed or wounded.

Fortunately for the fleet, its especially precious ships, the aircraft carriers, had been away. The *Enterprise* and *Lexington* were delivering aircraft to Wake and Midway islands, and the *Saratoga* was being repaired on the West Coast. Moreover, the Japanese task force commander, Admiral Nagumo, had not sent in a third wave to destroy Hawaii's huge oil tanks and repair facilities. The attackers lost 29 aircraft and five midget submarines.

Though the assault was a tactical success, strategically it was a disaster. President Roosevelt's depiction of it as an "unprovoked and dastardly attack" reflected the mood of the American public. According to Roosevelt's critics, he allowed the attack to occur (in order to justify his desire to enter the war) by withholding warning information from Kimmel and Short. The balance of evidence still refutes this theory as well as the arguments that Churchill withheld information about the imminent attack.

Pearl Harbor engendered a lasting desire to apportion blame. Afterward, Kimmel and Short were relieved of command and condemned by a commission of inquiry for dereliction of duty.

The Pearl Harbor attack led to the merging of the aggressive wars of Japan and Germany and the involvement of the United States in a global war. The cry "Remember Pearl Harbor" resonated throughout the war, as well as in postwar American foreign policy.

Attack on Pearl Harbor At 8 a.m. on Sunday, December 7, 1941, the first wave of 353 carrier-based Japanese bombers and other combat aircraft struck the U.S. Pacific Fleet's base in Hawaii. The U.S. naval and military garrison was almost completely surprised, and the devastation was extensive. Japan's dramatic entry into the Second World War was a remarkable strategic accomplishment, notwithstanding its political repercussions, the adverse propaganda, and the absence of the U.S. aircraft carriers from Hawaii that day.

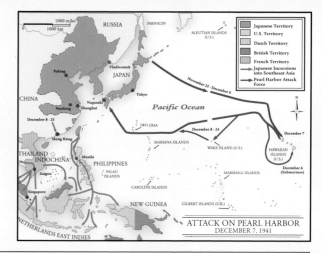

ATTACK ON PEARL HARBOR
DECEMBER 7, 1941

1941

November 3: As tensions mount between the U.S. and Japan, American women and children leave Guam, Wake, and Midway Islands.

November 6: The U.S. National Academy of Sciences reviews the technology behind the invention of fissile nuclear weaponry and calls for the immediate development of the atomic bomb. • Japan's military command prepares for planned attacks throughout the East Indies and South Asia, including Thailand and the Philippines.

November 7: Stalin rallies his war-weary subjects with his inspirational "Mother Russia" speech, recalling the heroics of great Russians from years past.

November 9: Working off intercepted intelligence information, the Royal Navy destroys two Italian shipping convoys.

November 10: Underscoring his commitment to Britain's partnership with the United States, Churchill insists he will declare war "within the hour" if Japan and the United States engage forces.

November 14: The British aircraft carrier *Ark Royal* sinks two days after being torpedoed in a German U-boat attack. The crippled ship is making its way back to England from its post off the coast of Gibraltar when it finally goes down. • The beleagured city of Leningrad gets a lifeline with the first airlift of supplies.

November 17: Congress allows for the arming of merchant ships with its repeal of key sections of the Neutrality Act, a move that Roosevelt lobbied hard to achieve. • The Japanese high command signs off on Admiral Yamamoto's plan to bomb Pearl Harbor.

1,177 die in *Arizona* bombing The USS *Arizona*, whose wreckage is pictured, was commissioned by the Navy in October 1916. It was docked on "Battleship Row" in Pearl Harbor on December 7. Minutes after the attack began, the *Arizona* was hit by a 1,760-pound armor-piercing bomb. The explosive penetrated the deck and ignited more than a million pounds of gunpowder, tearing the ship apart and killing 1,177 of the crew. A sailor on another ship saw the *Arizona* "jump at least 15 or 20 feet...upwards in the water and sort of break in two."

HORRIFIED

When that big bomb blew up and they put the fire out, I looked down in that big hole that went down three or four decks. I saw men all blown up, men with no legs on, men burned to death, men drowned in oil, with oil coming out of their eyes and their mouth and their ears. You couldn't believe it was happening. You could see it in front of your eyes, but you couldn't believe it. Here it was, a beautiful day—a beautiful Sunday morning—and you see everything blowing up and ships sinking and men in the water. And you think, we're at peace with the world. This can't be happening.

—Seaman Second Class Eddie Jones,
USS *California*

Volunteers come to the rescue On the morning of December 7, an alarm sounded across Oahu directing all civilian shipyard workers to report to Pearl Harbor, even as the battleships were still under attack. One group of civilians under the direction of Julio DeCastro, on board the USS *Oklahoma*, was credited with saving the lives of 32 crewmen trapped in the ship's hull. Many other civilians, both men and women, worked for hours fighting fires on the ships and docks. One civilian, George Walters, was cited for risking his life by running a crane up and down its tracks, shielding three battleships from enemy fire.

1941

November 17: Lewis Clark Grew, the U.S. ambassador to Japan, sends a message to U.S. secretary of state Cordell Hull. He emphasizes the need "for guarding against sudden military or naval actions by Japan in areas not at present involved in the China conflict."

November 18: Operation Crusader, the first British counteroffensive launched on the North African front, pits seven British divisions against 10 divisions of Axis soldiers.

November 19: In the biggest battle of the West African desert to date, British commandos raid Rommel's headquarters but fail to kill him as planned.

November 20: Japan issues an ultimatum to the United States, demanding American noninterference in Japanese relations in Indochina and China. Roosevelt will submit an equally unlikely program for peace in the Pacific.

November 24: Rommel makes one last unsuccessful attempt to outflank the British, while the Allies capture the key supply depot of Gambut, Libya. • Congress approves an expansion of the Lend-Lease Act to include French who are not living under Nazi rule.

November 25: The Axis renews the Anti-Comintern Pact for five years. Signatories include Italy, Japan, Spain, Croatia, Bulgaria, Romania, Hungary, Slovakia, Denmark, Finland, Manchukuo, and Japan's puppet government in Nanking. • Nearly 860 sailors die when the British battleship *Barham* sinks off the coast of Crete after being torpedoed by a German U-boat.

B-17s caught in line of fire On the morning of December 7, 12 unarmed B-17s were on a mission to the Philippines as part of the American effort to build up that area's defenses in the hope of deterring a Japanese attack. The planes' crew members planned to stop in Hawaii for refueling and the mounting of their guns. Chillingly, they did not realize that they were on a collision course with the Japanese attack force. The B-17s arrived at Oahu during the attack and had to dodge enemy and American antiaircraft fire. Miraculously, even though they were strafed by gunfire that wounded crew members, all of the B-17s landed intact except for the one pictured here. Although it split in half, its crew survived the landing.

1941

November 26: The Japanese Hawaii task force leaves the Kurile Islands, bound for Pearl Harbor, Hawaii. Later in the day, in a note to the Japanese ambassador, U.S. secretary of state Cordell Hull demands the complete withdrawal of all Japanese troops from China. Japanese prime minister Tojo will refer to this as "an ultimatum."

November 27: With the fall of Gondar, Ethiopia, the 350,000-man Italian army has been routed by about 20,000 Allied troops, marking the final stand of Italy in East Africa. • Believing that Japan is likely to attack within a matter of days, the United States military is placed on high alert.

December 1: In a unanimous vote, Japanese leaders officially endorse plans to enter the war against the United States.

December 4: Britain calls for unmarried women, ages 20 to 30, to serve in public service jobs, primarily on the home front.

December 5: At the end of a massive Russian campaign that has seen the elimination by death or injury of more than 750,000 Axis soldiers, Hitler calls for a temporary halt in the offensive. • In the interest of protecting wartime intelligence, U.S. naval facilities throughout Asia are ordered to destroy almost all documents and communications codes.

December 6: General Zhukov launches a successful counterattack around Moscow, pushing back the cold and starving German troops. It is the *Wehrmacht*'s first major defeat. • Roosevelt promises more than adequate funding for an atomic bomb research project.

December 6: British sailor John Capes makes a miraculous escape from the submarine *Perseus*, which had been sunk by a mine. Despite injuries, he ascends from a depth of 170 feet and swims to the Greek coastline. • Britain declares war on Finland, at the request of the Soviet Union. • Citing his doubt that Japanese troops in Indochina are there for defensive purposes, Roosevelt asks Emperor Hirohito to withdraw his forces.

Japan bombs naval yard in Philippines Flames rise from the Cavite Naval Yard in Luzon, Philippines, following a Japanese bombing raid on December 10, 1941. Japanese air superiority had been assured two days earlier when their planes caught much of the U.S. Far East Air Force, including a number of valuable B-17 bombers, on the ground at Clark Field. The Japanese followed with multiple landings on Luzon and later Mindanao. Deprived of his airpower and facing multiple enemy advances, U.S. general Douglas MacArthur abandoned plans to defend all of Luzon. On December 23, he ordered his forces to withdraw to the Bataan Peninsula for what would turn out to be their final stand.

The Philippines

Home to 17 million people in 1941, the Philippine Islands had been dominated by regional foreign powers since the third century A.D. European control arrived with the Spanish in the 1500s and lasted until 1898, when the islands were ceded to the United States following the Spanish-American War.

Possession of the Philippines placed the United States along crucial trade routes between Japan, China, and the oil-and mineral-rich regions to the south. Manila Bay on the island of Luzon was the finest natural harbor in the Far East.

During the 1930s, U.S. military planners correctly assumed that the islands would be a prime enemy objective in any war with Japan. U.S. defense plans, code-named "Orange," went through several versions over the years. They essentially called for American and Filipino forces to hold out against a Japanese invasion until the U.S. fleet could steam to the rescue. Anticipating this strategy, the Japanese called for attrition attacks on the U.S. fleet as it passed through imperial possessions in the central Pacific. Theoretically, the remainder of the American fleet would then be destroyed in battle off the Philippines.

By 1939, U.S. planners were backing

American and Filipino soldiers in Luzon, Philippines

away from Orange. Any war with Japan would clearly be part of a wider conflict, presumably involving Germany. The feasibility of projecting sufficient force 5,000 miles across the Pacific in the event of a two-front war was questionable at best. A new plan, Rainbow 5, conceded it might be necessary to abandon the Philippines. Meanwhile, Japanese plans also changed. In October 1941, Japan abandoned a reactive naval engagement in favor of an offensive strike against the U.S. Pacific Fleet at Pearl Harbor with a simultaneous invasion of the Philippines.

Rainbow 5 notwithstanding, the stunning Japanese success at Pearl Harbor on December 7, 1941, made relief of the Philippines a military impossibility. Not until October 1944 did U.S. forces finally return to wrest control of the islands from Japan.

1941

December 7: Hitler issues the "Night and Fog" decree, calling for the convenient disappearance of anyone who threatens the security of Nazi Germany. • Japanese planes attack American ships and planes at the U.S. base at Pearl Harbor, Hawaii. More than 2,300 American sailors and soldiers are killed.

December 8: Hitler acknowledges that the Soviet campaign will be neither quick nor easy. • Calling December 7 a "day that will live in infamy," Roosevelt calls for a congressional declaration of war on Japan. • Japanese troops occupy Shanghai, China, and capture a small U.S. garrison.

December 10: Britain's naval force is dealt a heavy blow when the Japanese sink the battleship *Prince of Wales* and the battle cruiser *Repulse*. • Guam quickly capitulates when overwhelmed by 6,000 Japanese troops.

December 11: Germany and Italy declare war on the United States. Congress responds by declaring war on those two nations.

December 13: The American policy of preventive internment is launched with the confinement of nearly 600 Japanese and 200 Germans.

December 16: Japanese troops land on Borneo in Southeast Asia.

December 17: Admiral Chester Nimitz is appointed commander of the U.S. Navy's Pacific Fleet.

December 19: Hitler himself becomes commander-in-chief of the German army, replacing Walther von Brauchitsch. • Amending the Selective Service Act, the U.S. Congress requires all men ages 18 to 64 to register. Those 20 to 44 are eligible for military service.

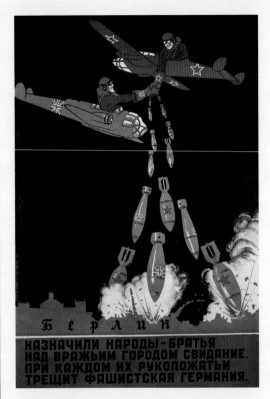

Soviet-British alliance The Soviet Union began the war as a virtual ally of Germany, due to the Soviet-German nonaggression pact. But Operation Barbarossa changed this situation completely. The Kremlin rarely promoted publicly the contribution of its Anglo-U.S. allies to the defeat of Germany, as it directed most of its propaganda to self-promotion and to motivating the Russian people. Nevertheless, this 1941 poster recognizes Britain's involvement in the war. It was produced when the Soviet Union was particularly dependent upon receiving large quantities of Anglo-U.S. war materiel to fight the "Great Patriotic War."

Allied Aid to Russia

In June 1941, the British stood alone in their fight against Germany. The United States had not yet entered the war, France had fallen to the Nazis a year earlier, and Italy had partnered with Germany in the fight to control Europe and North Africa. When the Nazis broke their alliance with the USSR by invading Russia on June 21, the British were quick to accept the Soviets as an ally in their fight against Germany. While many skeptics in Britain questioned the Soviet Union's intentions, they had little choice in their support. The Soviets provided much-needed assistance.

President Franklin Roosevelt also recognized the importance of nurturing the relationship with the USSR. The Lend-Lease Act, which authorized the U.S. to sell, exchange, or trade $50 billion in war materials to its Allies, did not include the USSR when it was passed in March 1941. It was not until November 7, 1941, that Congress finally declared the Soviets eligible to receive materials through the Lend-Lease Act.

Almost $11 billion worth of war materials were shipped to the USSR during the war, including combat aircraft, tanks, trucks, and jeeps. These supplies were especially needed at the beginning of the war when the Soviets did not yet have the ability to manufacture sufficient amounts of war materials. The United States and Britain also gave food and clothing through the Russian War Relief and the Red Cross.

British women selling flags to aid USSR

To avoid capture by German or Japanese troops, much of the Soviet aid was shipped via the Persian Gulf and Iran. Most of the remaining supplies were transported across the Pacific Ocean to Vladivostok and the North Atlantic to Murmansk.

When the end of the war was near, Soviet leader Joseph Stalin acknowledged the importance of Allied aid. "Lend-Lease," Stalin said, "is one of Franklin Roosevelt's most remarkable and vital achievements in the formation of the anti-Hitler alliance."

Japan takes Hong Kong Japanese infantrymen engage in the fight for Hong Kong in December 1941. Though British strategists originally considered Hong Kong too isolated to defend, they hoped that a show of force in 1941 would deter Japanese aggression and preserve British control of the colony. This effort to save face proved to be a miscalculation. Elements of the

Japanese 38th Division attacked on December 8. With the advantage of air and artillery superiority, veteran Japanese troops quickly overwhelmed the British defenders. Governor Sir Mark Young surrendered the colony on Christmas Day, 1941. Many Japanese atrocities followed.

1941

December 20: The soon-to-be legendary pilots of the U.S. Air Force Flying Tigers engage in their first combat mission, dominating their Japanese counterparts in the skies over Kunming, China.

December 22: The 23-day Arcadia Conference begins in Washington, D.C. The United States and Britain agree that defeat of Germany is their No. 1 objective. They also agree to combine military resources under one command.

December 23: With the United States officially among the world war belligerents, American military leaders hold their first joint war council with the British. They create the Combined Chiefs of Staff to craft Allied strategy. • The last American base in the Pacific between Hawaii and the Philippines is lost with the Japanese conquest of Wake Island. • American and Filipino officials evacuate Manila. • The Japanese take Jolo Island, the capital of the Philippines' Sulu province.

December 25: India's Congress Party offers its support to Britain, causing Mohandas Gandhi to resign his leadership post in protest. • Britain surrenders Hong Kong to Japan.

December 30: Most of Borneo falls to the Japanese.

Japan's potent Zero-sen When the Japanese naval air force became engaged in the conflict, first against China in 1937 and then in December 1941 against the Western allies, its opponents were shocked by the superior quality of its aircraft. Typical of these was the pictured Mitsubishi Zero-sen (Zeke), which entered service in 1940. A light, highly maneuverable, and well-armed fighter, the Zero outclassed Allied fighters in the Pacific Theater in 1941. It maintained its technological edge into 1942, when design weaknesses such as its light armor protection and non-self-sealing fuel tanks made it increasingly vulnerable to the new types of Allied fighters.

Germans unprepared for winter As autumn 1941 drew to a close on the Eastern Front, mud froze solid—as did most lubricating oils. Many vehicles, weapons, and equipment became useless. For Germans soldiers, winter clothing was not generally available, as the high command had confidently planned for Barbarossa to conclude within four months. Soldiers began to suffer respiratory diseases, and sentries literally froze to death. Frostbite and cold-burn injuries escalated in -40°F temperatures. Meanwhile, increasingly erratic deliveries of food, fuel, and ammunition via overextended supply lines affected operations and morale alike.

Canadian escorts From September 1939, convoys left Nova Scotia for Great Britain every eight days. The escorts were usually comprised of a large British warship (*pictured*) and two Canadian destroyers. At about longitude 20° west, the escort group handed the convoy to escorts from Britain, then usually took a westbound convoy to Halifax. Though the Royal Canadian Navy began the war with just six destroyers and five minesweepers, it expanded to more than 40 times its original size and contributed immensely to the Battle of the Atlantic.

THE AXIS SMASHES FORWARD

JANUARY 1942–JULY 1942

On February 15, 1942, the British Empire suffered one of its most humiliating defeats. At 6:15 p.m., in a makeshift conference room in the Ford Motor Company factory in Singapore, General Arthur Percival surrendered the island to Lieutenant General Yamashita Tomoyuki. The Japanese made the island the headquarters of the Southern Army, which conquered Southeast Asia, and renamed Singapore "Shonan," meaning "Light of the South." Of the 50,000 white troops captured, 18,000 would die of disease and/or mistreatment before war's end.

The Japanese armed forces aimed to capture a broad area in the south. They would defend the perimeter while the rich resources of the region were incorporated into the Japanese war effort. Resistance was limited. In the Dutch East Indies, the 140,000-man colonial army was overwhelmed. The northern Philippines, with a mixed native and American force, was quickly overrun except for the Bataan Peninsula, where 100,000 soldiers and refugees were bottled up. The Japanese captured the peninsula in

April. The American headquarters in the fortress of Corregidor, in Manila Bay, fell on May 6, 1942, after a fierce defense. By early June, nearly all American forces in the Philippines had surrendered. Further west, a Japanese force overran Burma and entered the capital, Rangoon, on March 8. A Japanese aircraft carrier raided the northern Australian port of Darwin on February 19, and in April Japanese aircraft sank British shipping on the Indian coast.

This was the limit of Japanese expansion, though the assault had been so successful and rapid that senior commanders sought to capitalize on their advantage with further advances. In early May, a naval force sailed south to seize the southern peninsula of New Guinea while Admiral Yamamoto planned a mid-Pacific offensive. This was designed to destroy what was left of U.S. naval power in the ocean and cut off American aid to the South Pacific.

The prelude to the final Japanese assault was the seizure of Port Moresby in southern New Guinea. The task force that was dispatched south in early May was attacked by a small Allied force in the Coral Sea. The battle was a strategic setback for Yamamoto, who was obliged to abandon his plan to seize Port Moresby and isolate Australia. This was the first hint that Japanese expansion was nearing its limit. A month later, Yamamoto dispatched a huge task force to Midway Island, hoping to lure what was left of the U.S. Pacific Fleet to battle and then annihilate it. With a small force of carriers and sufficient secret intelligence on Japanese intentions, the Pacific Fleet commander, Admiral Chester Nimitz, planned a daring interception. As the Japanese carrier fleet neared Midway, it was attacked by American dive-bombers. Only a few of their bombs struck, but they sank all four fleet carriers. Yamamoto ordered a return to Japan. His plans had been frustrated by America's intelligence successes, astute leadership, combat skills, and luck.

Elsewhere, the global war remained balanced on a knife edge. China's long, drawn-out conflict with Japan had become a formal state of war on December 9, 1941, following Pearl Harbor. Although the Japanese army controlled much of eastern and northern China, Chinese hit-and-run tactics made it difficult for Japan to pacify and control even those areas under occupation. In May 1942, Japanese commanders embarked on a ruthless policy of pacification—"kill all, steal all, burn all"—

Japan's capture of the island fortress of Singapore in February 1942 shocked Britain and other European colonial powers. The unthinkable had happened: What had been generally regarded as a second-rate Asiatic power had comprehensively defeated and humiliated the military forces of one of the world's greatest empires.

to try to deter further Chinese resistance. Roughly 250,000 Chinese were killed in 1942.

In North Africa, British Empire forces based in Egypt had moved forward successfully across Libya against weak Italian resistance. But in January 1942, against an Axis force strengthened by a German corps under General Erwin Rommel, the British Empire Forces began a long retreat back to Egypt. Tobruk fell to the Axis on June 21, and by the end of June Axis forces were a few miles from El Alamein, Egypt, within striking distance of the Suez Canal.

The British position at sea—in the Mediterranean and the Atlantic—remained precarious. In 1942 they lost 7.8 million tons of shipping. Britain was able to import only one-third of what it took in before the war. The Allies' persistent bombing of German naval installations and submarine building sites achieved almost nothing.

The most dangerous situation remained in the Soviet theater. With the successful defense of Moscow in December 1941, the Soviets launched further offensives, trying to find a weak spot in the German line. In the south, the Red Army created a large salient in German defensive lines south of Kharkov. But when Stalin ordered the Red Army to capture the city in May 1942, the German front first absorbed the attack and then encircled and annihilated the attackers. In the Crimea, the Germans successfully repulsed a Soviet counteroffensive on the Kerch Peninsula. In July, they captured Sevastopol after an assault with the world's largest artillery piece: "Big Dora."

Germany's central ambition was the final defeat of the Soviet Union in 1942. Hitler planned to attack the less well-defended southern front toward the Volga River and the Caucasus oil fields. Their capture would give his forces huge new oil supplies and deny them to the enemy. On June 28,

Germany launched Operation Blue with substantial success. The Soviet southern front retreated. So successful was the assault that Hitler divided the force in two. He sent the Sixth Army, under General Friedrich Paulus, to seize Stalingrad and cut the Soviet Union off from the resources of the south. By August, German forces had reached the oil city of Maikop and were advancing toward the rich oil fields around Grozny.

In midsummer 1942, the war was poised in the balance. The strategic dream of the Axis powers was to link up in the Middle East. They would seize the Suez Canal and the oil that lay beyond it from one side, and they would sweep down from the Caucasus on the other side. With Japan threatening India and the United States not yet fully armed, the ambition seemed less fantastic at the time than it now appears. Yet the summer of 1942 saw the high-water mark of Axis aggrandizement. Over the next year, the Allies would find not just greater resources but also more effective ways of fighting. They were poised to reverse the long series of defeats that had until then littered their war effort.

1942

January: In a directive that is important for troop morale, British General Claude Auchinleck reminds his Eighth Army that Erwin "Desert Fox" Rommel is an ordinary, though successful general, and not an invincible, supernatural force.

January 1: The United Nations is born from an agreement among 26 Allied nations not to make separate peace with the signatories of the Tripartite Pact. • Auto dealerships across the United States close their doors after steel conservation measures force a moratorium on new car and truck sales. • Twenty-three Czech partisans are murdered by the Nazi occupation force on suspicion of sabotage.

January 2: The rampaging Japanese army occupies the Philippine capital of Manila.

January 3–12: China emerges victorious in a battle for Changsha, Hunan. The Chinese drive some 70,000 Japanese troops into full retreat.

January 4: New Japanese bases in Thailand are now operational.

January 6: Washington and London announce plans to station American troops in Britain to help further Allied military goals in Europe. • In a victory that is Britain's first against German troops in this war, the Eighth Army routs a division of Rommel's Panzer Corps, inflicting nearly 40,000 casualties.

January 10: The Japanese launch a propaganda war in the skies over the Philippines, dropping leaflets on Allied troops that press for their surrender.

January 11: Japan invades the Celebes Islands, part of the Dutch empire, and declares war on the Netherlands. • Japan continues its campaign of conquest with the seizure of the Malaysian capital of Kuala Lumpur.

Borneo falls to Japan Japanese infantry go on the assault in British Borneo. Mountainous and heavily jungled, with a limited network of roads, Borneo was strategically important due to its position on the main routes between Japan and Malaya. It also offered large supplies of oil and raw materials to the resource-starved Japanese (though for Japan to successfully transport oil along shipping lanes that would see increased Allied activity would be difficult). For the moment, though, the possibility of Japanese access to additional oil was unappealing to the Allies. British strategists had long realized that Borneo could not be held. Nevertheless, the only Allied ground unit on Borneo, an outnumbered Indian battalion of the 15th Punjab Regiment, managed to resist for 10 weeks before it was overwhelmed.

1942

January 12: The Inter-Allied Conference meets in London and resolves to try Axis officials with war crimes at the end of the conflict.

January 13: The first 700 of 10,000 Polish Jews from the city of Łódź scheduled for "resettlement" are shipped to the newly established Chelmno death camp in Poland. • The Germans launch Operation Drum Roll, a U-boat offensive along the American East Coast.

January 14: American and British war planners, meeting in Washington, D.C., agree to focus on Hitler's defeat before turning their attention to Japanese domination in the Pacific. • Nearly 2,000 European companies with Axis interests are barred from doing business with any American entity, public or private. • The tanker *Norness*, flying Panamanian colors, is torpedoed off North Carolina's Cape Hatteras. It is the first ship attacked off the U.S. East Coast by a German U-boat.

January 20: At the Wannsee Conference in Berlin, the Nazis draw most German government agencies into the European portion of the "Final Solution" for the Jews. Reinhard Heydrich suggests that they should be worked to death, and those that don't succumb should be executed. • Facing a certain threat by Japan, Churchill calls on British troops to defend Singapore "to the death."

January 21: Rommel shocks his British foes by directing his *Afrika Korps* in a tactical about-face. He launches an offensive in Libya that will see him regain lost territory almost immediately.

January 22: The Soviets begin the evacuation of hundreds of thousands of people from the besieged city of Leningrad.

JAPANESE CONQUEST OF SOUTHEAST ASIA, 1941–42

A string of victories Soon after Pearl Harbor, Japanese forces invaded Thailand and Malaya. Landings also took place in the Philippines, North Borneo, and the Dutch East Indies. On December 26, the fall of Hong Kong ended an 18-day Japanese onslaught. During January 1942, Manila and Kuala Lumpur were occupied and the Solomon Islands invaded. From February to April, the British stronghold of Singapore fell, and Japanese landings were made at Bali, Mindanao, and Dutch New Guinea. Then, just as the overextended Japanese forces sought to consolidate their newly won territories, a series of U.S. victories from May to August—in the Coral Sea, at Midway, and at Guadalcanal—finally reversed the strategic situation.

Evacuation of Singapore Women and children arrive in Britain after evacuating from Singapore. Confident of the impregnability of the fortress and fearful of creating a panic, British authorities waited too long to begin the mass evacuation of civilians. As defeat loomed, all available ships were hastily loaded with fleeing civilians. The *Empire Star*, designed to carry a small number of passengers, was crammed with 2,000 refugees. As coordination broke down, the evacuation became a debacle. Enemy planes attacked the fleeing ships and thousands of civilians drowned. Others survived drowning only to be murdered by Japanese troops as they struggled ashore on Bangka Island.

1942

January 23: Australia sends an urgent request for assistance from the Allies after a series of conquests in the Southwest Pacific brings the Japanese within a thousand miles of Australian territory.

January 24: U.S. Supreme Court justice Owen Roberts reports that inquests into culpability for the Japanese attack on Pearl Harbor reveal indifference and neglect on the part of Navy and Army commanders—Rear Admiral Husband Kimmel and Lieutenant General Walter Short. • The first significant naval battle in the Pacific Theater, the Battle of Makassar Strait, ends with the Japanese losing four transport ships. Despite their losses, they will achieve their objective of securing the oil-rich port of Balikpapan, Borneo.

January 25: Thailand declares war on the United States and Great Britain.

January 26: The U.S. armed forces establish their British office in the capital city of London. • The Japanese gain a critical base with the capture of Rabaul, New Britain.

January 30: In a speech that leaves no doubt about one of Hitler's primary goals of the war, the *Führer* asserts that the conflict will end with the "complete annihilation of the Jews," calling them "the most evil universal enemy of all time."

February 1: The Reich institutes a policy of tobacco rationing in the Fatherland, allowing German women half a man's ration. • Nazi puppet Vidkun Quisling is named Norwegian premier for the second time. He will publicly accept his reappointment in a speech unapologetically delivered in German. • German U-boats adopt a new cipher called "Triton," meaning the Allies can no longer interpret their messages.

The Combined Chiefs of Staff

For the Allies to prosecute the war successfully, they needed to establish and maintain a sound working relationship between the national military staffs of the U.S. and Great Britain at the strategic level. To achieve this, the U.S. Joint Chiefs of Staff and the British Chiefs of Staff formed the Combined Chiefs of Staff in February 1942. Britain was represented in Washington by the British Joint Staff Mission.

The Combined Chiefs advised on, developed, modified, and directed Anglo-U.S. strategic policy on behalf of Churchill and Roosevelt. Heading the British mission was Field Marshal Sir John Dill (*pictured, seventh from left*), formerly chief of the British Imperial General Staff (CIGS). Although Dill's caution as CIGS chief had not endeared him to Churchill, his appointment to Washington proved to be a smart decision. There, working with his American colleagues, he was instrumental in circumventing or defusing numerous issues and policy differences that could have disrupted Anglo-U.S. relations.

Combined Chiefs of Staff at the 1943 Quebec Conference

Foremost among these was the recurring U.S. pressure for an unrealistically early Anglo-U.S. "Second Front" invasion of France.

The gentlemanly Dill was lauded for his diplomacy, intellect, and achievements in Washington. He also formed a great personal friendship with U.S. general George Marshall, the U.S. Army chief of staff. When Dill died in post in 1944, he was accorded the unique honor of burial in the Arlington National Cemetery.

1942

February 1: Japanese bases on the Gilbert and Marshall islands come under attack by more than 90 carrier-based U.S. warplanes.

February 4: In Egypt, British ambassador Sir Miles Lampson surrounds King Farouk's palace with Allied tanks to pressure the monarch into appointing a pro-British government. • Japan presses Britain to surrender control of Singapore, the crown jewel in the British Asian empire.

February 6: British and American officials meet in Washington, D.C., for the first conference of the Allied Combined Chiefs of Staff. • The United States counterattacks a reinforced Japanese force on the island of Luzon, Philippines.

February 7: A congressional call for $500 million in aid to the Nationalist Chinese gets Roosevelt's stamp of approval.

February 9: The Japanese capture Singapore's Tengah airfield, a vital supply link.

February 10: Axis sabotage is suspected when *Normandie*, the luxury French liner impounded in New York, catches fire and capsizes. No sabotage actually occurred.

February 11: London questions Vichy France's assertions of neutrality, revealing that France has supplied German forces in North Africa with more than 5,000 tons of fuel over the past three months.

February 11–13: The German navy humiliates the British with the perfect execution of Operation Cerberus, also known as the "Channel Dash." Unable to return from Brest, France, to their home ports via the British-controlled Atlantic route, the German battleships *Scharnhorst* and *Gneisenau* and the cruiser *Prinz Eugen* make an audacious escape up the English Channel.

The *Wehrmacht*'s youngest general Adolf Galland, probably the best-known *Luftwaffe* ace of the war, led a fighter group during the Battle of Britain that accounted for 103 aircraft "kills." By late 1941, he was commanding the *Luftwaffe* fighter arm. In late 1942, he became the *Wehrmacht*'s youngest general (age 31). Despite his youth, he consistently demonstrated impressive organizational and intellectual abilities. Galland's well-founded advocacy of using the *Luftwaffe* tactically rather than strategically was fully in line with the air-warfare policies of Göring and Hitler. He was dismissed in January 1945, and was later shot down and captured while commanding an Me 262 jet fighter squadron.

1942

February 13: After numerous delays, Hitler permanently cancels the German invasion of Britain, code-named Operation Sealion. • Japanese aviators inadvertently dive-bomb their own troops in a raid on the Bataan Peninsula in the Philippines.

February 14: The British government directs the RAF to begin a campaign that targets German civilians, shifting the focus away from exclusively bombing military and production facilities.

February 14–16: The Japanese score an important strategic victory with the seizure of the oil-rich island of Sumatra in the Dutch East Indies.

February 15: In a stunning defeat for the Empire, the British surrender Singapore to the Japanese, who will raise the rising sun flag over the governor's residence the following day.

February 19: The Canadian Parliament approves a resolution calling for a military draft. • In just one day, the unstoppable Japanese attack Bali, Mandalay, and Timor. They will install occupation forces in both Bali and Timor the following day.

February 20: Lieutenant Edward "Butch" O'Hare, Navy flying ace for whom Chicago's major airport will eventually be named, shoots down five Japanese bombers over a five-minute period.

February 22: The Allies launch a campaign against Japanese shipping when they seed the mouth of Burma's Rangoon River with 40 British magnetic mines dropped from USAAF B-24 bombers. • President Roosevelt reassigns General MacArthur, pulling him from his post in the Philippines and naming him commander of Allied forces in Australia.

Kondo among Japan's top commanders Vice Admiral Kondo Nobutake ranked among Japan's most outstanding fleet commanders in 1941 and '42. He led the naval forces that supported the invasion of Malaya, Java, and Singapore, and spearheaded the main "covering force" in the Battle of Midway. He later commanded the Second Fleet in the bitter—and ultimately unsuccessful—struggle to dominate the waters off Guadalcanal from August to November 1942. Following that defeat, he served as deputy commander of the Combined Fleet and briefly as commander following Admiral Yamamoto Isoroku's death in 1943. Kondo survived the war and died in 1953.

Japanese Americans report to camps In response to dire warnings from the military and rising panic among ordinary citizens, the U.S. government in February 1942 began evacuating people of Japanese ancestry from Pacific Coastal areas. About 8,000 Japanese Americans voluntarily left, and another 120,000—72,000 of whom were U.S. citizens—were forcibly relocated. Like the young people seen here, Japanese Americans were held under guard at assembly centers, where their baggage was inspected for forbidden items, such as cameras, shortwave radios, and guns. They were then bussed to camps east of the Sierra Nevada Mountains.

1942

February 23: In the first Japanese "attack" on the American mainland, a Japanese submarine surfaces at night off Ellwood, California, near Santa Barbara. It fires on an oil derrick, damaging a catwalk but little else. Much local panic follows for a few days.

February 26: Stalin makes the first of many requests to the American and British command to open a second European front against the Germans so as to relieve some of the pressure on the Red Army.

February 27: Japan launches an assault on the Andamans, a chain of islands on India's Bay of Bengal.

February 27–March 1: Ten Allied warships are sunk during the disastrous Battle of the Java Sea. With the Allies suffering one of the worst wartime defeats at sea, Japanese ships are left to roam Indonesian waters at will.

February 28: Pearl Harbor commanders Lieutenant General Walter Short and Rear Admiral Husband Kimmel retire. The U.S. military announces it will court-martial the two commanders at a later date.

March: The Allies lose 273 merchant vessels this month. • Desperate for metal to manufacture airplane engines, Germany begins to collect bronze and copper church bells for the smelter's fires.

March 2: The U.S. government bans all Japanese Americans from all of two and portions of three Pacific coastal states. • Nazis murder some 5,000 Jews in Minsk, Belorussia.

March 8: The Japanese take the Burmese capital of Rangoon.

March 9: The Japanese seize the Indonesian island of Java from the Dutch.

1942

March 10: Britain has already spent more than nine billion pounds on the war effort, more than was spent on the entire First World War.

March 11: The French Resistance blows up a Nazi troop train, killing about 250 German soldiers. • As compensation for their shipping losses to the Axis, Brazil seizes Axis property.

March 13: America enters the China-Burma-India theater with the arrival of U.S. Army Air Force airmen in Karachi, India.

March 14: Washington sets plans in motion to increase troop levels in Europe in preparation for an eventual attack on the heart of the Nazi Reich. • In response to the Japanese menace, the first contingent of American troops that will serve under General MacArthur lands in Australia.

March 17: General MacArthur assumes his new post as supreme commander of Allied forces in the southwest Pacific Theater. He lands in Darwin, Australia, a few days after his first group of men.

March 17–31: Some 20,000 prisoners, mostly Jews, are murdered in the new Belzec, Poland, death camp, which opened on March 13.

March 18: The American and British Combined Chiefs of Staff install Admiral Lord Louis Mountbatten as the chief of Combined Operations.

March 19: British home secretary Herbert Morrison accuses the London paper *The Daily Mirror* of "reckless indifference to the national interest" for its practice of publishing stories with an antiwar slant.

March 20: Japanese and Chinese troops clash along the Sittang River on the Burmese front.

Chinese medical care Throughout the war, the Chinese struggled to adequately treat wounded and diseased troops and civilians. The relatively few available hospital facilities suffered from a lack of supplies and equipment, and a shortage of doctors. Conditions were better at the center seen here, a U.S. missionary hospital run by Dr. Gordon Seagrave and his nurses in the Namhkam Valley, Burma, off the Burma Road. Seagrave had been recruited by the U.S. military, and may have had intelligence duties as well as medical responsibilities.

1942

Spring: Construction begins at the Dugway Proving Ground in Utah. The U.S. Army constructs simulated Japanese and German towns in order to test the effects of incendiary bombs and other weapons.

March 22: British and American air force units are left exposed to assault as they beat a retreat after the Japanese capture of Burma's Magwe airfield. The loss of the strategic landing strip leaves the Allies unable to call for air support. • *Abwehr* (German intelligence) captain and double agent Paul Thummel, a British MI6 asset on the ground in Czechoslovakia, is arrested by the Nazis.

March 24: Japan launches an offensive against Bataan.

March 26: The Nazi government orders that all Jewish homes in Germany and the occupied territories must be identified as such. • Admiral Ernest King, commander-in-chief of the U.S. Fleet, becomes the highest-ranking officer in the Navy with his appointment as chief of Naval Operations.

March 28: Allies deliberately slam the HMS *Campbeltown* into the gates at the Normandy dock at St. Nazaire on the French Atlantic coast, the largest drydock in Nazi-occupied Europe and the only one large enough to handle the German battleship *Tirpitz*. Once past the gates, Allied commandoes sabotage the facility. • The first of 6,000 Parisian Jews designated for "resettlement" at Auschwitz are loaded onto a train and sent to that extermination camp.

March 31: India's Congress Party demands immediate independence from Britain. It rejects a British offer made the previous day that included Indian independence but only after the conclusion of the war.

Bataan prisoners await grim fate Hands tied behind their backs, these three Americans were among 78,000 American and Filipino troops who went into captivity on Bataan on April 9, 1942. Their starving and diseased condition influenced Major General Edward King's decision to surrender, though he was unable to extract from the Japanese commanders a commitment to treat the prisoners compassionately. The Japanese decided to march the prisoners to Camp O'Donnell, some 65 miles away. The tragedy that would follow is encapsulated in the story of these three, all of whom apparently died in captivity. James Gallagher reportedly died on the day this photograph was taken.

1942

April 1: Vital supplies reach the Soviets, as 14 of the 19 ships of the first Arctic convoy successfully make it to the Russian port of Murmansk.

April 3: Some 2,000 Burmese civilians die during a Japanese air raid on Mandalay.

April 4: Hitler orders the Baedeker raids. Named after a series of tourist guides, the raids will be specifically targeted to inflict maximum damage on Britain's most important historic sites.

April 6: Japanese troops land at Bougainville in the Solomon Islands.

April 7: The air raid sirens on Malta sound for the 2,000th time since the beginning of the war.

April 8: In one of the most intense air raids of the war, the RAF attacks Hamburg, Germany, with more than 270 bombers. • A new lifeline is opened to China with the inauguration of U.S. Air Ferry Command service over the Himalayan mountain range.

April 9: Soviet general Mikhail Yefremov takes his own life rather than suffer the shame of surrendering to the Germans.

April 10: Japanese troops land on Cebu Island, Philippines. • The atrocity that will become known as the Bataan Death March begins with the surrender of more than 78,000 exhausted and starving American and Filipino troops in the Bataan Peninsula. In an effort to get them to the nearest railhead, their Japanese captors will force-march the prisoners some 65 miles. Eleven thousand of the captives will be killed or will perish along the way.

April 11: The first 8,000-pound bomb is dropped on Essen, Germany, by a Halifax bomber. It is not known if the bomb reached its target or what damage it caused.

The Baedeker Raids The 15th-century Old Boar's Head Inn in Norwich, England, was damaged (*pictured*) in an April 1942 *Luftwaffe* raid. Germany bombed the picturesque English towns of Exeter, Bath, Norwich, and York. Nazi propagandist Baron Gustav Braun von Sturm declared, "We shall go out and bomb every building in Britain marked with three stars in the [German-published] Baedeker [travel] guide." These Baedeker Raids on England—which included Canterbury and other nonstrategic historic sites—took lives and destroyed property. However, the heavy toll on the *Luftwaffe* revealed the German bombers' limitations.

Doolittle's Tokyo Raid

On April 18, 1942, 16 B-25 bombers lumbered off the deck of the American aircraft carrier *Hornet* and turned toward the Japanese coast, more than 600 miles away. Their top-secret mission: to carry out the first attack of the war on the enemy homeland.

B-25 bombers abord the USS *Hornet*

Leading the raid was 45-year-old Lieutenant Colonel James Doolittle, a modest but highly capable officer who owned all the major aviation racing trophies of his day as well as a Ph.D. in aeronautical engineering from MIT. Doolittle's airmen were volunteers who knew only that they had signed on for a "dangerous secret mission." Details would be revealed after they were at sea. The bombers were fitted with extra fuel tanks, and the fliers practiced taking off from shortened runways intended to simulate a carrier flight deck. Since the B-25s were too cumbersome to land on a carrier, their missions would be one-way, with the bombers continuing on to secret airfields in China.

Doolittle intended to launch about 400 miles from the coast, but an encounter with a Japanese picket vessel 600 miles out forced an earlier departure. All 16 B-25s got airborne and bombed various military and industrial targets, most located in Tokyo, before fleeing toward China. Short on fuel due to the early launch, the crews of 15 planes either crash-landed or bailed out. One bomber landed in Vladivostok, Russia, where the five-man crew was interned.

Of the other 75 raiders, one man was killed bailing out, two drowned after crash-landing in the water, and eight were captured by the Japanese. Three prisoners were executed. Another died of malnutrition while in captivity. The other fliers evaded the Japanese and found refuge with the Chinese Nationalists. Upon his return home, Doolittle was awarded the Medal of Honor.

While the material damage inflicted was minimal, the Doolittle Raid lifted Allied morale and stunned the Japanese, who had grown complacent with victory after victory. No longer could the Japanese pretend that the homeland was inviolate.

Bombers take off from aircraft carrier
A B-25 lumbers off the deck of the USS *Hornet* on its one-way bombing raid against Tokyo. The Army pilots had practiced short takeoffs from dry land, but none had ever tried it from a heaving carrier deck. The raiding force was comprised of 16 modified bombers, each carrying five crew members, four bombs, and extra fuel. An encounter with a Japanese picket boat forced the Doolittle Raiders to launch earlier than planned. Aided by a 50-mph headwind, all the B-25s got safely into the air, though many hung perilously close to the waves before gaining altitude.

Raid affects morale on both sides
This aerial photo, snapped during the Doolittle Raid, reveals ships moored in Tokyo Bay. Most of the B-25s arrived over Tokyo just after noon on April 18. They targeted an oil tank farm, steel mill, and power plants. Other bombers hit targets in Yokohama and Yokosuku. All the B-25s survived the actual raid, except for one that crash-landed in China after it ran out of fuel. Though minimal damage was done to the targets, the harm to Japanese morale was immense. By contrast, the raid lifted American spirits, which had been at low ebb following a string of Allied military defeats.

1942

April 14: The U.S. Navy "kills" its first U-boat when *U-85* is attacked by the destroyer USS *Roper* in the Atlantic Ocean. • With Japanese forces closing in, British troops torch Burma's Yenangyaung oil fields to keep them out of Axis hands.

April 15: Sobibór, the newest Nazi extermination camp in Poland, opens its gates. • In an effort to minimize textile-industry labor, Britain bans the manufacture of lace on women's underwear, effective June 1.

April 16: German field marshal Gerd von Rundstedt is appointed commander-in-chief of the Atlantic Wall defenses. • Britain presents the strategically critical island of Malta with the George Cross, a medal given for valiant service to the Empire.

April 18: Japan is blindsided by a carrier-based bombing raid on Tokyo by 16 B-25 bombers from the USS *Hornet.*

April 20: The *Luftwaffe* destroys 30 Spitfire planes on the island of Malta.

April 21: General Henri Giraud, captured by the Nazis when they occupied his native France, makes a daring escape to Allied territory.

April 24: German authorities issue a decree prohibiting Jews from using public transportation of any kind.

April 26: Hitler is empowered to act outside the laws of the Reich in dealing with his subjects when the *Reichstag* confers on him the ultimate title of "supreme justice," among others.

April 29: Hitler and Mussolini meet to decide how to address internecine border bickering between Hungary and Romania. • Nazi saboteurs are suspected when an explosion in a Belgian chemical plant claims some 250 lives. • A critical link to China is lost when Japan's capture of Lashio, Burma, closes the Burma Road.

Allies deliver tanks to Soviets When Germany sent its powerful army against the USSR in June 1941, Russia dismantled and moved some of its arms factories away from highly endangered areas. That disrupted production, and by fall the nation was in urgent need of tanks and aircraft. Britain and the U.S. began supplying Russia with 400 tanks and 500 aircraft per month—numbers that would rise as the war progressed. Here, British Valentine and Matilda tanks are loaded onto a train for shipment to Russia via ship convoy through the Arctic.

1942

April 30: By the end of the month, the squalor of the Warsaw Ghetto has claimed the lives of nearly 4,500 Polish Jews.

May 1: A strategic error by Britain allows the Japanese to take Mandalay by penetrating the Royal Army's exposed left flank.

May 2: Aid is promised to both Iran and Iraq under the provisions of the U.S. Lend-Lease Act.

May 4: The USAAF Flying Tigers shift their base of operations to Kunming, China, and out of Japanese-occupied Burma.

May 4–8: The Battle of the Coral Sea, the first carrier-to-carrier battle in history, results in a tactical Japanese victory, since they sink a major American carrier. But it marks a strategic Japanese reverse since the Japanese are unable to seize New Guinea and thus isolate Australia.

May 5: Nationalist Chinese general Chiang Kai-shek leads his troops in a major offensive against the Japanese occupation, striking seven key cities.

May 6: After 27 days of artillery barrage, the Americans surrender to the Japanese at Corregidor in the Philippines.

May 8: Japan's ability to produce fuel from its captured oil fields in the Dutch East Indies is seriously crippled when the ship carrying skilled production workers to the fields is sunk by an Allied torpedo.

May 10: Churchill sternly warns Germany against engaging in chemical warfare on the Russian front.

May 11: An Allied personnel transport ship is struck by a German U-boat that managed to make its way up Canada's St. Lawrence River undetected.

German E-boats The German fast patrol and torpedo-carrying *Schnellboot* was dubbed "E-boat" by the Allies. The MTB and PT boats were the Anglo-U.S. equivalents. E-boats were used extensively in the English Channel and North Sea littoral region for raids on Allied shipping, routine patrols, clandestine operations, and rescue of downed aircrew. By 1944 about 40 E-boats were operating in the Channel area. One of their most significant successes was on April 28, 1944, when two flotillas attacked a D-Day landing exercise in the Channel off Slapton, Devon, sinking two LSTs and killing 749 men of the U.S. Fourth Infantry Division.

Fighting in Madagascar British troops rush ashore from landing craft at Madagascar on May 5, 1942. Seizure of the Vichy French-controlled island was prompted by fears that Japanese long-range submarines might use it as a base to interdict Allied communication lines and shipping in the Indian Ocean. This was critical for supply lines to India, the Soviet Union, and the Middle East. Vichy forces, consisting mostly of Madagascan and Senegalese troops, offered more resistance to the operation than expected. Low-level fighting dragged on until November 5, when the Vichy commander finally surrendered.

1942

May 12: Thirteen German transport planes go down in the Mediterranean after an RAF engagement off the coast of North Africa. • Overwhelming monsoon-induced mud brings operations in Southeast Asia to a standstill.

May 14: Not entirely trusting British guarantees to return Madagascar to France at war's end, General de Gaulle sends troops under his command to force the issue. • Congress establishes the U.S. Women's Army Auxiliary Corps.

May 15: Fuel rationing begins in 17 cities along the United States' eastern seaboard. • Chinese troops retreat into China and British troops retreat into India, officially completing Japan's occupation of Burma.

May 16: Roosevelt appeases the Soviets by releasing Earl Browder from federal prison. Browder, the leader of the Communist Party in the U.S., had served 14 months for passport violations.

May 20: Thanks to outstanding work by U.S. intelligence cryptologists, the Allies possess advance knowledge of a Japanese attack on Midway Island and a simultaneous diversionary attack on the Aleutians. The U.S. command responds by deploying a defensive force to Midway.

May 21: Hitler delays a planned invasion of Malta indefinitely, as he is afraid of losses to airborne troops after the experience on Crete. He opts to focus on the conquest of Egypt.

May 22: Mexico declares war against the Axis.

May 25: A small Japanese fleet steams out of Hokkaido en route to Alaska. The Japanese stage an attack on the Aleutians that they hope will draw attention away from the real target of Midway Island in the South Pacific.

The deadly Mosquito Operational from 1942, the RAF's De Havilland Mosquito fighter bomber is generally regarded as the most successful and versatile combat aircraft of the war. With its revolutionary lightweight, wood-based construction, the "Mossie" could fly at 408 mph up to 2,206 miles while carrying its two-man crew and a total bomb load of 5,000 pounds. A Mossie could fly to Berlin and back twice in one night to deliver its devastating 4,000-pound "Blockbuster" bombs. When configured as a fighter bomber, it had four 20mm cannons and four machine guns and could carry 1,000 pounds of bombs or eight rockets.

Alternative Japanese Strategy

By March 1942, the Japanese had achieved nearly all of their initial goals. Their ultimate objective—to establish an impenetrable defensive perimeter to secure their vast Southeast Asian conquests—was impossible to achieve given the length of the perimeter and the limitations on the size of forces available to defend it. Yet the scale of their successes and their failure to destroy the Pacific Fleet at Pearl Harbor made them reluctant to surrender the initiative by taking a defensive stance.

Admiral Yamamoto still sought the long-cherished decisive sea battle with the American fleet, which led to subsequent plans to invade Midway Island. However, squabbling strategists—infected by what one admiral called "victory disease"—diffused Japan's strength with additional forays in the Aleutians, the Indian Ocean, and the South Pacific. The setbacks that followed at the Coral Sea, Midway, Guadalcanal, and Papua allowed Japan's enemies to regroup and permanently gain the initiative. Given its inadequate resources, Japan had little chance of ultimate success.

Japan did have other strategic options in 1942, none of which came to fruition. One option was to attack Australia, but this effort was halted at the Battle of the Coral Sea. Another was to attack Hawaii, but this attempt was halted at the Battle of Midway. A third option was to attack Britain's lifeline in the Indian Ocean. Such an offensive likely would have cut off Britain's oil supplies, cost it India, eliminated the supply route to the Soviet Union across Iran, and had an impact in North Africa and the Caucasus. But by the beginning of 1943, all such discussion was academic, since Japan's war had become defensive.

1942

May 27: The British Eighth Army shows off the American Grant M3 tank, its newest piece of high-tech weaponry, against Rommel's troops in Libya. • Damaged in the Battle of the Coral Sea, the carrier USS *Yorktown* returns to Pearl Harbor for repairs.

May 29: Effective today, all French Jews must wear the yellow Star of David badge. • Czech partisans sent from England attack the car carrying Bohemia and Moravia deputy *Reichsprotektor* Reinhard Heydrich, mortally wounding him.

May 30–31: Cologne, Germany is devastated by the first RAF raid to employ more than 1,000 bombers.

June: Eight German secret agents arrive via U-boat in the U.S., four in New York and four in Florida. They plan to destroy a cryolite factory in Philadelphia, but two of the members betray the operation to the FBI.

June 1: The *Luftwaffe* inflicts heavy damage on Canterbury, England.

June 2: More than 130 Czech citizens are murdered to avenge the attack on Reinhard Heydrich.

June 4: Reinhard Heydrich dies in Prague of an infection stemming from his injuries at the hands of Czech partisans.

June 4–6: The momentum of the Pacific war shifts to favor the Allies when they achieve a stunning victory at the Battle of Midway. The Japanese lose 3,500 men and four of their six largest aircraft carriers, permitting the Allies to go on the offensive.

June 5: Forty-nine civilians die in an accidental explosion at an Elmwood, Illinois, ordnance plant. • The United States formally declares war on Axis satellites Bulgaria, Romania, and Hungary, each of whom had declared war on the U.S. in December 1941.

Japanese subs attack Sydney area A shattered Japanese midget submarine is hoisted from the waters of Sydney Harbor following an attack on Allied shipping on the night of May 31, 1942. Three of the two-man midget subs, launched from standard submarines, participated in the attack. All were lost. One became tangled in an anti-torpedo net and blew itself up. The crew members of the second committed suicide after their sub was damaged in a depth-charge attack. The third sub fired two torpedoes, one of which sank a depot ship. Though never found, it too failed to return to the mother sub. One week later, a Japanese sub attacked the Sydney area, damaging houses but causing no serious injuries.

Reinhard Heydrich and the SD

From fall 1941 to spring 1942, Reinhard Heydrich was regarded as a potential successor to Hitler. He had played a key role in the development and implementation of the "Final Solution" to exterminate Europe's Jews—a policy enthusiastically expounded by him at the Wannsee Conference in January 1942.

Heydrich's time as one of the most powerful men in the Third Reich actually began in 1934 when he became head of the Gestapo, from which he shifted in 1936 to become chief of the *Sicherheitsdienst* (Security Service, SD). His assassination by Czech partisans in May 1942 reflected not only his personal status but also his new role as the German official in control of occupied Czechoslovakia.

Formed in 1932, the SD was the intelligence and security branch of the SS. Initially, the SS was responsible for the security of Hitler, other prominent Nazis, and the wider NSDAP organization. Later, it assumed responsibility for security throughout the Third Reich. The SD was the intelligence branch of the SS. It helped to implement Nazi policies concerning Jews, Communists, and other socially or politically "undesirable" groups, in parallel with traditional security and intelligence-gathering activities. The SD played a significant role in the *Einsatzgruppen*, which conducted counter-partisan operations. The *Einsatzgruppen* carried out many thousands of executions in German-occupied territories, and played a part in the clearance of Jewish ghettos in Eastern Europe.

Heydrich's assassination In September 1941, Reinhard Heydrich became the governor of German-occupied Bohemia and Moravia (today's Czech Republic). The overly confident governor often rode in an unescorted, open-roofed car. On May 27, 1942, two British-trained Czech resistance fighters successfully ambushed him in Prague, wounding him with a grenade. Seen here is the car in which he was attacked. After several days of agony, Heydrich died on June 4.

Battle of Midway

Flush with victory in the spring of 1942, Japan turned its attention to tiny Midway Island, 1,100 miles northwest of Hawaii. Seizure of U.S.-held Midway would provide a useful outpost for the subsequent occupation of Hawaii. Furthermore, the operation was expected to bring out the U.S. Pacific Fleet, which could then be totally destroyed.

Commanded by Admiral Yamamoto Isoroku, the attacking force consisted of several groups and subgroups and included a secondary thrust into the Aleutian Islands of Alaska. The striking force, with four aircraft carriers, would hit Midway. The main body, which included a light carrier and three battleships—one of them the fearsome *Yamato* with its 18-inch guns—would follow. Other groups included battleships, cruisers, destroyers, and transports. When the U.S. fleet sortied from Hawaii, these groups were to close in and destroy the Americans in a complicated pincer movement.

There was one fatal flaw. U.S. cryptologists had broken the Japanese naval code and knew Yamamoto was coming. Armed with details of the enemy plan, the Americans set a trap. When the Japanese arrived on June 4 and began their aerial attack on the island's defenders, the U.S. carriers *Yorktown*, *Enterprise*, and *Hornet* were waiting in ambush.

The Japanese suddenly found themselves under attack not only from land-based aircraft from Midway, but from torpedo bombers, dive-bombers, and fighters from U.S. carriers that they had not suspected were in the area. Initial attacks by the torpedo bombers, carried out by Americans flying obsolete aircraft, failed as whole squadrons were shot down. But the unrelenting pressure created openings for the carrier dive-bombers, which proceeded to sink Japanese aircraft carriers *Akagi*, *Kaga*, *Soryu*, and *Hiryu*. Stunned by these losses, Yamamoto ordered a withdrawal.

Midway cost the Americans the carrier *Yorktown*, a destroyer, 147 aircraft, and 307 dead. Yamamoto lost four carriers, a cruiser, 322 aircraft, and 3,500 dead, including irreplaceable air crews. Also lost forever was the once overwhelming Japanese naval initiative in the Pacific.

Japan's important aircraft carrier The Japanese aircraft carrier *Hiryu* takes evasive action while under attack by U.S. B-17 bombers during the Battle of Midway. Commissioned in 1939, the 20,250-ton carrier was involved in the raid on Pearl Harbor in December 1941 as well as in operations in the East Indies and Indian Ocean. At Midway, its planes heavily damaged the U.S. carrier *Yorktown* on June 4. Hours later, *Hiryu* was attacked by 13 dive-bombers from *Enterprise*. Struck by four bombs, it was abandoned when massive fires could not be brought under control. The *Hiryu* was subsequently scuttled by torpedoes from the destroyer *Makigumo*.

Yorktown **sunk at Midway** Smoke billows from the USS *Yorktown* following Japanese air attacks at Midway. The carrier survived three bomb hits and returned to action before coming under renewed attack by enemy torpedo planes. Struck by two torpedoes, the carrier lost headway and began listing to port. Fearing the carrier was about to capsize, the crew was ordered to abandon ship. Hours later, with the *Yorktown* still stubbornly afloat, efforts were underway to salvage the ship when a Japanese submarine sent two more torpedoes into the carrier. Mortally wounded, *Yorktown* sank in 3,000 fathoms the following morning.

The reliable Dauntless A U.S. Navy Douglas SBD Dauntless dive-bomber releases part of its payload. Considered obsolete when war broke out, the Dauntless was underpowered, slow, noisy, and fatiguing to fly over long distances. On the plus side, it handled well, could absorb considerable punishment, and was very accurate. These attributes transformed the Dauntless into the mainstay of the U.S. Navy's air fleet from 1941 to 1943. In fact, it was credited with sinking more Japanese warships than any other U.S. aircraft type. At Midway alone, Dauntless dive-bombers sank four Japanese carriers and damaged two heavy cruisers.

1942

June 7: The *Chicago Tribune* states that the U.S. Navy had advance knowledge of the Midway strike. The article jeopardizes years of intelligence collection and cryptology work. • Japanese forces occupy the Aleutian islands of Attu and Kiska in the war's only Axis occupation in North America.

June 10: The entire Czechoslovakian village of Lidice is razed in reprisal for the killing of Reinhard Heydrich. More than 400 residents are driven from their homes; the men are executed while the women and children are sent to concentration camps.

June 11: The office of SS *Reichsführer* Heinrich Himmler calls for the transfer of some 100,000 Jews from occupied France to "relocation" camps. • German U-boats launch a mine-laying campaign in eastern U.S. coastal waters. • U.S. officials sign a new Lend-Lease agreement with Soviet ambassador Litvinov.

June 12: The oil-producing region around Ploesti, Romania, is strafed by U.S. Army Air Force B-24 bombers.

June 13: British troops suffer a major defeat at the hands of General Rommel when Lieutenant General Neil Ritchie orders an attack against a well-entrenched German Army in Libya.

June 15: The tanker *Robert C. Tuttle* runs aground on Virginia Beach after hitting a German mine, making it the first American ship lost to enemy mines at home.

June 18: A six-hour gun battle in a church ends with the deaths of seven Czech partisans who took part in the Heydrich assassination. • Bernard Robinson becomes the first African American U.S. naval officer (an ensign in the Reserves).

June 20: Roosevelt and Churchill agree to move forward with an invasion of the French colonies in northwest Africa.

The expanded role of the FBI The Federal Bureau of Investigation (FBI) was established in 1908 and led by J. Edgar Hoover beginning in 1924. Primarily a crime-fighting agency during its early years, the FBI was authorized to investigate subversive organizations beginning in 1936. When war broke out in Europe in 1939, the FBI's role was expanded to include sabotage and espionage investigations. With the added responsibilities came an increase in agents, from 391 in 1933 to 3,000 in 1942 to 4,886 in 1944. Hoover publicized the successes of his department, increased the confidence of civilians, and expanded the FBI's responsibilities well beyond its prewar assignments.

1942

June 21: German General Rommel pushes east after conquering Tobruk, Libya. His troops capture supplies, along with 33,000 prisoners of war.

June 22: Fort Stevens, Oregon, escapes harm when it is shelled by the Japanese.

June 23: Rail-transported Parisian Jews are the first to go through the selection process for the Auschwitz gas chambers.

June 25: Roosevelt appoints Dwight Eisenhower to the post of U.S. Army chief in Europe.

June 26: The important U-boat base of Bremen, Germany, is in flames following a massive RAF attack.

July 1: Some 250 alien saboteurs are arrested in the U.S. when the FBI uncovers a plot to blow up the Pennsylvania Railroad.

July 4: After eight months, the Germans finally prevail in the Battle of Sevastopol, the site of the Soviets' main naval base on the Black Sea. Germany's 11th Army takes 90,000 Soviets as prisoners. • American bombers undertake their first independent raids of the war, attacking four German air bases in Dutch territory.

July 5: Russia yields the Crimea to Germany. • Britain angers Stalin by imposing a moratorium on convoys to northern Russia. This follows a devastating German attack that sank 23 of 33 Allied ships in a convoy on the Barents Sea.

July 7: The British send Nazi spies Jose Keys and Alphonse Timmerman to the gallows.

July 8: U.S. Pacific Fleet commander Admiral Nimitz orders the invasion of the strategically significant Solomon island of Guadalcanal. His aim is to take an airfield being built by the Japanese, who have seized this island.

Germany's railroad guns From 1937, the German manufacturer Krupp designed and built two enormous railroad guns: "Gustav" and "Dora." The guns were arguably vulnerable to air attack. However, the existence of Europe's extensive railroad system and the ability to utilize poor-quality and rapidly repaired rails generally validated the railroad gun concept. Eventually, Dora was test-fired in 1942. It was manned by 1,420 men commanded by a brigadier general. Subsequently, it was employed to good effect in the Crimea, where it fired 40 seven-ton shells almost 30 miles into Sevastopol in mid-1942. It later fired 30 rounds into Warsaw during the 1944 uprising. The Gustav was never used in action.

The "Mosquito Army" The Long Range Desert Group (originally the Long Range Patrol Group) was founded by Major Ralph Bagnold in 1940 to assist British military efforts in North Africa. Sometimes called the "Mosquito Army" and the "Libyan Taxi Service," the group's purpose was to disappear behind enemy lines in order to scout routes, gather intelligence, and launch raids. Members such as the ones pictured here sometimes spent weeks or even months on dangerous missions in oppressive desert heat. LRDG teams were so cunning and skillful that, as Bagnold observed, raids seemed to come from "a fourth dimension," leaving German and Italian forces baffled and paralyzed.

American POWs stick together American prisoners celebrate the Fourth of July in 1942 in the Malaybalay camp in Mindanao, Philippines. The Japanese regime in Malaybalay seems to have been relatively benign, but this gathering was against regulations and dangerous. At Malaybalay, rations were far better than at Davao, where by October the U.S. prisoners had been moved. Prisoners of war of all nations sought to maintain a sense of national unity and to find diversions from the boredom and suffering of imprisonment. Mutual support was crucial to survival.

U.S. begins production of war goods Laborers in the Lockheed plant in Burbank, California, work on a B-17 Flying Fortress. One of the tasks facing President Roosevelt in the early days of the war was to dramatically shift the focus of American manufacturing from domestic to war goods. To oversee that process, the president called for the creation of the War Production Board, whose job would be to oversee the manufacture of war materials. The first decision of the board, which was formed in January 1942, was to ban the production of all cars and light trucks after that month. By the middle of the year, production of consumer durable goods decreased by 29 percent. America's shift to a wartime economy had begun.

1942

July 9: Teenaged diarist Anne Frank goes into hiding along with her family and friends as the Nazis begin to purge Amsterdam of its Jewish population.

July 10: In a disturbing new facet of Nazi inhumanity, 100 female Auschwitz inmates are selected for medical experimentation.

July 11: RAF bombers fly to Danzig to bomb U-boat pens.

July 13: President Roosevelt approves the creation of the Office of Strategic Services (OSS), the forerunner to the Central Intelligence Agency.

July 15: In the first deportation of Holland's Jews, some 2,000 are sent to Auschwitz under the guise of being relocated to a German labor camp. • Rommel must postpone his Egyptian offensive to assist two Italian divisions under Allied attack at El Alamein.

July 17: The United States begins its campaign to convince Britain to launch an invasion of mainland Europe in 1942. The British will resist, opting to build their strength for a major invasion at some unspecified future date.

July 19: The Germans attempt to limit French partisan violence by imposing a law calling for the slaughter and deportation of male family members of known "terrorists" that evade capture by Nazi authorities.

July 22: The Nazis open the Treblinka death camp outside of Warsaw, Poland. Like Belzec, Treblinka's mandate is exclusively extermination, not confinement and labor.

July 23: The German army captures some 240,000 Soviet troops at the fall of Rostov. • A German U-boat lays mines in the Mississippi River delta.

Operation Magic

By 1941 American cryptanalysts had broken the Japanese "Purple" cipher, enabling them to read Tokyo's diplomatic traffic. Dubbed Operation Magic, this intelligence coup yielded a wealth of information regarding Japanese political aims.

Military codes, such as the Japanese navy's JN-25, proved more difficult to crack. Introduced in 1939, JN-25 remained in effect in various versions throughout the war. U.S. cryptanalysts broke the early version of JN-25, but a second version introduced in late 1940 remained largely unsolved until 1942.

The attack on Pearl Harbor prompted a determined Allied assault on enemy codes. By May 1942, about 40 percent of intercepted Japanese navy radio traffic was being deciphered, though only 10 to 15 percent of each message was readable. While Japanese code changes periodically shut off the flow of information, the U.S. advantage was incalculable. This advantage grew in early 1943 when cryptanalysts also managed to penetrate the Japanese army code.

Information from decrypts, code-named Ultra, provided intelligence on every aspect of the Japanese war effort: operations, ship sailings, troop movements and strategy, even the promotion of junior officers. Such information enabled the U.S. to ambush the Japanese fleet at Midway in June 1942—one of the greatest victories in the history of naval warfare. Foreknowledge of Admiral Yamamoto's planned visit to Bougainville in 1943 allowed U.S. fighter pilots to intercept his aircraft and send him to his death. Armed with enemy ship departures and schedules, U.S. submarines proceeded to destroy the Japanese merchant fleet, delivering a mortal blow to the enemy war effort. Reports from Japanese diplomats in Europe provided critical information on German defenses, new weapons, and other topics.

Incredibly, the Japanese never realized that the string of disasters and hemorrhaging ship losses were largely caused by the compromising of their codes. Like the Germans, each time they became suspicious, they decided that since they themselves could not break Allied machine codes, the Allies—who they deemed less intelligent—could not accomplish such a feat. As a result, U.S. code-breakers continued to "read Japanese mail" until the end of the war.

1942

July 23: *Judenrat* president Adam Czerniakow, who is charged by the Nazis with delivering 6,000 Jews a day for "resettlement" from the Warsaw Ghetto on penalty of the death of his wife and some 100 other Jewish hostages, takes his own life. A day earlier, he was unable to convince the Nazis to spare the ghetto orphans from being sent to Treblinka as part of a mass deportation of Jewish children.

July 26: British minister of food Lord Woolton institutes a sweets and chocolate rationing program that allows a half pound for every man, woman, and child every four weeks.

July 27: Hamburg is once again bombarded by the RAF. This time, some 600 planes participate in the attack.

July 28: According to President Roosevelt, no less than four million Americans are serving in the military.

July 30: The First Battle of El Alamein in Egypt, fought mostly between British Commonwealth and German troops, ends in a stalemate, thereby halting the German advance. • With the Germans on the move on two separate Russian fronts, Stalin issues a directive forbidding retreat. • The U.S. Navy begins a reservist program for women called the Women Appointed for Voluntary Emergency Service, better known as WAVES.

July 31: The approaches to the harbor at Charleston, South Carolina, are mined by a German U-boat. • American planes bomb Japanese positions on Guadalcanal and Tulagi in the Solomon Islands. • A Nazi "scientific" organization calling itself the Institute for Practical Research in Military Science begins to collect corpses from the Oranienburg concentration camp in an effort to study Jewish skeletons.

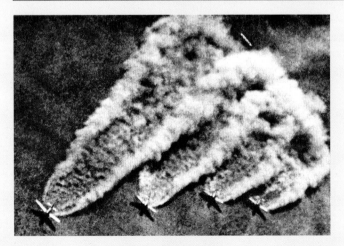

Hitler's bad judgment in the Caucasus Germany's insatiable need for oil-based products meant that the capture of the oil fields at Maikop, Baku, and Grozny remained a key strategic objective. Here, four German dive-bombers take off in the Caucasus. This strategy was ostensibly sound and could have succeeded. However, from mid-1942 German combat power in the Caucasus was dissipated by Hitler's ill-judged decisions to redirect forces to the competing operations at Leningrad, Moscow, and Stalingrad. Thus, the Caucasus advance lost momentum. Characteristically, Hitler blamed his generals for this failure.

THE ALLIES STRIKE BACK

AUGUST 1942–JANUARY 1943

The German armies that moved relentlessly toward Stalingrad in summer 1942 were confronted with a bleak terrain. "A barren, naked, lifeless steppe," wrote Johann Wieder, who survived the conflict to write his memoirs, "without a bush, without a tree, for miles without a village." For a time, the advance appeared to be a repeat of the summer of 1941. The Sixth Army of General Friedrich Paulus pushed the Soviet forces in front of it. By August 19, they had reached the outskirts of Stalingrad. On August 23, the first formations reached the banks of the Volga River. Paulus promised Hitler that the city would fall within a few days.

In reality the attempt to seize Stalingrad turned into one of the epic battles of World War II. During the five months in which the battle for the city raged, the advance of the Axis powers was halted and crushed. By the time Paulus surrendered in early February 1943, the tide had begun to turn not just on the Eastern Front but also in the Middle East and the Pacific.

Following the Japanese defeat at Midway Island in June 1942, the Allies found it possible to begin the long and brutal campaign to dislodge Japan's forces from the string of islands they had occupied around the ocean perimeter of the Empire. This was a difficult and costly campaign for both sides. Men and equipment had to be transported over long oceanic supply lines, thousands of miles from the home countries, and in terrain where tropical heat and disease took a high toll on the combatants, as did some of the bitterest fighting of the war.

The first battles were fought in southern New Guinea and the Solomon Islands, deemed by Japanese planners to be areas in the new perimeter that needed to be consolidated. In New Guinea, Japanese forces attempted, by an overland campaign, to seize Port Moresby, which they had tried to secure three months earlier by sea. The battle against Australian and American forces continued for six months until finally, on January 22, 1943, the last Japanese troops were cleared from the central portion of the huge island.

American forces landed on Guadalcanal and Florida Island in the southern Solomons on August 7, 1942. There, against fierce resistance, they captured the port of Tulagi and the airfield on Guadalcanal. The U.S. needed six months to secure these modest gains against fierce resistance that was repeatedly reinforced. However, the American capacity to supply large numbers of planes and trained pilots slowly tilted the conflict toward the Americans. All Japanese efforts to destroy the tenuous American foothold were beaten off. At the end of December 1942, the Japanese high command decided to abandon the contest, having lost more than 20,000 men, 600 aircraft, and 15 warships in the attempt. Though Allied gains on New Guinea and in the Solomons had been modest, it was now clear to both sides that Japan was fully stretched by commitments in the Pacific and China, and lacked the capacity for further advance.

In the Middle East, German general Erwin Rommel advanced into Egypt and toward Palestine. However, this apparently disastrous position for the Allies was stabilized and then reversed. As in the Pacific, both sides were fighting far from the home base and at the end of supply routes, which were regularly threatened by submarine and air action. By autumn 1942, British Empire forces had succeeded in building up large reserves while Axis supplies were regularly interrupted by submarine action in the Mediterranean. North Africa mattered differently to each side as well. For Hitler,

North Africa was a sideshow. For the Allies, it was a vital part of their global strategy; the Middle East and Mediterranean should not be abandoned to the Axis.

Nevertheless, Rommel had achieved a great deal. On August 31, 1942, he began a final offensive designed to bring him into Egypt and Palestine so that the Jews there could be killed before the area was turned over to Italy. Like the Japanese, he discovered that his overstretched resources had reached their limit. The British Eighth Army, which was dug in on a line near the small Egyptian city of El Alamein, absorbed Rommel's assault. On October 23, with overwhelming materiel advantage, a new British commander—General Bernard Montgomery—launched a counteroffensive. His 1,030 tanks proved too large an obstacle for the 500 or so Axis tanks that opposed him, and by November 4 Axis forces were in full retreat.

Montgomery did not cut off the Axis retreat, but by early February, Axis forces had been pushed back into Tunisia. Many of the Italian units were destroyed, and thousands of soldiers were taken prisoner. Once again, as in the Solomons, airpower had played a critical role in the Allies' success.

The change in fortunes owed something to the willingness of the Allies to collaborate. The three Axis powers made little attempt to coordinate their strategies, share economic resources, or divulge military or technical secrets. The Western Allies recognized earlier how important it was to share resources. They also understood how vital it was to mobilize their extensive manufacturing and scientific capacity as fully as possible to compensate for their lack of a large and experienced army.

The United States sent large amounts of food, raw materials, and equipment to Britain. So too did Canada, whose contribution is often overlooked. The Soviet Union was the beneficiary of a rich flow of resources from both North America and the British Empire, including a half-million vehicles and a million miles of telephone cable. The Soviets received few weapons, but the provision of food, manufactured products, and materials allowed the Soviet economy—which had lost around 60 percent of its capacity in 1941—to concentrate on the mass production of armaments.

The help was sourly acknowledged, because Stalin wanted his allies to open a second front in 1942 to take pressure off the Red Army. In August 1942, Winston Churchill flew to Moscow to discuss Allied strategy face-to-face. It was a difficult meeting. Stalin implied that the British were simply afraid of the Germans. Churchill's furious rebuttal finally won over Stalin. He was told of Western plans for an expanded bombing campaign against German targets and of a still-secret operation, code-named "Torch," of Allied landings in northwest Africa, planned for November.

Ideologically, Churchill and Stalin were diametrically opposed to each other. However, war had made them comrades in adversity. In mid-August 1942, at the First Moscow Conference, they met face-to-face for the first time. Despite their philosophical differences, they developed the unique personal relationship that subsequently ensured the Allied victory.

The invasion of North Africa began on November 8, 1942. Like operations in the Pacific, the American task force sailed the whole width of an ocean to reach the Moroccan coast on November 7. British forces landed at Oran and Algiers. After brief fighting with French colonial forces, the whole area was secured three days later. The Allied armies rushed toward Tunis to cut off the retreating Rommel. The Germans deployed enough forces into the pocket from Italy to create a stable front line, and the battle for Tunisia began in the last week of November.

In retaliation, Hitler ordered German forces to occupy the whole of Vichy France, which was absorbed into the German New Order. Jewish refugees who had managed to hide in the unoccupied zone were now pursued with a new vigor. As Axis forces found themselves pressed on all fronts, the mass murder of Jews reached its crescendo in the death camps at Auschwitz, Sobibór, Belzec, Chelmno, and Treblinka.

The gains in other theaters paled in comparison to the struggle that had engulfed the southern front in the Soviet Union. German expectations that the city of Stalingrad would quickly fall were frustrated by many factors: German forces had to be supplied along a single rail track into the battlefield. The destruction of the very large city by German bombers created ideal conditions for a determined infantry defense. Most of the buildings were modern steel and concrete structures with bunkers and cellars beneath them, which meant that not even regular shelling and bombing could easily flatten what was left of the twisted structures.

Into this wrecked landscape, the remnants of Soviet divisions retreated. They hid in the crumbled buildings and underground hiding places, attacking in small groups, often at night. Soviet sharpshooters pinned down German forces, which for most of the battle greatly outnumbered their opponents.

The commander in Stalingrad was a young Soviet general, Vasily Chuikov. The son of a peasant, Chuikov was robust and unflinching in the face of battle. His 62nd Army was scattered in pockets of what remained of the center of Stalingrad. It was supplied across the Volga River from the east bank, from which came waves of artillery and rocket fire, a stream of Soviet air attacks, and large numbers of soldiers. On several occasions, his weakened forces were close to collapse, but Paulus lacked the means to launch a knockout blow. The last major German offensive, designed to sweep Chuikov's remaining troops into the river, began during the second week of November. On the 8th, Hitler told the party faithful in Munich that in days he would be "master of Stalingrad."

The swift retreat on the southern front had been a shock to Stalin, who was determined to hold the city which now bore his name. In mid-September, his deputy commander-in-chief, General Georgi Zhukov, worked with the army staff on a possible way out of the crisis. Rather than throw more troops into the Stalingrad pocket, he suggested building up massive reserves on the German flanks that could be used to cut the German line of advance and encircle Paulus's troops. As long as Chuikov could hold the city, the plan—Operation Uranus—would work.

Further north, Zhukov planned Operation Mars, another large assault on the German line. This operation would prevent any German reinforcement of the south and might unhinge the whole German front line in Russia. This was the first time Soviet commanders had been able to plan, with Stalin's approval, a large-scale counteroffensive. Preparations were made under the strictest secrecy.

On November 19, Soviet armies fell on the unprepared Axis forces. Because they lacked adequate forces to guard the flanks of their advance, the Germans had pushed their Romanian, Italian, and Hungarian allies to increase their commitment of troops to the Eastern Front. Since the Germans had failed to provide these troops with proper equipment, the Romanian front was torn apart and Paulus was encircled. German field marshal Erich von Manstein launched a counterattack to break the ring, but failed. The Axis forces retreated back across the steppe. In the Caucasus, Soviet armies drove the southern German front back as well, though they failed to close off all avenues of escape. The success of Operation Uranus masked the mixed fortunes of Operation Mars, in which the Red Army suffered very heavy casualties for virtually no strategic gain.

After another two months of bitter fighting, Paulus and his shrunken army of diseased, hungry, and frostbitten soldiers finally surrendered on February 2, 1943. The remnants of the remaining Axis forces in the north of the city surrendered two days later. Some 91,000 Axis soldiers were taken prisoner. This defeat, far more than the victories elsewhere, signified to the world that the Axis was not invincible.

1942

August: As many as 400,000 Jews will be murdered in occupied Europe during this month alone.

August 1: In an attempt to conserve oil for the war effort, President Roosevelt asks residents of the coal-rich states in the East to use that source of fuel instead of oil at every opportunity.

August 4: Auschwitz receives the first trainload of Jews from occupied Belgium to be designated for "resettlement."

August 7: Lieutenant General William "Strafer" Gott is killed by a German air assault in Egypt one day after reporting to his new post as commander of the British Eighth Army. • For the first time, the United States seizes control of territory occupied by Japan when the 19,000-man First Marine Division lands on Guadalcanal and Tulagi.

August 8: The United States executes six of eight German spies caught after coming ashore in Florida and Long Island. Two are given life sentences instead of death sentences after testifying against their comrades. • The day after a local victory on Guadalcanal, the Allies suffer a stunning setback offshore in the Battle of Savo Island, losing more than 1,000 sailors and four cruisers.

August 9: German operatives mark the ground near Long Island's Mitchell Field so that the important air base can be easily seen from the air. • In India, Mohandas Gandhi is arrested for impeding the war effort, three days after promising to engage his people in widespread civil disobedience if Britain continued to deny India immediate independence.

August 11: Vichy prime minister Pierre Laval claims that France will be liberated "when Germany wins the war."

Germans advance toward Stalingrad During the first half of July 1942, German infantry and armored forces battled to the Don River near Voronezh (a key city in the supply line to Moscow), Rostov, and other towns. Soviet resistance was initially disorganized but determined, and it delayed the Germans' crossing of the Don (*pictured*) long enough to move Red troops away from danger of capture. By mid-month, Stalin realized that the ultimate objective of this German drive was Stalingrad. Soviet resistance stiffened accordingly.

Amphibious Assault Doctrine

By the opening of the Pacific war, the Japanese had mastered the art of unopposed landings against undefended or lightly defended coastlines. This skill was repeatedly demonstrated on Southeast Asian coasts in the first few months of the Pacific war.

The Japanese, in fact, were the first practitioners of modern amphibious landings using purpose-built craft. In the initial Pacific campaigns, the hallmarks of Japan's highly effective amphibious doctrine were thorough planning, local air and naval superiority, and surprise, achieved notably through night landings. What the Japanese never developed was a capability in amphibious *assault*, such as that developed by the U.S. Marine Corps.

The disastrous Gallipoli campaign of 1915 largely discredited amphibious operations. But in the interwar years, the U.S. Marine Corps—looking for a distinctive role to justify its separate existence—decided to specialize in amphibious assault, coordinated landings in the face of a heavily defended shoreline. The Marine Corps Schools published a *Tentative Manual for Landing Operations* in 1934. In the remaining prewar years, the corps won some interservice support for its increasingly refined doctrine. Moreover, some actual landing craft were developed.

Guadalcanal marked the Pacific debut of U.S. amphibious forces. The Marine landing there was hastily planned and executed, and the failure to secure lines of communication might have been disastrous for inferior troops. General Douglas MacArthur in the South West Pacific Area and Admiral William Halsey in the South Pacific improved the doctrine through increasingly large and sophisticated operations, and the development of better and, especially, bigger vessels. Both leaders employed "leapfrogging": bypassing strongly defended outposts, which became isolated and strategically irrelevant. General Tojo later identified this amphibious strategy as a key factor in Japan's defeat.

Bypassing enemy forces was often impractical in the central Pacific, where routines had to be developed for attacking heavily fortified beaches where surprise was impossible. The bloody experience of Tarawa helped improve this doctrine, which involved preliminary bombardment of the enemy positions, for days or even weeks, then armored amphibious landings in daylight. By 1945 the routine was so effective that the Japanese gave up resisting the beach landings and instead tried to stop the attackers inland.

Marines land on Guadalcanal
American Marines storm ashore from a
landing craft at Guadalcanal in August
1942. After U.S. Intelligence discovered
a Japanese airfield under construction on
Guadalcanal, the First Marine Division
interrupted its training in Australia
and hastily shipped out to seize the
island. Planners saw the airfield as an
unacceptable threat to supply lines
to Australia and New Zealand and
a possible preliminary to a renewed
enemy advance to the south. The landing
by more than 11,000 Marines took
the 2,571 Japanese—mostly laborers
working on the airfield—by surprise.
Most of the enemy fled into the jungle
as the Marines stormed ashore.

America's first modern battleship
The USS *North Carolina*, the
first of the U.S. Navy's modern
battleships, participated in the
invasion of Guadalcanal in
August 1942. Though damaged
by a torpedo on September 15, it
returned to action, participating in
operations throughout the Pacific.
Its role was to screen carriers from
air and surface attack and use its
big guns to soften enemy island
defenses prior to amphibious
assault. The *North Carolina*
received 15 battle stars for service
during the war, more than any
other U.S. battleship. It was
decommissioned in 1947.

1942

August 12: Churchill arrives in Moscow for a summit with Stalin, who will be disappointed with Churchill's assertion that U.S. and British forces will concentrate on driving Rommel out of North Africa rather than relieving the pressure on the Soviets with a second European front. • Japan goes on the offensive in China's Shantung Province, capitalizing on internal strife between Chinese Nationalist and Communist troops.

August 16: The United States Army Air Force (USAAF) sees its first action in the skies over Egypt, staging raids against Rommel's troops.

August 17: USAAF high-altitude "Flying Fortresses" attack Rouen, France, in the first all-American air raid of the war. • A contingent of Marine commandos known as Carlson's Raiders attacks Japanese units and a seaplane base on Makin Island, killing the entire Japanese garrison.

August 19: A racing pigeon named Tommy finds its way back to England from the Netherlands. It carries a message from the Dutch resistance that reveals the location of an important U-boat base.

August 20: With a portion of Guadalcanal in the hands of the Allies, 31 American fighters land safely on that island at Henderson Field.

August 21: The Nazi swastika is planted at the 18,500-foot summit of Mt. Elbrus in the Soviet Caucasus Mountains. • The Japanese suffer 800 casualties in an attempt to retake the airfield on Guadalcanal.

August 22: In the past two weeks, some 75,000 Jews from the Polish city of Lvov have been murdered at the Belzec death camp.

Japan's unwise assault Dead Japanese soldiers lie half-buried on an Ilu River sandbar after Colonel Ichiki Kiyono's ill-fated assault on Marines defending Henderson Field on Guadalcanal on August 20–21, 1942. Grossly underestimating the number of U.S. defenders, Ichiki ordered a frontal assault with only 900 men. Nearly 800 Japanese were killed by the dug-in Marines. It was a mistake Japanese commanders repeated throughout the campaign. First Marine Division commander General A. A. Vandegrift wisely kept his forces in a defensive posture to protect the valuable airfield, moving reinforcements to critical points as needed.

Disaster at Dieppe

In 1942 raids by British Combined Operations on the coast of occupied Europe intensified. Commando raids at Bruneval and St. Nazaire, France, showed the value of an aggressive strategy in anticipation of an eventual invasion and liberation.

Canadian soldiers awaiting medical assistance near Dieppe

For the summer of 1942, the Combined Operations (under Louis Mountbatten) and the Home Forces (under Bernard Montgomery) planned a powerful raid, 10 times the size of St. Nazaire, against the French port of Dieppe. The purpose of the raid remains unclear. It may have been to test the practicality of seizing a port, to alarm the Germans, to "blood" the untried Second Canadian Division, or to reassure the Soviet Union.

Montgomery wished to cancel the upcoming raid, but after he left to command the Eighth Army, Mountbatten revived the plan. On August 19, 1942, 5,000 Canadians, 1,000 British troops, and 50 U.S. Rangers landed. They were covered by 237 warships and 70 squadrons of medium bombers and fighters.

The scale of support did not guarantee success. Poor planning and intelligence compounded by bad luck turned the attack into a disaster. Photographic reconnaissance failed to find powerful German batteries, and the attackers had lost surprise when detected in the Channel.

Only on the right flank, where commandos neutralized German batteries, were the landings successful. Shocked soldiers, who had been safe in Britain the day before, were marched off into captivity.

The raid failed disastrously, with heavy losses. Fifty percent of the Canadians became casualties. The raid at least showed the difficulties of a cross-channel invasion, and it persuaded Operation Overlord's planners of the need to bring their own port with them. It also convinced the Germans to place their big guns near the ports.

Many Canadians never forgave Churchill for Dieppe, and debate continues over the necessity of a raid that was likely to fail.

Fighting among the rubble When German troops reached the suburbs of Stalingrad on August 23, 1942, they found little more than ruins. But German claims to victory were cut short by Russian soldiers and civilians fighting back from those remains. The war broke down into smaller battles in which, as a German general said, "The mile, as a measure of distance, was replaced by the yard...." Here, in the fall of 1942, Soviet soldiers fight the enemy in an area already devastated by warfare.

1942

August 23: The fortifications around Stalingrad are beginning to succumb to the endless German onslaught, as some 600 *Luftwaffe* planes bomb the city.

August 25: The plane carrying the Duke of Kent (brother of King George VI) crashes in Scotland en route from Britain to Iceland. He becomes the first member of the modern Royal Family to die on active duty.

August 26: As many as a half-million German and Romanian soldiers attack the Red Army near Stalingrad.

August 28: The first of thousands of Japanese-launched incendiary balloon bombs fall on an Oregon forest.

September 2: British commandos raid a lighthouse off the Channel Islands (in the English Channel), seizing seven German operatives and secret codebooks.

September 3: Rommel's troops come under heavy Allied fire as they attempt an overnight retreat from Alam el Halfa in the North African desert.

September 5: Allied leaders determine that the invasion of northwest Africa, code-named Operation Torch, will include the landing of troops near Casablanca, Morocco, as well as Oran and Algiers, Algeria. • Soviet air raids bring nightly blackouts to the Hungarian capital of Budapest.

September 8: In a national broadcast, Roosevelt characterizes the global conflict as "the toughest war of all time."

September 10: In a speech before the House of Commons, Churchill reports that troops have been sent to India to quell the revolutionary impetus of the Congress Party. • Germany makes a renewed attempt to disrupt American East Coast shipping when a U-boat plants 12 mines in and around the Chesapeake Bay.

"Those who have seen Stalingrad from the air in the moonlight say it might be an impressionist's concept of craters on the moon. But when the sun is full and bright, Stalingrad from the air seems to be a dazzling desert of rhinestones—a mirage caused by tons of scattered glass."

—Time-Life correspondent Richard Lauterbach

Stalingrad resisters refuse to quit German soldiers enter a captured factory in Stalingrad, where they find little left to reward their victory. Even when the Germans had taken most of Stalingrad, they met strong resistance in the city's northern industrial areas. Factory workers joined militias, produced tanks and weapons (which they sometimes took into battle themselves), and repaired damaged Soviet tanks near or on the battlefield. Raging conflicts at the Red October steel factory, Dzerzhinsky tractor factory, and Barrikady gun factory lasted far beyond Nazi expectations.

SAVAGERY AT STALINGRAD

On the flat plain were thousands of bodies, tossed like broken dolls onto the ground. Most were Russians, victims of German artillery and Stukas. At the height of the bombardment, Petrov saw a tiny figure, no more than three feet high, waving his arms wildly. Amazed, Petrov looked more closely and saw that it was the upper body of a Russian soldier. Beside it on the ground lay a pair of legs and hips, neatly severed by a shellburst.

The man was looking at Petrov and his mouth opened and closed, sucking air, trying to communicate one last time. Petrov gaped at the apparition until the arms stopped flailing, the mouth slackened and the eyes glazed. Somehow the soldier's torso remained upright and forlorn.

—Historian William Craig, describing a moment during the Battle of Stalingrad, December 1942

1942

September 10: Düsseldorf is in flames following an intense, one-hour RAF raid that dropped more than 100,000 firebombs on the German city.

September 12: The British liner *Laconia* is torpedoed and sunk off Ascension Island in the South Atlantic. To the horror of the attacking U-boat crew, some 1,500 Italian POWs are among the victims. The U-boat crew attempts to rescue the Italians but comes under heavy American aircraft fire, leading Germany to decide to repudiate a 1936 accord calling for the rescue of vanquished crews.

September 13: Operation Torch planning gets underway in London, with U.S. general Dwight Eisenhower in command. • Some 1,200 Japanese die in a desperate bid to wrest control of Guadalcanal's Henderson Field from the U.S. Marines. • All Vichy French men 18 to 50 years of age, and single women ages 20 to 35, are ordered to labor for the Reich's war machine.

September 14: The U.S. emerges victorious from the Battle of Bloody Ridge at Guadalcanal when a large Japanese contingent is forced into retreat by 11,000 U.S. Marines.

September 15: The carrier USS *Wasp* goes down in waters south of Guadalcanal after being torpedoed by a Japanese submarine.

September 18: The shipping lanes into Charleston, South Carolina, are mined by a German U-boat.

September 20: General Eisenhower and his military team decide to schedule Operation Torch, the invasion of the French protectorate of Morocco and the colony of Algeria, for November 8. • The situation in Stalingrad has so deteriorated that German and Soviet troops are engaging in house-to-house combat on the streets of the devastated city.

The *Enterprise* survives bombing A gun position lies in ruins after bombs struck the USS *Enterprise* on August 24, 1942. A veteran of Midway and the Doolittle Raid, the "Big E" survived thanks to efficient damage control. The carrier was struck again in the Battle of the Santa Cruz Islands, but went on to participate in the Naval Battle of Guadalcanal, the "Great Marianas Turkey Shoot," the Battle of Leyte Gulf, and numerous other engagements, receiving 20 battle stars for World War II service. Though struck by a *kamikaze* off Okinawa in May 1945, the *Enterprise* survived the war and was decommissioned in 1947.

The Japanese Army's Fatal Flaw

The Japanese Army had spent decades preparing for confrontation with the Soviet Union on the plains of Manchuria. The China war and the war in the Pacific brought not only different battle environments but different enemies—one the Japanese failed to fully understand.

In the Pacific, the Japanese war plan called for a wave of attacks on American, British, and Dutch forces throughout the Pacific. Planners anticipated a short, intense conflict that would end to their advantage with a negotiated peace. Little consideration was given to the possibility of failure or to contingency planning should Japan unexpectedly find itself involved in a protracted war.

This heady optimism was inherent in the very fiber of the Japanese army. Rank and file were certain that their "warrior spirit" would prevail over weak-willed Westerners, even if faced by superior numbers or firepower. Emphasis was largely on offensive action. The Japanese soldier—whether a general conducting a campaign or a private manning a machine gun—was expected to fulfill his duty or die in the attempt. To question orders was a shameful sign of weakness. Since failure was not allowable, there was little call for tactical flexibility or deviation from the plan once underway.

The result was disaster. Campaigns such as those in Guadalcanal and New Guinea were pressed long after they were lost. Japanese troops in the field launched attacks that followed failed plans and satisfied their warrior code but had little impact beyond their own destruction.

The absence of long-range programs such as army pilot rotation also began to bear bitter fruit as the war dragged on past expectations. Lack of search-and-rescue capability meant that highly trained pilots who went down with their planes were lost. As the small pool of experienced pilots died in combat, they were replaced by rookies who were easy game for enemy fighters.

In their failure to appreciate their enemy's resolve and their own flawed mind-set, the Japanese contributed to their own defeat.

最後の幕

Japan firebombs Oregon On September 9, 1942, the Japanese submarine *I-25* surfaced off the coast of Oregon. The sub carried a Yokosuka E14Y, a small, folding-wing seaplane type dubbed a "Glen." Not long after the aircraft was catapulted from the *I-25*'s deck, Chief Warrant Officer Fujita Nobuo and Petty Officer Okuda Shoji dropped two incendiary bombs on Mount Emily, near Brookings, Oregon. Their hope was to ignite colossal forest fires and create panic. However, the incendiaries had little effect. A Glen is depicted in this John Meeks painting, *The Last Act*.

1942

September 21: The women and children of Stalingrad are evacuated from the dying city. • Boeing Field in Seattle is the site of the maiden voyage of the Boeing B-29 Superfortress, a high-altitude, long-range bomber.

September 24: Russian pilot Olga Yamschchikova becomes the first woman to record an aerial "kill" when she downs a German plane over Stalingrad.

September 25: Madagascar becomes controlled by British forces after Vichy governor general Armand Léon Annet refuses to accept peace terms and the British gain control of the island nation's main port.

September 29: The RAF's Eagle Squadrons, comprised of American pilots, are officially transferred to U.S. command.

September 30: In a speech delivered at the Berlin *Sportpalast*, Hitler mocks the Allies, calling them "military idiots."

October: Britain and the United States begin sending troop and materiel convoys to North Africa in preparation for Operation Torch. • Both Britain and the United States lower their military induction minimum age to 18.

October 1: Bell test pilot Robert M. Stanley puts the XP-59 Airacomet, the first U.S. jet, through its paces in the skies over the Mojave Desert. • The *Lisbon Maru*, a Japanese ship carrying 1,816 Allied prisoners of war, goes down with its human cargo when the USS *Grouper* torpedoes it and the Japanese crew seals the exits before abandoning ship.

October 2: The *Queen Mary*, sailing in an evasive zigzag pattern off the coast of Ireland, accidentally slices through its escort, the *Curacao*, which sinks, claiming 338 lives.

Hitler ousts the respected List Competent field marshal Wilhelm List was commander-in-chief of Army Group A in the Caucasus in 1942 when Hitler unreasonably commanded him to push on to the Soviet city of Grozny and its nearby oil centers. Faced with fierce Russian resistance along a sprawling front, List failed to carry out the *Führer*'s orders. Hitler angrily relieved List of his command on September 9, creating a rift between himself and some of his highest officers.

The massive Tigers The Tiger I was Germany's most famous and feared tank. After its introduction on the Leningrad and Tunisian fronts in 1943, Allied soldiers' first instinct was to identify every enemy tank as a Tiger. This huge, fearsome weapon's 88mm gun could destroy any Allied tank at long range, and its armor was virtually impenetrable frontally. Its elite crews appreciated these qualities, but because it was underpowered and mechanically unreliable, they nicknamed it "furniture van." By war's end, the Henschel company had built about 1,350 Tigers.

Allied raids over Ruhr By late 1942, American assembly lines were able to build enough bombers and fighter planes to support the United States' entry into the air war over Europe. Allied commanders began formulating a plan for around-the-clock bombing over the industrial centers in the Ruhr area of western Germany. In this new campaign, the Royal Air Force continued its blanket bombing of German cities at night while American planes struck industrial centers that were important to the German war effort during the day. In this picture, American bombers fly over the Ruhr after an attack on a rubber factory.

1942

October 3: Wernher von Braun, the Nazi rocket scientist who will ultimately go to the U.S. after the war and become one of the greatest minds at NASA, sees Germany successfully launch one of his earliest creations, the A4 ballistic missile.

October 4: Underscoring the Nazi obsession with Jewish genocide that will eventually contribute to the fall of the Reich, *Reichsmarschall* Hermann Göring claims that the war is "not the Second World War, [but]...the War of the Races."

October 5: Nationalist Chinese leader Chiang Kai-shek calls for the withdrawal of all Soviet forces from Sinkiang Province.

October 7: In a concept that will develop into the Nuremberg Trials, Roosevelt says that the perpetrators of mass murder and other wartime atrocities will be judged at the conclusion of the war.

October 10: Citing the "splendid showing the Italians in America" have made during the war, U.S. attorney general Francis Biddle suspends the "enemy alien" status of some 600,000 resident Italian citizens.

October 11–12: The Allies have an open supply line to Guadalcanal in the wake of Japan's defeat in the Battle of Cape Esperance.

October 12: The RAF's new long-range Coastal Command Liberator sinks its first U-boat in the North Atlantic.

October 14: Guadalcanal's Henderson Field is badly damaged in a bombardment by the Japanese battleships *Kongo* and *Haruna*. • The Red Army manages to stand against yet another intense, five-division German attack in Stalingrad.

France's Laval aligns with Germany "If the Germans are beaten, General de Gaulle will return," predicted Pierre Laval, prime minister of the Vichy government, in September 1942. "He will be supported by...the French people, and I shall be hanged." After the Germans invaded France in 1940, Laval was named vice premier in Philippe Pétain's Vichy government. Laval, convinced Germany would win the war, pressed for a German-French military alliance. Suspicious of his subordinate, Pétain had Laval dismissed, but Laval came back even stronger with the support of Germany and was named prime minister. When the Vichy government fell in 1945, Laval was shot by a firing squad—not hanged.

America's Aircraft Carriers

The United States entered World War II in 1941 with seven fleet carriers. By war's end, those numbers had quadrupled; the aircraft carrier had replaced the battleship as the preeminent surface ship of the Navy.

Airpower played a key role in the naval campaign against Japan, and the aircraft carrier provided the means to deliver that power over the vast distances of the Pacific. To that end, U.S. carriers were built without heavy armor or big guns so that they could carry more planes and fuel, and to maximize their speed and mobility.

The Essex Class aircraft carrier, introduced in 1943, was a 27,000-ton, 32-knot vessel capable of operating 90 to 100 aircraft. The complement generally included a mix of fighters, torpedo bombers, and dive-bombers. The proportion of fighters increased from about 25 percent of the total to 75 percent by the end of the war.

Though loaded with antiaircraft guns, the carriers also relied on escort ships—destroyers, battleships, and cruisers—for protection against enemy air and surface attack. Defense was enhanced by the carriers' own fighter protection—known as Combat Air Patrol— which remained overhead to deal with enemy air attacks.

Naval officers eventually realized that three or four carriers organized into groups with supporting battleships, cruisers, and destroyers offered the best combination of offensive punch and defensive firepower. These Task Groups could operate independently or in combination as a Fast Carrier Task Force, which provided considerable flexibility. Radar and combat information centers allowed the various ships and aircraft to coordinate offense and defense. These task groups benefited from a logistical supply system that made around-the-clock offensive air operations against land targets possible. This put the Japanese, who were capable only of quick raids, at a distinct disadvantage.

Despite the prominence of the aircraft carrier, only five carrier-to-carrier battles were fought during the entire war. Most carrier operations were conducted against shipping and island bases and in support of amphibious landings. Combining speed, mobility, and fearsome power, the Fast Carrier Task Forces made the island-hopping campaign of the Pacific war possible.

French town harbors Jews "Things had to be done, and we happened to be there to do them. It was the most natural thing in the world to help these people." This sentiment was shared by the citizens of Le Chambon-sur-Lignon, a small mountain town in southern France. Under the leadership of a local minister, Andre Trocme, and his wife, Magda, the citizens of the town began hiding Jews in their homes. A network of informants warned Trocme when searches of the town were to be made. Trocme encouraged a cousin, Daniel Trocme, to run a refugee house for children, but Daniel and his wards were discovered and shipped to the Majdanek concentration camp, where Daniel died. The townspeople saved nearly 5,000 lives.

1942

October 16: The supply line to the Burma front is crippled by a cyclone that claims 40,000 lives and devastates India.

October 18: Hitler issues a directive calling for the execution of all British commandos who fall into Nazi custody.

October 21: With defense expenses skyrocketing, Roosevelt signs legislation calling for an all-time high $9 billion tax bill.

October 23: The American M4 Sherman tank, equipped with high-explosive shells and capable of speeds up to 24 mph, makes its battlefield debut in the Second Battle of El Alamein in Egypt.

October 29: An overland military supply route to Alaska is opened with the completion of the 1,500-mile Alaska Military Highway through the Yukon Territory.

October 30: As a U-boat sinks, two British sailors rescue a German Enigma machine. Before they drown, the sailors pass it into Allied hands.

October 31: The cathedral city of Canterbury, England, suffers extensive damage in a retaliatory raid for the RAF bombing of the Italian city of Milan.

November 2: Operation Supercharge, a massive Allied attack on Rommel's line in Egypt, is successfully launched. Defeated Axis forces will retreat by November 4. • Some 100,000 Polish Jews from Bialystok and the surrounding area are marked for deportation to the Treblinka death camp. • Berlin's so-called Ancestral Heritage Institute, a quasi-scientific organization searching for biological "proof" of Jewish inferiority, obtains the corpses of 150 Jewish Bolsheviks for dissection.

Hitler overextends his forces
German troops advance in the Caucasus in October 1942. Hitler attempted to seize this oil-rich region while other German troops advanced on Stalingrad. His decision vastly overextended his forces; German men and tanks in the Caucasus quickly outpaced their supply lines. Moreover, they faced impossibly narrow roads and impenetrable walnut forests. In one pointless act, alpine troops scaled 19,500-foot Mount Elbrus and planted a German flag at the summit. Hitler raged at this, and in the end the Caucasus misadventure destroyed whatever respect he retained for his generals.

Oil fields burn in the Caucasus
With their eye on the region's oil reserves, the Germans began their ill-fated invasion of the Caucasus on June 28, 1942. In response, the Soviets, as they retreated, carried out the scorched-earth tactics that they had followed in 1941. When the advancing Germans captured the North Caucasus oil center of Maikop, they found themselves faced with the demoralizing spectacle of burning oil fields, such as the one pictured here in October 1942.

House-to-house fighting The Soviet tactic of "hugging"—keeping their soldiers close to or even intermingled with the enemy—nullified Nazi air and artillery superiority. It reduced the war to house-to-house fighting, which the Germans called *Rattenkrieg* (rat war). In October 1942, a German officer wrote, "We have fought for fifteen days for a single house with mortars, grenades, machine-guns and bayonets." He added that the battlefront had become "a corridor between burnt-out rooms" or "a thin ceiling between two floors." Here, Soviet troops storm through smoking ruins toward an apartment block in Stalingrad.

1942

November 5: General Eisenhower opens the operational headquarters for the Allied invasion of North Africa on the British island of Gibraltar.

November 6: Angling one more time for a second European Front, Stalin complains that the Soviets are dealing with the far greater Axis force while the British and Americans concentrate on the comparatively quiet North African front. • General MacArthur arrives in Port Moresby, the capital of Papua New Guinea, to supervise operations in that sphere of the Pacific Theater.

November 8: Allied forces land at their North African targets, with Algiers capitulating almost immediately. The U.S. and Britain plan to use occupied North Africa as a base for launching operations against Southern Europe. • Vichy France announces the severing of diplomatic ties with the United States following the invasion of French North Africa.

November 9: Units of the German and Italian armies occupy Tunisia without opposition by the French colonialists.

November 10: In a Mansion House speech covering Britain's victory over Rommel, Churchill famously quips, "This is not the end. It is not even the beginning of the end. But it is, perhaps, the end of the beginning." • All traffic into and out of one of the world's busiest ports ceases for two days when it is discovered that the Germans have mined the waters off New York Harbor.

November 11: Hitler ends the armistice between Free and Vichy France, occupying the entire country north of the Riviera. • The Moroccan city of Casablanca falls to the Allies.

The dependable P-40s The Curtiss P-40 won international fame in late 1941 when the "Flying Tigers," American-manned versions painted with shark teeth, fought the Japanese in China. P-40 fighters were built in the United States and flew with virtually every Allied air force. They proved valuable in France and with the RAF over the North African desert, and they shot down Japanese aircraft at Pearl Harbor in December 1941. Though not especially fast, they were stable and tough. More than 14,000 were built, and numerous versions and designations existed, including Hawk, Mohawk, Tomahawk, Kittyhawk, and, most commonly, Warhawk (*pictured*).

The Persian Corridor The Soviet Union and the British government became allies following the German invasion of the USSR. The Soviets were in desperate need of supplies, but a secure supply line had to be opened. They chose the newly completed Trans-Iranian Railway as the Persian Corridor to open the supply line from the Persian Gulf to the Soviet Union. Necessary permissions were secured from Iraq and Iran to use the corridor. Once the United States entered the war, it sent troops to guard and maintain the railway.

1942

November 12–15: The United States loses nine ships and the Japanese lose five in the waters off Guadalcanal. This is one of the most ferocious naval battles of the war, and a tactical victory for the United States.

November 15: The cruiser USS *Juneau* sinks off Guadalcanal, claiming the lives of five Sullivan brothers of Waterloo, Iowa. Despite popular myth, no law or executive order inspired by the Sullivan tragedy is created that would prohibit family members from serving together. However, the practice is discouraged.

November 20: The RAF launches its most destructive raid against Italy in this war, devastating the northern industrial city of Turin. • In an address to the French people, Vichy prime minister Pierre Laval encourages the Vichy alliance with the Third Reich in the face of continued threats from "Jews and Communists."

November 22: In a stunning turnaround, some 270,000 soldiers of the German Sixth Army are surrounded by the Red Army in Stalingrad.

November 23: The U.S. Women's Coast Guard Reserve is established.

November 24: The Japanese begin construction of a new airfield at Munda, New Georgia, their new base of operations in the Solomon Islands.

November 25: The U.S. government selects a site in Los Alamos, New Mexico, to build a lab devoted to the development of the atomic bomb.

November 27: Citing betrayal by Vichy France, Hitler disbands the Vichy army.

November 28: Against the recommendation of Rommel, his accomplished general on the ground, Hitler insists that his beaten German forces fight to the death in the North African desert.

"As there wasn't time to dig graves the bodies were simply laid out and covered with sand. Near one with a rough wooden cross marked 'Unknown German' lay pieces of vertebrae."

—AMERICAN WAR CORRESPONDENT WALTER GRAEBNER, DESCRIBING THE FRONT DURING THE BRITISH OFFENSIVE AT EL ALAMEIN, NORTH AFRICA, FOR *LIFE* MAGAZINE, 1942

Rommel's desert retreat Allied soldiers watch two German vehicles go up in flames. On October 23, 1942, British lieutenant general Bernard Montgomery's Eighth Army struck Germany's *Afrika Korps* near the village of El Alamein, Egypt. After 12 days of desperate fighting against an army twice the size of his own, German general Erwin Rommel finally ordered his corps to retreat—in defiance of Hitler's command to fight until they won or died. In those 12 days, the Germans lost 12,000 men and 350 tanks. Rommel had no more than 80 tanks remaining for the 1,400-mile retreat through the desert to Tunisia, where he hoped to find reinforcements and supplies.

Higgins Boats and the Beaches

American plans to liberate Europe depended on amphibious assaults. A shortage of landing craft hamstrung initial planning. General George Marshall eventually overcame the U.S. Navy's skepticism of the need for landing craft threatening to make landing craft production an Army responsibility.

Marines landing at Guadalcanal

A classic problem of amphibious warfare was getting troops from ship to shore; from the vessels in which they left port to the enemy-held beach. Andrew Higgins, a Louisiana boat builder, resolved this problem with his Higgins boat, which would evolve into the LCVP (Landing Craft, Vehicle, Personnel). Transported by ship, then released near the target area, the Higgins boat took troops to the beach and released them through bow ramps. More than 20,000 Higgins boats of many types were built. General Eisenhower later said: "If Higgins had not designed and built those LCVPs, we never could have landed over an open beach. The whole strategy of the war would have been different."

The 1942 landings in French North Africa involved more than 500 vessels and 65,000 men. The landing craft included early-model Higgins boats, some without ramps. However, British craft (largely makeshift) predominated.

The 1943 landings in Sicily and Italy were more sophisticated. Complex planning was required to ensure the optimum balance of men and materiel in each vessel; to coordinate air and naval support before, during, and after the landing; and to meet the logistical challenges of consolidating and swiftly expanding the beachhead. In both campaigns, amphibious forces made "end runs" to cut the enemy's lines of communication: successfully in Sicily, but without the desired outcome at Anzio.

The intricacy of amphibious operations peaked in the planning for D-Day (June 6, 1944), when more than 130,000 men hit five Normandy beaches. For months afterward, those beaches operated as ports. The last major amphibious landings in Europe—in southern France in August 1944—had typical outcomes: Formidable Axis defenses were virtually negated by Allied air and naval superiority. The troops reached shore with relatively few casualties.

1942

December 1: The United States institutes a gasoline-rationing program across the nation.

December 2: In a breakthrough that will make atomic weaponry a reality, University of Chicago physicists Enrico Fermi and Arthur Compton achieve the first nuclear chain reaction.

December 3: Attacking American bombers hamper the efforts of Japanese engineers to build an airfield on New Georgia in the Solomon Islands.

December 4: Long-range U.S. Liberator bombers sink ships in a raid on Naples, Italy.

December 5: The German hospital ship *Graz* sinks after being torpedoed off the coast of Libya.

December 7: More than 700 young German Edelweiss Pirates, a group formed in response to the rigidity of the Hitler Youth movement, are arrested by the Gestapo in Düsseldorf, Cologne, and several other cities. • The USS *New Jersey*, the largest battleship in the U.S. fleet, is launched from the Philadelphia Navy Shipyard on the first anniversary of the Japanese attack on Pearl Harbor.

December 8: Spanish dictator General Francisco Franco delivers a speech in Madrid. He defends his Axis alliance by claiming he'd rather be a Fascist than a Communist.

December 11: Hitler orders that the surrounded and besieged German Sixth Army may not retreat from Stalingrad.

December 13: The "Shark" Enigma code, which was especially difficult to crack due to its use of an extra rotor, is finally deciphered. This intelligence breakthrough allows the Allies to resume intercepting German communications to U-boats in the Atlantic.

The Flying Fortresses B-17 Flying Fortresses bomb Lae, New Guinea. Many B-17s were destroyed on the ground by Japanese attacks in the opening days of the war, and the heavy bombers that survived attempted to interdict enemy shipping, with mixed results. Pacific-based B-17s proved more useful in attacks against enemy bases in the island-hopping campaign that followed Midway. The B-17 was tough, though early models were vulnerable to attack from the rear. The "belly gunner" also faced a horrifying fate if the plane was forced to land without its landing gear.

African American Soldiers

In April 1944, nine African American soldiers were denied service at several establishments in Texas. As they left, "about two dozen German prisoners of war, with two American guards came to the station," remembered Corporal Rupert Trimmingham,

Fighter pilot Lieutenant Andrew D. Marshall (left)

one of the black soldiers. "They...had their meals served, talked, smoked, in fact had quite a swell time....I could not help but ask myself why they are treated better than we are?"

In the 1940s, the segregation of African Americans was not limited to civilian life. About 909,000 black Americans served in the Army during WWII, but most of these recruits were assigned to support details because military leaders questioned their ability to perform effectively in combat.

Two all-black infantry divisions, the 92nd and 93rd, were led by white officers, some of whom were openly racist. Morale was low in these units due to substandard facilities, poor training, low pay, and inferior commanders. The 93rd was shipped to the Pacific and showed promise in its first few fights. It was later split up, with its troops assigned to support positions.

The 92nd Division, nicknamed the Buffalo Division, had mixed success in Italy. By the end of fighting, the division had suffered about 22 percent casualties while earning about 12,000 decorations. Its erratic performance in the field, due primarily to ineffective leadership, damaged the division's reputation and reinforced the stereotype that African Americans were unfit for combat.

Tuskegee, Alabama, became the training site for black pilots. The 99th Fighter Squadron and the 332nd Fighter Group were two of the units formed from its graduates. The 99th was inadequately trained when it was sent into combat, and its poor performance placed the Tuskegee program in jeopardy. Given a second chance, these airmen eventually proved themselves in combat. By the end of the war, almost 1,000 pilots had graduated from Tuskegee and earned more than 850 medals. The 332nd Fighter Group, nicknamed the "Red Tail Angels," earned fame as the only escort group that did not lose a bomber to the enemy.

1942

December 14: Despite an airlift of supplies, the German Sixth Army remains trapped, inadequately equipped, and under siege in Stalingrad. The airlift is hindered by the weather, the Red Air Force, and the need to use many transport planes to support Axis forces in Tunisia.

December 16: Hitler issues a directive that Germany is to be purged of Gypsies, and anyone with any amount of Gypsy blood is to be sent to "resettlement" camps in the East.

December 17: An Allied official makes the first public statement confirming the Nazi death camps when British foreign secretary Anthony Eden tells the House of Commons that Hitler has begun to make good on his threat to annihilate Europe's Jews. • Vichy admiral François Darlan announces that French ships and resources at North African ports will be at the disposal of the Allied cause.

December 22: A group of Jewish partisans sets off bombs in two Kraków cafés, killing 20 German army officers.

December 26: Former German prisoner of war general Henri Giraud succeeds Admiral Darlan as high commissioner for French North Africa following Darlan's assassination in Algiers two days earlier.

December 28: Despite the wartime alliance between the two nations, Roosevelt admonishes the Los Alamos science-research team against sharing atomic secrets with the British.

December 31: In the Barents Sea north of Norway, German ships attack a British convoy that is attempting to deliver materiel to the Soviet Union.

Soviets punish German POWs During the winter of 1941–42, and again the following winter (*pictured*), German mechanized transport, tanks, artillery, and aircraft froze up, while frostbite killed and maimed inadequately clothed soldiers. Since Hitler still banned retreat, capture must have seemed a better option to many Germans, including those surrendering here. However, the Soviets took revenge for the crimes that Germans had committed against civilians during the invasion. The Soviets executed some POWs and sent others to work camps, where many died of exposure, starvation, and overwork during forced labor. Nearly 500,000 of the more than three million prisoners taken by Russia died in captivity.

Beasts of Burden

In 1939 Poland's cavalry famously fought against the invading Germans. Both Germany and the Soviet Union used large cavalry forces on the broad steppes of Russia and the Ukraine, including Cossacks fighting on both sides. A Soviet cavalry corps once operated behind German lines for four months. Italian mounted cavalry had some success in Russia. Two cavalry divisions served in the *Waffen-SS*, and the German army formed more units later in the war.

Red Army calvaryman on the Eastern front

Though the popular image of the *Wehrmacht* is of panzers, it remained dependent upon 5,000-plus horses in each infantry division for the war's duration. More than 600,000 animals drew German artillery and transport wagons in the advance into Russia. They suffered terribly, with 180,000 dying in the winter of 1941–42 alone. In July 1944 in France, British and Canadian troops in the Falaise Pocket saw the horrific effects of Allied air attacks on the congested horse-drawn transport of Panzer Group West.

While the U.S. Cavalry was mechanized by the end of 1941, the 26th Cavalry Regiment of the Philippine Scouts is said to have made the last American charge, on the Bataan Peninsula in January 1942. Britain mechanized its last cavalry division in Palestine in 1941, but the Burma Frontier Force made a suicidal charge against the Japanese at Toungoo in March 1942. The Japanese in turn used cavalry regiments in China and mule transport in the rugged terrain of New Guinea and Burma, as did their opponents there and in Italy.

Nuclear breakthrough A number of scientists and dignitaries gathered together on December 2, 1942, on a platform next to a large oblong structure of bricks and wooden timbers. They were in a racquet court under the west stands of Stagg Field at the University of Chicago. Physicist Enrico Fermi closely monitored a set of instruments, and at 3:25 p.m. directed a colleague to withdraw a rod from the structure. For 28 minutes, Fermi and onlookers witnessed the first artificial self-sustaining nuclear chain reaction. The experiment produced only about a half watt of controlled energy, but it was the first step in developing the atomic bomb.

1943

January: The German Sixth Army, trapped in Stalingrad, is in desperate need of food and supplies the men need to survive.

January 1: Americans' annual salaries are capped at $25,000, part of a short-lived plan designed to curb inflation. The law will be repealed within the year.

January 4: After forcing the Japanese to quit Guadalcanal, the U.S. Navy attacks Japan's new Solomon Islands base at Munda, New Georgia.

January 5: In an effort to put a stop to the Axis practice of seizing property and goods from occupied nations, 18 Allied nations agree that property transfers and similar business conducted under German or Italian occupation can be declared null and void at the discretion of the occupied government.

January 6: Ion Antonescu's forces detain and execute scores of disbanded Fascists after another attempt by the Iron Guard to wrest away control of Antonescu's Romanian government.

January 10: A Soviet force of nearly 300,000 men closes in on the surrounded German Sixth Army at Stalingrad following the refusal of German general Friedrich Paulus to negotiate a surrender.

January 11: The Chinese Nationalists form an official alliance with the United States and Britain. This comes two days after their Japanese-puppet counterparts in Nanking declared war against the Allies.

January 13: The Germans brutally suppress dissent in occupied Bulgaria, executing 36 anti-Nazi protestors in the capital of Sofia.

Tanaka's claims to fame Rear Admiral Tanaka Raizo was the leading tactical commander of Japanese destroyer forces during the war. His finest hour came during the Battle of Tassafaronga off Guadalcanal on November 30, 1942, when his eight destroyers were ambushed by U.S. warships. Heavily outgunned, Tanaka sank one American cruiser and damaged three others with "Long Lance" torpedoes, while losing only a single destroyer. Tanaka also gained fame for his tenacious effort to resupply Japanese troops on Guadalcanal via the so-called "Tokyo Express." He was exiled to a shore command in 1943 because of his criticism of Japanese strategy and tactics in the Solomons.

Manstein's successes
Generalfeldmarschall Erich von Manstein devised the *Sichelschnitt* (sickle-cut) plan that allowed troops to move past France's Maginot Line in 1940. Sent into Russia in late 1942 to rescue the trapped Sixth Army, Manstein fought through blizzards to within 30 miles of Stalingrad on December 19 before being stopped by the Red Army. Put in charge of Army Group

South, Manstein halted the Red Army offensive and went on to capture Kharkov. A strong supporter of the Nazi Party, he accepted huge bribes from Hitler. However, the *Führer* relieved him of command in 1944.

1943

January 14: The RAF raids German U-boat ports at Lorient and Cherbourg in occupied France.

January 14–24: The Allied leadership meets in Casablanca, Morocco, to strategize the next phase of the global war. First priority is assigned to the defeat of the U-boats. In addition, Roosevelt and Churchill announce publicly that they will demand the unconditional surrender of the Axis countries.

January 15: Acting on assurances from Hermann Göring, Hitler calls for the daily delivery of 300 tons of supplies to the trapped Sixth Army in Stalingrad. While 300 tons would meet the needs of the men on the ground, it is far beyond what the *Luftwaffe* can accomplish.

January 16: For the first time in months, the RAF bombs Berlin.

January 18: After two and a half years, the siege of Leningrad comes to an end. With some 20,000 civilian deaths a day, relief has come too late for many of the city's residents. • The German army fields its new weapon, the Mark VI Tiger heavy tank, in a battle on the outskirts of the Tunisian capital of Tunis. • Realizing that the German concept of "resettlement" is a charade designed to lead them quietly to their deaths, the Jews of the Warsaw Ghetto fight back for the first time.

January 21: Dr. Nahum Goldmann, president of the World Jewish Congress in New York, receives a telegram from prisoners in the Warsaw Ghetto. They plead for aid and say, in part, that they are "poised at the brink of...annihilation" and that they "live with the awareness that in the most terrible days of our history you did not come to our aid."

Japanese Rivals: Army vs. Navy

The effectiveness of the Japanese military during the war was seriously diminished by the dissension—even outright hostility—between the Imperial Army and Imperial Navy. This conflict was rooted in a history of fierce competition for funding, endless battles for political influence, a fundamental difference in worldview, and disagreement on strategic policy.

Some Japanese naval officers tended to be more cosmopolitan in outlook, while most of the Army remained provincial and deeply conservative. Militarily, the Navy placed strategic emphasis on Southeast Asia, while the Army focused almost exclusively on China and Russia.

The Japanese command structure exacerbated interservice squabbling by allowing the two services to function as antagonistic equals. No authoritative joint command structure existed. Nor was there a meaningful recourse to a higher authority or method for resolving interservice differences.

The result was an almost pathological mutual mistrust. The services consistently failed to pool information, coordinate operations, or cooperate on the battlefield. With few exceptions, they did not share research, supplies, materiel, or resources, even when faced with disaster.

Squabbles could descend to astonishing pettiness. At the Mitsubishi factory at Nagoya, locked doors were put in place to conceal each service's contract work from the other. On a more serious level, some Army officers were not informed about the extent of the 1942 naval catastrophe at Midway until as late as 1945.

The outcome of this fratricidal relationship was inescapable: an impaired war effort and the speedier defeat of both services.

Americans listen in on Japanese An NBC technician mans a listening post in North Hollywood, California, monitoring shortwave radio broadcasts from the Far East. Numerous listening posts were maintained by American press associations, broadcasters, and government agencies—such as the Federal Communications Commission—to monitor foreign broadcasts. Though such broadcasts tended to be heavily laced with propaganda, they also provided clues about enemy intentions, policy changes, and other useful information.

1943

January 21: Six teachers and 38 students, most under the age of seven, are killed when the *Luftwaffe* destroys the Catford Central School for Girls during a bombing raid of London.

January 22: Hitler refuses to consider the surrender of his forces at Stalingrad despite a desperate message from General Friedrich Paulus reporting dire conditions on the ground.

January 23: The British Eighth Army captures Tripoli, the capital of the Italian colony of Libya. • The United States seizes control of Kokumbona and Mount Austen, Japan's last two strongholds on Guadalcanal.

January 27: American bombers attack the critical port at Wilhelmshaven, Germany, causing extensive damage. It is the first air raid against Germany conducted exclusively by American forces.

January 29: Dr. Ernst Kaltenbrunner takes the post in Hitler's inner circle vacated by the assassinated Reinhard Heydrich. Kaltenbrunner will oversee the death camps, the *Einsatzgruppen*, the SS, and the Gestapo.

January 30: As Germans in Berlin gather to observe Hitler's 10th anniversary as *Führer*, RAF bombers sweep down over the city in their first daytime raid on the German capital. • The H2S bombing radar, a device that displays the contours of the ground below a bomber, is made operational by the RAF.

January 31: To Hitler's disgust, newly promoted field marshal Friedrich Paulus surrenders to the Red Army at Stalingrad. Hitler made the promotion because no field marshal in German history had surrendered.

U.S. in control of Guadalcanal Rowdy American servicemen celebrate Christmas on Guadalcanal in a scene far removed from the perilous early days of the campaign. By January 1943, the Japanese conceded defeat and started to evacuate surviving troops from the island. As the war moved on, U.S. engineers transformed Guadalcanal into a bustling rear-area base, complete with full amenities. The campaign had cost Japan nearly 25,000 dead, irreplaceable resources, and control of the central portion of the Solomon Islands. At a cost of approximately 1,600 Marines and soldiers killed, the U.S. had turned the tide of the ground war in the Pacific.

Paulus surrenders In November 1942, surprise Soviet offensives isolated the German Sixth Army in Stalingrad, led by General Friedrich Paulus. Hitler refused to allow Paulus to break out while escape might have been possible, even though the German forces were not equipped with sufficient clothing, food, or medical supplies to withstand the Soviet winter. On January 30, 1943, the *Führer* promoted Paulus to *Generalfeldmarschall*, assuming that a man of such rank would either fight to the death or commit suicide rather than surrender. Paulus, hoping to save some of his men, is seen here surrendering to the Soviets on January 31.

The casualties of Stalingrad These German soldiers were taken captive by the Soviets following the surrender. The Battle of Stalingrad has been called the bloodiest battle in history. More than a million Germans and Soviets (combined) were killed, wounded, or captured. The 91,000 taken as Russian POWs were already exhausted, starving, and weakened by disease and untreated wounds. Only 6,000 of them would survive the overwork and malnutrition of Russian labor camps and return home after the war. Some of the 22 captive senior officers, including General Paulus, signed anti-Hitler statements that were used in Soviet propaganda broadcasts.

THE TIDE TURNS

FEBRUARY 1943–DECEMBER 1943

Allied victories on Guadalcanal and at Stalingrad have to be put into perspective. In both cases, the overwhelming bulk of enemy armed forces remained undefeated. In each case, victory was geographically remote from the enemy heartland. The Allies understood that winning the war would be a long, drawn-out, and costly endeavor.

The turning points that are familiar to us now were less clear-cut at the time. In most cases, small victories were important in order to keep the Allied populations committed to an otherwise demoralizing and indecisive war. In February 1943, Hitler's propaganda minister, Joseph Goebbels, asked an audience in Berlin, "Do you want total war?" His audience clamored approval, but the mood among Germany's non-Nazi loyalists was somber and fearful. The changing expectations on both sides also played an important part in determining an outcome that was still more than two years away.

Just days before the German surrender at Stalingrad on January 31, 1943, Franklin Roosevelt and Winston Churchill met for a high-level conference in the Moroccan city of Casablanca, recently captured in Operation Torch. There they discussed the future direction of the war. They gave the European Theater priority, but they would not commit to an invasion of Northern Europe until the Atlantic could be made safe for the mass transport of men and supplies. While the naval struggle continued, they agreed, the two Western states would capitalize on success in North Africa by continuing a Mediterranean strategy against Mussolini's Italy. They would also maintain a relentless bombing campaign against the European Axis states to ease the pressure on the Red Army. This Combined Bomber Offensive was the Allies' substitute for a second front, which was deemed too risky in 1943.

At the final press briefing of the conference, Roosevelt—in agreement with Churchill—announced that the enemy states had only one option open to them: "unconditional surrender." Though secret contacts were occasionally made between individuals on both sides with a view to brokering an agreement, Roosevelt's public statement committed the Allies to a fight to the finish. No room was put aside for maneuver or compromise.

After a year in which the Allies lost 7.8 million tons of shipping, the submarine threat was expected to get worse during 1943. But a fortunate set of tactical changes tilted the balance in the Allies' favor. Most important was the adoption of new forms of radar on ships and aircraft as well as the transfer of adequate numbers of long-range planes to patrol the sea lanes. In May 1943, the German navy lost 41 submarines while Allied merchant vessel losses dropped sharply. Over the next two months, a further 54 submarines were sunk, prompting the German naval commander-in-chief, Admiral Karl Dönitz, to withdraw from the North Atlantic. The Allies' victory over the submarine menace was a critical one, for it made possible the full extension of American military and economic power into the European Theater.

That power was principally represented in the air in 1943. The Combined Bomber Offensive was officially launched as Operation Pointblank in June 1943, although British Bomber Command and the U.S. Eighth Air Force had begun around-the-clock bombing—the British by night, the Americans by day—from the winter of 1942–43. The offensive was aimed at the enemy's military-economic complex—the source of German airpower and the morale of the urban workforce.

Efforts to attack identifiable industrial or military targets could not be achieved with prevailing technology without a high cost to civilians. From July 24 to 28, a succession of attacks on the northern German port city of Hamburg resulted in the first "firestorm," which killed an estimated 40,000 people. Over the course of the war, more than 420,000 German civilians would die from the bombing attacks; a further 60,000 civilians would be killed in attacks on Italian cities. The bomb attacks immediately affected German strategy. The Germans established a large air defense sector. To do so, they had to withdraw valuable resources of manpower, artillery, shells, and aircraft from the military front line. There, German armies were forced to fight with shrinking air cover. Though military production continued to rise in Germany during 1943, the increase was much lower than it would have been otherwise. Bombing placed a ceiling on the German war effort and brought the war to bear directly on German and Italian society.

The Allies capitalized on these growing advantages. In North Africa, the Axis forces that were bottled up in Tunisia were slowly starved of supplies by Allied naval and air power in the Mediterranean. By May 13, when the battle was over, 275,000 Italian and German troops had surrendered. As had been decided at Casablanca, the Western Allies launched an attack on Sicily on July 9–10, 1943. During the capture of the island, Mussolini's regime was overthrown by the Fascist Grand Council and the monarchy. On September 3, an armistice was agreed upon, and on September 8, Italy surrendered.

That same week, American and British Commonwealth forces landed in southern Italy against limited German resistance. However, German forces were reinforced as the battle took shape. Though Naples was liberated on October 1, Allied progress slowed in the difficult mountain terrain. By the end of 1943, the German army—which had formally occupied Italy as an enemy state—consolidated a strong line of defense, the Gustav Line, south of Rome.

The Allies' pressure at sea, in the air, and on the southern front made the Axis task in the Soviet Union more difficult. Following the collapse of the German assault on the Caucasus and Stalingrad, the Red Army became overly ambitious. After the Soviets pressed the German army back, a swift counteroffensive around Kharkov in early 1943 was a reminder that the huge German army remained a formidable foe. Hitler listened to the advice of his generals, who argued that in summer weather, with good preparation, they could smash a large part of the Soviet army in a single pitched battle. They chose a large salient that bulged into the German front line around the city of Kursk as their battleground.

Operation Citadel lacked the geographical scope of previous operations, but it became one of the largest set-piece battles of the whole war. It followed a classic German pattern: Two heavily armored pincers would close around the neck of the salient, trapping the Soviet armies in the salient and creating conditions for a possible drive into the areas behind Moscow. Manstein, who commanded the southern pincer, wanted to attack in April or May, before the Red Army had time to consolidate its position. But Hitler, in agreement with General Model (who commanded the northern pincer), ordered a delay until German forces were fully armed with a new generation of heavy tanks and guns—the Panthers and Tigers.

The Soviets, for the first time, guessed the German plan correctly. Stalin had to be persuaded by Georgi Zhukov and the General Staff that a posture of embedded defense was better strategy than seeking open battle against a powerful mobile enemy. Stalin accepted it only because the defensive stage was to be followed by a massive blow struck by Soviet reserves against the weakened and retreating German armies.

In May and June, a vast army of Soviet civilians turned the Kursk salient into a veritable fortress. Six separate defense lines were designed to absorb the expected shock of the German armored assault. The Red Army numbered 1.3 million, the Germans 900,000. Each side had approximately 2,000 aircraft and more than 2,500 tanks. On July 5, German forces began the attack. They made slow progress over the first week against determined Soviet resistance. Zhukov's plan worked, and for the first time in the two years of fighting on the Eastern Front, a large-scale German campaign was held and then reversed without the crisis and retreat that had preceded other victories.

On July 13, Hitler canceled Operation Citadel after news of Allied landings in Italy. But at just the moment that German forces pulled back, the Soviet punch into the rear of the northern pincer was delivered. The German army had not expected a counterstroke of such ferocity. Over three months, they were pushed back across southern and central Russia. On November 6, Russian forces reentered the Ukrainian capital of Kiev. The Battle of Kursk, more than any other single engagement of the war, unhinged the German war machine and opened the way to victory in the East.

In the midst of the euphoria of victory, Stalin traveled to the Iranian capital of Tehran for the first summit conference with his Western partners. The central issue was a second front in the West. Though Stalin now privately argued that his forces could finish

A Russian T-34 tank rolls through a burning village during the Battle of Kursk in July 1943. Anticipating the German offensive, the Soviets absorbed the blow with a network of well-prepared defensive lines, then counterattacked. The counterblow drove the German army out of central and southern Russia and opened the way to victory in the East.

the job without Western help, the Red Army continued to suffer a terrible level of loss that could not be sustained indefinitely in a single-front ground war. After two days of argument, in which Churchill tried to insist on a strengthened Mediterranean strategy at the expense of invasion, Roosevelt was able to promise Stalin an operation in the spring of 1944 that would bring American and British forces in strength into northwestern Europe. One witness recalled a sober, pale-faced Stalin replying, "I am satisfied with this decision."

In the atmosphere at Tehran, it was easy to forget that another war was being fought

President Franklin Roosevelt meets with Soviet foreign minister Vyacheslav Molotov in Tehran in November 1943. Though their situation was improving, the Soviets continued to suffer terrible losses in their single-front ground war against the Axis. Roosevelt promised that the Allies would open a second front in the spring of 1944 with an invasion of Europe.

in Asia and the Pacific that was quite distinct from the conflict in Southern and Eastern Europe. There, it was still possible for the Japanese to attempt further expansion. In October 1943, the Japanese army undertook military operations in central China designed to erode the spread of Chinese communism. The Communist forces were led by Mao Zedong, who had devoted much of the Communist efforts to maintaining independence from the Chinese Nationalist army of Chiang Kai-shek.

In the Pacific Theater, the Japanese defeat on Guadalcanal was followed by a slow American advance through the

Solomon Islands and a combined American and Australian campaign in New Guinea. Japanese air and naval strength could not match the United States' huge production programs. And though the Allies' move through the islands of the southern and central Pacific, code-named Operation Cartwheel, was slow and costly, it proved unstoppable. By the end of 1943, the central Solomons had been occupied and progress had been made on New Guinea. Japan's major base at Rabaul was bypassed.

Throughout the region, Japanese garrisons were left to themselves in strategically unimportant places, increasingly hungry and sick but supplied by submarines. In the rest of the Japanese empire of occupation, imperial rule was consolidated. Anticolonial and anti-European movements were encouraged. The Japanese encouraged the formation of the Indian National Army under the leadership of nationalist Subhash Chandra Bose, who recruited 18,000 Indian prisoners of war to the cause in Southeast Asia. They were tolerated only as long as they fought for the Japanese. For millions of others in the so-called Great East Asia Co-Prosperity Sphere, one form of domination had been exchanged for another. In China, more than 10 million people died during the course of the war with Japan in a conflict largely unnoticed by the rest of the world.

1943

February: Along several fronts in Tunisia, Allied forces clash with German units in heavy fighting. Germany's Mark VI tanks battle the Allies' Churchill and Sherman tanks.

February 3: Germans observe the first of three official days of mourning for the loss of the Sixth Army at Stalingrad. Of a force of about 270,000 men, nearly 150,000 were killed and 90,000 taken prisoner.

February 4: The RAF Bomber Command receives orders that the next phase of the German bombing campaign is to focus on the destruction of Germany's U-boat manufacturing capabilities. • American General Dwight D. Eisenhower assumes command of the Allies on the North African front. • The British Eighth Army, fresh from victory in Tripoli, rolls into Tunisia.

February 5: Mussolini relieves his son-in-law, Count Galeazzo Ciano, of his duties as Italy's foreign minister, reassigning him to the ambassadorship at the Vatican. *Il Duce* will appoint himself to fill the vacant ministry post.

February 8: The Russians retake Kursk, a vital operations base, from the German occupation force that has held the city for almost 14 months.

February 9: President Roosevelt orders a 48-hour minimum workweek in several U.S. industries that are key to the war effort. • After six months of desperation, disease, and brutal fighting, the U.S. declares Guadalcanal secure the day after the last Japanese soldier quietly evacuates the island.

February 10: Civilians evacuate the town of Lorient, France, site of an active German U-boat base, in the face of a heavy RAF bombing campaign.

Hundreds of thousands die at Treblinka
Before Jews and other enemies of the Third Reich were exterminated at the Treblinka death camp in Poland, their shoes (and other possessions) were confiscated. This image alone suggests that a huge number of people met their fates at Treblinka. In fact, more than 700,000 Jews died at the camp, a death toll exceeded only at Auschwitz. Most of the victims came from such major ghettos as Warsaw (250,000 in the summer of 1942) and Bialystok, while others endured (or died during) long train rides from Czechoslovakia, Greece, and other countries. Deportations to Treblinka ended in May 1943.

The "White Mouse" Nancy Wake used her position as wife of a wealthy French businessman to help the French Resistance. She served as courier, obtained false papers, bought an ambulance to aid fleeing refugees, and helped get some 1,000 escaped prisoners and downed Allied fliers out of France. By 1943 Wake—called the "White Mouse" because she was so hard to catch—topped the Gestapo's most-wanted list. She fled to Britain, was trained by the SOE (Special Operations Executive, a spy agency), and then parachuted back into France. There she served as liaison between London and the Maquis, and also led guerrilla raids.

A warning to U.S. workers Allied propaganda typically portrayed the Japanese as nearsighted, bucktoothed caricatures or as monkeys, alternating between a subject of ridicule and an object of fear. This particular piece, probably made to be posted in U.S. defense plants, reminds workers that goldbricking hurts productivity and aids the enemy. It also links Japan to its Axis partner, Germany, through the subject's swastika collar medallion.

Allies lose fewer merchant ships In February 1943, a triumphant German submarine crew watches its prey—a U.S. merchant ship—sink. During the early war years, Allied merchant ships in the Atlantic were destroyed faster than they could be built. But by May 1943, Allied shipping losses dropped sharply due to increased air protection, the relocation of some U.S. warships from the Pacific to the Atlantic, and tremendous progress in antisubmarine technologies. Even though enemy air attacks still could be devastating, Allied merchant ship losses in 1943 were half those of 1942.

Bomber gunners U.S. Army Air Force machine gunner Sergeant William Watts fires at enemy planes from a bomber over Europe in 1942. Almost 300,000 aerial gunners were trained during World War II—a substantially greater number than were trained as pilots, navigators, or bombardiers, and for good reason. A bomber's very survival depended upon the gunners' skill at fending off enemy planes. Gunners also held the crew's most dangerous and physically disagreeable positions. They were unprotected by armor, and because of high altitudes, they sometimes had to endure temperatures as low as –60°F.

1943

February 10: Mohandas Gandhi stops eating in protest of Britain's detention of India's independence-seeking Congress Party leaders. He vows to consume only diluted fruit juice for the next three weeks.

February 11: The Allied assault on the U-boat program continues with the first of a series of intense RAF raids on the German port of Wilhelmshaven.

February 14: The RAF launches a nighttime bombing raid against the northern Italian city of Milan. • The Allies suffer a setback in Tunisia, as the Axis drives back Allied forces with the capture of the city of Sidi Bou Zid.

February 15: A German panzer unit withdraws from the Russian city of Kharkov in defiance of an order from Hitler to stand against the Red Army. The Soviets will retake the city the next day.

February 16: Radio Risorgi, an anti-Mussolini radio show broadcast from Britain and staffed by Italian detainees, begins operation. • The Vichy French government institutes a mandatory labor program to which young adults must devote two years of their lives.

February 18: A prototype B-29 long-range bomber crashes into the Frye Packing Plant during a test-flight near Boeing's Seattle headquarters. The accident kills 31 people. • Madame Chiang Kai-shek makes a state visit to Washington. In a speech before Congress, she expresses confidence in a Japanese defeat.

February 21: The *Wehrmacht* attacks the Red Army in an attempt to retake the Russian city of Kharkov.

February 22: University of Munich students Christoph Probst and Hans and Sophie Scholl die at the guillotine for leading the "White Rose" anti-Nazi resistance movement.

The White Rose From left to right are Hans Scholl, his sister Sophie, and Christoph Probst, students at the University of Munich who helped found the White Rose, a nonviolent resistance movement against the Nazi regime. Using a hand-operated mimeograph machine, the White Rose distributed thousands of leaflets eloquently denouncing Hitler's tyranny. On February 18, 1943, Sophie impetuously threw leaflets from the top of a university staircase, leading to the prompt arrest of the group's active members. On February 22, the same day as their conviction for treason, Hans, Sophie, and Probst bravely faced their deaths by guillotine.

Tresckow involved in Hitler murder plots "Hitler is not only the very enemy of Germany, but the enemy of the world." This sentiment was expressed by German major general Henning von Tresckow, chief of staff of the German Army Group Center. Although an officer, Tresckow hated Hitler and was a leader in the military resistance. An attempt to blow up Hitler in a plane in March 1943 was unsuccessful. Another attempt at a meeting in July 1944 also failed. Learning of this latest failure and realizing it could be traced back to him, Tresckow killed himself a day after the attempt.

1943

February 22: The Bulgarian government authorizes the deportation of 11,000 Jews from the annex areas of Thrace and Macedonia. Most will die in the gas chambers of Treblinka.

February 25: The Allies enjoy 24-hour bombing capability with the implementation of a schedule that assigns daytime raids to the USAAF and nighttime bombing to the RAF.

February 27: Allied commandos sabotage the Vemork power plant, a German plant on Norwegian soil that produces heavy water used in atomic weapons research. Engineers will get the facility back on line by summer.

February 28: The Allies outline the ELKTON Plan, with the goal of seizing and occupying the southwest Pacific region of New Guinea, New Ireland, and New Britain.

March: Spring mud bogs down both the *Wehrmacht* and the Red Army on the Soviet front, leading to a relative (though temporary) peace. • The Nazis begin the deportation of Greek Jews from their zone of occupation. Most are bound for Auschwitz, though the fortunate ones escape to Palestine via Turkey and a small number are rescued by Spanish and Turkish diplomats.

March 1: The Polish government is put on notice that the eastern part of the country that was occupied by the Soviets following Germany's 1939 invasion will be incorporated into the Soviet Union. • The Allies convene the Atlantic Convoy Conference in Washington. They agree on a plan in which the U.S. Navy, the Royal Navy, and the Royal Canadian Navy will share the escort of convoys on the Atlantic.

March 2: Berlin threatens retaliation against New York and Washington after the most punishing Allied air raid to date on the German capital.

Reprisals in Yugoslavia Serbia, Croatia, Slovenia, and other territories were joined together to create Yugoslavia in December 1918. From the beginning of its occupation in 1941, insurgents mounted stiff resistance against the German army. On October 16, 1941, rebels killed 10 Germans and wounded 26 in Serbia. In retaliation, the commander of German forces in Kragujevac reported on October 21, "For every dead German soldier, 100 residents have been executed, and for every wounded German soldier, 50 residents have been executed...all totaling 2,300." Thousands of other civilians were murdered by German troops. This Serbian partisan was hung from a lamppost in April 1943.

The Katyn massacre On April 13, 1943, German commanders announced over Berlin Radio that they had discovered a mass grave of 4,000 Polish officers in the Katyn Forest near Smolensk, Poland. They later discovered the number to be about 4,400 bodies, each shot in the back of the neck with his hands tied. The Germans accused the Soviet Union of carrying out these executions. The Soviet government denied the charge, accusing Germany of the killings. In 1944 an international commission determined that the killings took place in 1940 when Poland was under Soviet control.

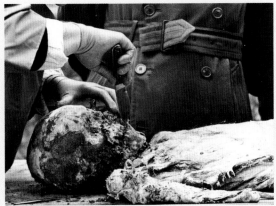

1943

March 2: In the wake of a devastating defeat at the hands of the Red Army, Mussolini pulls Italy's surviving troops from the Eastern front. • An Allied attack on a Japanese troop convoy en route to New Guinea culminates in the Battle of the Bismarck Sea. The Japanese will suffer heavy losses.

March 3: Nearly 180 Londoners die after a woman trips entering an Underground station serving as an air raid shelter. The crowd rushing to get under cover presses in and suffocates the fallen.

March 5: The RAF introduces its latest weapons technology, the OBOE navigation system, in an air raid over Essen, Germany, home of the Krupp plant. • The Reich war machine orders the Vichy government to deliver an additional 100,000 slave laborers. • The RAF conducts test-flights of the Gloster Meteor, its first fighter plane powered by a jet engine.

March 6: General George Patton assumes control of the U.S. Second Army Corps on the same day that German general Erwin Rommel loses his last North African battle. Rommel, accused of "pessimism" by the *Führer*, will be succeeded by General Jürgen von Arnim. • The Allies lose 13 supply ships when a North Atlantic convoy is attacked by German U-boats.

March 10: Congress moves to extend the Lend-Lease Act, which would allow the United States to continue to supply the Allies with war materials without any expectation of repayment.

March 13: Some 14,000 Jews are sent to Auschwitz and other death camps as the Nazis begin to shut down the Jewish ghetto in the Polish city of Kraków. • An attempt on Hitler's life fails when the chosen weapon, a bomb made of plastic explosives, fails to detonate.

Jews revolt in Warsaw Ghetto By late 1942, Jews in the Warsaw Ghetto realized that those among them who were deported usually went to death camps, not to labor camps as the Nazis had claimed. On January 9, 1943, SS chief Heinrich Himmler ordered that another 8,000 Jews from the ghetto be deported. On January 18, Warsaw resistance groups began fighting back with weapons smuggled in through the sewers. Ordered to quell the uprising, SS officer Jürgen Stroop (*center*) did so in April. He claimed to have caught or killed 56,065 Jews with a loss of only 15 Germans. *The Stroop Report* bragged that "the Warsaw Ghetto is no more."

Nazi Death Camps

The words "*Arbeit Macht Frei*" ("Labor Liberates"), displayed prominently above the entrance of the camp at Auschwitz in Nazi-occupied Poland, exemplified the deceitfulness and hypocrisy of the Nazi regime. Auschwitz was a facility dedicated not to the liberation of its inmates but to their systematic extermination in accordance with the plan for a "Final Solution" of the "Jewish question."

Auschwitz was the most notorious of the Nazi death camps in Poland, whose overall purpose was the extermination of Europe's Jews, together with Gypsies, homosexuals, and many other groups considered socially, politically, or racially undesirable. Treblinka, Sobibór, Majdanek, Belzec, and Chelmno were the other main extermination camps, aka death camps (not to be confused with the concentration camps, which had primarily penal, economic, and slave-labor functions). These extermination camps were designed to kill on an industrialized scale, this being achieved most efficiently through the use of gas chambers. The resulting corpses were burned in purpose-built crematoriums.

The victims usually arrived at the death camps by rail, often after days traveling in sealed cattle wagons under the mistaken impression that they were being "resettled"—an illusion scrupulously maintained by the Nazi guards and camp staff until the very end. Europe's extensive rail network readily

Jews at Auschwitz

facilitated the mass movement of these people, with railway lines that often terminated at the very gates of the camps.

On arrival, those chosen for immediate extermination—the aged, the infirm, children, and men and women deemed useless—were separated from those assessed as suitable for slave labor. Thereafter, those destined for immediate death were led to the camp "bathhouse," where they were ordered to store their personal effects and then strip to "shower" after their long journey. Any remaining illusions were finally shattered as the "bathhouse" doors were locked behind them. At that point, the deadly Zyklon B gas crystals were dropped into what was in reality the gas chamber, or carbon monoxide was pumped in. About four million people died in the extermination camps.

Allied gains in North Africa In the fall of 1942, General Montgomery's Eighth Army inflicted a significant defeat upon General Rommel's *Afrika Korps* at El Alamein in Egypt. At last the tide of German successes had turned, as Alamein now opened the way for a general advance westward by the British. Simultaneously, Anglo-U.S. landings (Operation Torch) at Casablanca, Oran, and Algiers were largely unopposed by the Vichy

THE CAMPAIGN IN NORTH AFRICA, 1942–43

French defenders. Tripoli fell on January 28, 1943, and in February the Allies entered Tunisia—where U.S. forces suffered a costly reverse at Kasserine Pass. However, the end was in sight, and the remaining Axis forces in North Africa surrendered on May 12.

1943

March 15: The Germans prevail in the Third Battle of Kharkov, the last major local victory for the Germans in the war.

March 16: Tired of having the burden of the entire Eastern Front placed on the shoulders of the Red Army, Stalin demands a second European front from the U.S. and Britain.

March 16–19: The Allies suffer serious losses when 21 merchant ships and a convoy escort are lost in a three-day battle with nearly 40 German U-boats.

March 18: General Henri Giraud, a French war hero and new leader of the Free French, restores full citizenship, rights, and property to French Jews. • The government of French Guiana aligns itself with the Free French, repudiating Vichy France.

March 20: Another attempt to assassinate Hitler, this time via suicide bomber, fails when Hitler leaves the vicinity before the bomb can be detonated.

March 22: The Nazis open a new, diabolically efficient death chamber at Auschwitz. Crematorium IV will allow the Nazis to drive their victims into an underground gas chamber equipped with a lift that conveys the corpses into the crematorium.

March 26: The U.S. Navy prevents Japan from reinforcing its troops on Alaska's Aleutian island of Attu, as it attacks and repels a Japanese naval convoy.

March 30: The suspension of Allied convoys to the Soviet port of Murmansk, due to very heavy ship losses, drives a wedge between the Soviet Union and its allies.

April 2: Hermann Göring orders every able-bodied man and woman in Germany to take part in anti-air raid civil defense, manning antiaircraft guns and partaking in similar duties.

The air war in North Africa A German Messerschmitt Me-109 is camouflaged to blend in with the African desert. Prior to February 1941, the fight for North Africa was waged between British and Italian forces. The arrival of German divisions commanded by General Erwin Rommel tipped the scales in Italy's favor. The equalizer for British troops was the superiority of its air force over the German *Luftwaffe*. Squadrons based in Malta and occupied areas of North Africa attacked German supply lines and supported ground troops across North Africa. The greatest threat to both Allied and Axis aircraft was the damage inflicted by sand and the torrid climate.

Armored cars From the outset, the main belligerents' armored forces included armored cars. Their primary roles were reconnaissance and scouting, so they needed to be faster and quieter than tanks, and to have a better range. Typically they had thin armor, light or nonexistent armament, and limited cross-country performance. This vehicle, a British Daimler, fires its two-pounder (40mm) gun near Tripoli in January 1943. Daimler armored cars performed well in the desert from their introduction in 1941. They served throughout the war, with nearly 2,700 produced.

The Battle for Cassino Early in 1944, Axis-occupied Cassino, Italy, stood in the path of the Allied advance toward Rome. On February 15, Allied bombers destroyed the city's historical abbey of Monte Cassino (founded by St. Benedict in 529), on the assumption that it was occupied by Axis forces. After the bombing, German troops moved into the ruins and defended them. During the brutal months that followed, the Allies demolished Cassino, finally capturing the city in May. Here, victorious British and South African soldiers and engineers pose amid Cassino's ruins with a captured Nazi flag.

1943

April 5: The German SS murders 4,000 Jews at the Ponar Woods near Vilna, Lithuania. • USAAF pilots staging a raid on a *Luftwaffe* facility in Antwerp, Belgium, miss their targets by more than a mile and kill more than 900 Belgian civilians. • The Allies launch their most intense air raid to date on both sides of the Mediterranean, hitting Axis targets in Italy and North Africa. • Japanese troops overrun British headquarters on the Mayu Peninsula in Burma.

April 7: A downcast Mussolini meets Hitler in Salzburg to discuss the string of recent Axis defeats and to lobby for a separate peace with the Soviet Union, but Hitler convinces him that their setbacks are temporary. • The British government releases the Keynes Plan, named for economist John Maynard Keynes, which calls for the establishment of a world bank.

April 12: Thousands of bodies—Polish army officers massacred by the Soviet secret police—are found in Russia's Katyn Forest. The grim discovery is seized upon by German propagandists and denied by the Soviets.

April 14: Joseph Stalin's oldest son, Yakov, dies in a German POW camp. Captured in 1941, he was offered back to Russia in a prisoner trade, but Stalin declined.

April 15: The Allies attack the important German manufacturing center of Stuttgart with aptly named bombs called "factory-smashers" and "blockbusters." • The U.S. high command is reorganized, as General Patton is needed to plan the American portion of the invasion of Sicily. General Omar Bradley will take Patton's place as the commander of the U.S. Second Army Corps.

The Dam Busters

On May 16–17, 1943, the British Royal Air Force launched Operation Chastise. With a new type of bomb, the RAF attacked three dams (the Möhne, Eder, and Sorpe) that supplied water to the German industries of the Ruhr.

Invented by aeronautical engineer Barnes Wallis, the cylindrical "bouncing bomb" needed to be released precisely and at a very low level. The bomb needed to "skip" across the lake surface to slide down the dam wall and explode.

The bombs were delivered from specially modified Lancasters, which were crewed by experienced (and very brave) British and dominion airmen.

The Eder dam after it was bombed

A newly formed 617 Squadron, led by Wing Commander Guy Gibson, trained over the dams of England, perfecting the technique, which needed to be performed in the face of intense flak. Of the 19 attacking aircraft, eight were lost. Gibson received the Victoria Cross, while his crews were decorated and celebrated. The dams, however, were repaired within months.

The dam raids boosted British morale more than they damaged the German war effort. Perhaps the most significant result was the creation of the elite 617 Squadron, demonstrating the value of giving highly trained aircrew specialized weapons. Later, 617 Squadron achieved striking success in attacking industrial targets and railroad viaducts with "Tallboy" bombs and in sinking the last German battleship, the *Tirpitz*, in its Norwegian fjord.

1943

April 16: As Allied air raids against German U-boats continue unabated, France evacuates from several key ports all citizens who are not staffing critical war-related jobs.

April 18: In the midst of calls by the Polish government-in-exile for an investigation into the Katyn massacre, the Soviets attempt to save face by blaming the Nazi Gestapo. • The Allies shoot down 69 *Luftwaffe* planes en route to Tunisia into the Mediterranean in a 10-minute dogfight. The Allies lose just nine of their own planes in the process. • Japan's Admiral Yamamoto, commander in chief of the Japanese Combined Fleet and the mastermind behind the attack on Pearl Harbor, is shot down and killed over the Solomon Islands by American P-38 Lightnings.

April 19: A force of more that 2,000 SS men under General Jürgen Stroop, sent by SS chief Heinrich Himmler to empty the Warsaw Ghetto, are unexpectedly driven out by lightly armed Jewish residents.

April 21: Responding to rumors that the Japanese are executing American POWs, President Roosevelt promises to follow through with his plan to prosecute war criminals.

April 23: Hitler demands "utmost severity" from his SS troops in their suppression of the Warsaw Ghetto uprising. • The Allies establish a London-based command under British lieutenant general Frederick Morgan to plan an invasion of Axis-controlled Europe.

April 24: A U.S. Navy fleet departs San Francisco en route to Alaska's Aleutian Islands to reclaim the Japanese-occupied island of Attu.

April 25: Turncoat Chinese army commander Sun Tien-ying joins the Japanese.

Japanese fight to the death on Attu A Japanese soldier who bound his own wounds and fought to the death lies sprawled in a defensive position on the island of Attu. The Japanese occupied Attu in June 1942. This operation was designed to divert American forces from the defense of Midway and Hawaii. Since the Japanese expected to annex Alaska, a base in the Aleutians would have been a good place to start.

Chinese, Japanese battle in Burma
Chinese soldiers battle Japanese units along the Salween River in Burma in June 1943. Spurred by American insistence, 16 Chinese divisions commanded by General Wei Li-Huang crossed the river on the night of May 11–12. Their mission was to trap enemy forces by seizing key terrain north and south of the Burma Road. Fierce Japanese resistance slowed the attack. Chinese forces to the south reached the outskirts of Lung-ling on the Burma Road in early June before a counterattack pushed them back. Lacking adequate supplies, the Chinese offensive finally stalled.

Race riots rage in U.S.
Federal troops patrol Detroit in June 1943 after 34 people were killed in a race riot. Detroit defense industries had recruited African Americans from the South, but the city's segregation limited housing and services available to blacks. That month, riots broke out in Los Angeles when returning servicemen marched against Mexican American "Zoot Suiters." In August, another race riot erupted in New York City's West Harlem. The U.S. Army—itself accused of racial prejudice—intervened in all three conflicts. Concerned about possible protests from the southern wing of his party, President Roosevelt avoided comment on the riots.

U.S. bonds finance the war Treasury Department workers such as these received, checked, and counted a million Series E bonds daily, sealing them into packages of 4,000 for distribution. Sold at 75 percent of its face value, a "war bond" matured in 10 years to $25, $50, $75, $100, $200, $500, $1,000, or $10,000. War bonds were promoted on posters, in ads contributed by radio stations and print publications, at sports events, and via celebrity appearances. More than 85 million Americans (most of the population) spent a total of more than $185 billion on War Bonds —at a time when the median annual income was about $2,000. The bonds helped finance the war effort and took cash out of the economy to control inflation.

1943

April 26: Angered by the investigation and accusations surrounding the Katyn massacre, Soviet officials sever diplomatic relations with Poland's government-in-exile. • A United States force reaches Alaska and begins its assault on the Japanese-held Aleutian island of Attu.

April 28–30: German panzer units attack Djebel Bou Aoukaz, Tunisia, in what will be Germany's last offensive armored maneuver in North Africa.

April 30: The British launch Operation Mincemeat by releasing a corpse—which is dressed as a British officer and carries falsified war plans—off the coast of Spain. The "plans," which indicate that the Allies will attack Greece and Sardinia, and not Sicily as long suspected, will successfully divert Axis defenses from several key fronts.

May: War shortages affect civilians on both sides of the Atlantic, as Canada introduces meat rationing while Germany further reduces the size of existing rations. • Due to improved Allied interception technology, Germany will lose a third of its U-boats out on patrol this month. This leads German admiral Karl Dönitz to implicitly concede an Allied victory in the Battle of the North Atlantic when he repositions his fleet to the south.

May 1: German and Italian forces retreat in Tunisia.

May 2: The war reaches Australian shores once more when Japanese aircraft pound the port city of Darwin in the Northern Territory.

May 7: A day after destroying Germany's 15th Panzer Division, the Allies score a major victory with the fall of the Tunisian capital of Tunis. Approximately 250,000 Axis soldiers will surrender in the upcoming days.

Nisei Troops

"Before World War II," U.S. admiral Chester Nimitz recalled, "I entertained some doubt as to the loyalty of American citizens of Japanese ancestry in the event of war with Japan. From my observations during World War II, I no longer have that doubt." The admiral's lack of trust in Japanese Americans had been shared by many at the beginning of the war.

Following the attack on Pearl Harbor, Japanese Americans were widely viewed as potential spies and saboteurs. Those of draft age were classified 4-C (enemy alien). Federal officials were more accepting of Nisei—second-generation Americans of Japanese descent—than of first-generation. After taking an oath of allegiance, the 100th Infantry Battalion, comprised of more than 1,400 Nisei, was activated. It fought in Italy in 1943, and suffered so many casualties that it was called the "Purple Heart Battalion."

In 1943 the 100th was assigned to the 442nd Regiment Combat Team, a segregated unit of Japanese Americans. The 442nd's motto was "Go for Broke." In 1944 the regiment saved the 141st Infantry Regiment, the "Lost Battalion" that had been surrounded by German forces in northern France. By the end of the war, the 442nd had suffered more casualties and won more medals

Color guard of the 442nd Regiment Combat Team

than any other outfit of its size and length of service.

Japanese Americans also served the American armed forces in the Pacific Theater as interpreters. About 60 Nisei were being trained at the Military Intelligence Service Language School in San Francisco when Pearl Harbor was attacked. By war's end, 2,000 Nisei had served in Pacific combat zones as interpreters, interrogators, and translators. They earned the moniker "Yankee Samurai."

"Don't rush me. I'm going to enjoy this. It's the last meal I'll eat in this world."

—Soviet tank crewman to a comrade, minutes before the momentous tank battle at Kursk, Russia, early July 1943

Million-man armies clash at Kursk Following its defeat at Stalingrad, the German Army formed a massive line of defense, with Leningrad to the north and Rostov in the south. It had a 118-miles-long and 75-miles-deep salient, with Kursk at its center. It was no surprise to the Soviets that the Nazis intended to attack them within the salient in an attempt to trap hundreds of thousands of Red troops. By the beginning of May 1943, more than a million Soviet soldiers and 3,600 tanks faced almost a million Germans with 2,700 tanks. Here, Soviet soldiers and tanks advance during the battle.

1943

May 7: Japanese dominance on the Burma front continues unabated, as they handily capture Buthidaung from the Allies.

May 8: Operation Retribution, an Allied naval operation designed to prevent the Axis from safely retreating from the North African front, is staged in the Strait of Sicily. • British women ages 18 to 45 are now required to fill part-time national service jobs.

May 9: Three days after the Allies launch what will prove to be their last offensive against Axis positions in North Africa, several *Wehrmacht* units in North Africa surrender. All Axis forces in North Africa will officially surrender on May 12. • Concerned by an apparent increase in resistance activities among the Dutch, the German occupation force imposes martial law throughout the Netherlands. • The Allies score an intelligence coup when a German flight crew defects.

May 12: Thoroughly fooled by Operation Mincemeat, Hitler orders Axis reinforcements to Greece's Peloponnese while relaxing defenses on Sicily.

May 13: As a prelude to a full-scale assault in Sicily, the Allies attack Pantelleria, a small Italian island about 30 miles off the Tunisian coast and strategically located in the Strait of Sicily.

May 15: The Axis launches Operation Black in Yugoslavia, a military action designed to crush Josip Broz Tito's Communist partisans.

May 16–17: An RAF raid causes extensive damage to two of Germany's largest dams and important sources of hydroelectric power. Nearly 1,300 people die in the ensuing floods.

Soviets halt German advance Soviet tanks, troops, and artillery stubbornly fought the advancing Germans, inflicting heavy casualties for each mile gained. As the Second SS Panzer Corps advanced on July 12 out of the town of Prokhorovka, it was met by the Soviet Fifth Guards Tank Army. About 1,200 tanks participated in this battle, the largest tank fight of the war. Although the Soviets suffered many more casualties than the Germans, the advance was halted. The Allied invasion of Sicily caused Hitler to order the Second SS Panzer Corps to Italy. Facing weakened resistance, the Soviets launched an offensive, which they would maintain until the end of the war.

Scorched-earth policies As the German Army pushed the Soviets through the Ukraine in 1941 and 1942, Stalin ordered his army and civilians to destroy anything that could be useful to the Germans, including industrial facilities, rail lines (*pictured*), communication lines, and shelter. The Germans practiced their own scorched-earth policy in 1943 and 1944 as they retreated through Russia and Europe. As his country was collapsing in March 1945, Hitler ordered his armaments minister, Albert Speer, to destroy any German resources not yet in Allied hands. Unknown to Hitler, Speer never carried out the order.

UNSTOPPABLE CARNAGE

Then it happened. It was about six o'clock in the morning. Our tanks and our cavalry suddenly appeared and rushed straight into the thick of the two columns. What happened then is hard to describe. The Germans ran in all directions. And for the next four hours our tanks raced up and down the plain crushing them by the hundreds....Hundreds and hundreds of cavalry were hacking at them with their sabers, and massacred the Fritzes as no one had ever been massacred by cavalry before. There was no time to take prisoners. It was a kind of carnage that nothing could stop till it was all over.

—Recollection of the February 17, 1943, Soviet rout of German forces in the Korsun salient, central Ukraine, by Red Army major Kampo

Sex and War

War notoriously disrupts traditional morality, and such was the case during the biggest war of all. From female teenagers jitterbugging with British airmen in Alberta, to brothels condoned or organized by armies, to rapes committed with or without official knowledge, World War II affected sexual behavior across the globe.

The demands of war made millions of lonely, fearful men and women mobile. Many found solace in relations that were more accessible than they had been in peacetime, mixing at dances or in bars. Traditional moralists decried the spread of disease and out-of-wedlock pregnancies. (Military commanders regarded sexually transmitted diseases as an efficiency problem.) Propaganda stigmatized the "good-time girl" as dangerous, although many women felt liberated by wartime sex. Gays in the military found that service gave them unprecedented opportunities to discreetly meet other homosexuals.

In previous wars, armies in enemy territory had frequently, if tacitly, condoned rape. In this

RAF officer with a French woman

war, sex crimes involving people from Allied nations were often punished severely. However, some Allied forces (especially French colonial troops and New Zealand Maoris in Italy) gained a reputation for sexual brutality. Soviet troops in Germany used rape as a weapon of terror and revenge against literally millions of hapless German women in 1945.

When large numbers of well-paid servicemen arrived in impoverished countries, prostitution became rampant. The practice was common in Egypt, Italy, and India (especially around Calcutta), as well as in Germany after its defeat.

Axis soldiers generally raped without retribution, notably in Nanking, China, in 1937, where Japanese soldiers raped tens of thousands of Chinese women. The Japanese army operated officially sanctioned brothels, in which tens of thousands of Asian women, mainly from occupied Korea, were used, mostly against their will. In 2007, Japanese prime minister Abe Shinzo formally apologized for Japan's treatment of Asian "comfort women" during the war.

Allies invade Sicily After the Axis defeat in North Africa, the Allies' next objective became the enemy's airfields and ports in Sicily. They also hoped that the fall of Sicily would force Italy out of the war. The plan called for American and Allied paratroopers to jump on the evening of July 9–10, followed the next morning by one of largest amphibious landings of the war with 160,000 British troops, 600 tanks, and 1,800 artillery pieces. These are two of the 26,000 Canadians who participated in the landing.

Allies ship materiel through Iran At the beginning of World War II, the Allies were aggravated by supposedly neutral Iran's coziness with Germany. On August 26, 1941, Britain and the Soviets invaded Iran, forcing Reza Shah to abdicate. The Allies then were free to move what ultimately amounted to more than five millions tons of materiel across Iran into Russia. The Soviet troops seen here operated horse-drawn wagons fitted with machine guns, as part of a joint Russo-British military exercise.

American cargo ships This painting by American artist Thornton Oakley shows a U.S. cargo ship unloading scrap materials—indicating both Nazi and U.S. air force losses—to be recycled. In the background, more ships wait. Cargo ships carried food, ammunition, clothing, guns, and troops. These U.S. merchant vessels came in all sizes and were outfitted with cranes for loading and unloading. They were subject to destruction by mines, battleships, bombers, submarines, and kamikaze attacks. During the war, 733 cargo ships were lost and more than 5,000 U.S. merchant seamen were killed.

1943

May 29: Chinese forces arrest the progress of the Japanese army.

May 30: Almost 20 days after U.S. troops first landed on the Aleutian island of Attu, it is finally recaptured from the Japanese, who lose some 2,000 soldiers in the battle.

June 2: Pope Pius XII sends a pointed message to the Allies in which he implicitly condemns the routine targeting of civilians in "terror" bombing campaigns, although he has not commented on German bombing.

June 3: German mining operations sink *Halma*, a cargo ship sailing under the Panamanian flag, off the coast of Halifax, Nova Scotia. • French generals Charles de Gaulle and Henri Giraud join forces in Algiers to create the French Committee of National Liberation. Their organization will act as the French authority wherever the French empire exists beyond the reach of the Nazis. • The Michelin tire plant in Clermont-Ferrand, France, is sabotaged by the Resistance, costing the Reich some 300 tons of tires. • The plane carrying British serviceman Leslie Howard, the actor who played Ashley Wilkes in the screen version of Margaret Mitchell's *Gone With the Wind*, is shot down by Axis planes over the Bay of Biscay.

June 6: In a speech ironically delivered a year to the day prior to the Allied invasion of Normandy, General de Gaulle insists that France does not want assistance throwing off the Nazi yoke, claiming, "We intend to win our liberty ourselves."

June 7: The Axis discovers the "Comet Line," an underground network of safe houses established in 1940 to rescue Allies trapped behind enemy lines. The houses stretched from Belgium through France, Spain, and Gibraltar.

Allies slowed by intense heat, resistance
Rough terrain and the stubborn resistance of German troops slowed the Allied advance across Sicily. Oppressive heat (100°F) also affected the advance. More than 10,000 Allied soldiers became sick with heat exhaustion and malaria. Those Allied troops who could still fight found that the enemy would not go down easily. The British capture of the town of Centuripe exemplified the intensity of combat. The British 78th Division launched its attack on the town on July 31, and needed four days of treacherous house-to-house fighting to finally capture it.

The Axis defense of Sicily Sicily was defended by some 300,000 Italian and 40,000 German troops with 50 tanks and 200 pieces of artillery. The Germans were formidable foes for the Allies, but the Italians were ill-equipped and badly trained, and had poor morale. German commanders realized that, given an opportunity, many Italians would surrender to the Allies. Lacking equipment and manpower to launch an effective counterstrike, Axis coastal troops encircled the island. In addition, German and Italian divisions were concentrated at the most likely Allied landing sites to prevent them from establishing a beachhead. Here, an Italian soldier mans a gun post on the coast.

Cunningham stars in Mediterranean British admiral Sir Andrew Browne Cunningham, the naval commander-in-chief in the Mediterranean, aggressively destroyed Italian warships and ran supplies to Malta. Using obsolete Swordfish aircraft, he mounted the first all-aircraft naval attack in history at Taranto in November 1940, cutting the Italian fleet in half. When Germany seized Crete in May 1941, Cunningham insisted on evacuating 16,500 trapped Allied troops in the face of heavy *Luftwaffe* opposition. He commanded the Naval Task Forces during Operation Torch—the November 1942 British-American invasion of French North Africa—under General Dwight Eisenhower, who praised Cunningham for his intelligence, devotion, and selflessness.

The power of the Browning The Browning automatic rifle (BAR), seen here on its bipod, was used by U.S. infantry throughout World War II. A lightweight, gas-operated weapon with a 20-round magazine, the WWII model of the Browning (unlike earlier versions) did not include a semiautomatic, single-fire option. Instead, it was solely automatic with an adjustable rate of fire. It therefore functioned more like a light machine gun than a traditional military rifle. Despite its drawbacks (including difficult cleaning, a tendency to overheat, and a recoil mechanism with a tendency for corrosion), the BAR was extremely useful for spreading heavy fire, and was standard at the squad level.

"Nobody ever defended anything successfully. There is only attack and attack and attack some more."

—U.S. Army general George Patton

The audacious General Patton "All real Americans love the sting and clash of battle," declared General George Patton in an otherwise largely unprintable speech to soldiers in 1944. Profane, mystical, flamboyant, and audacious, Patton was undoubtedly America's most controversial general during World War II—especially when he slapped and verbally abused two shell-shocked soldiers for what he considered their cowardice. His skills as a tank commander, honed during World War I, proved valuable in North Africa in 1942—and in Sicily the following year. He showed his most dazzling leadership during the Battle of the Bulge of 1944–45, in which his Third Army's incredibly swift, bold movements drove back Germany's desperate last offensive on the Western Front.

1943

June 8: Japanese military leaders order their troops to evacuate the Aleutian island of Kiska.

June 11: SS chief Heinrich Himmler orders the resettlement of all remaining Jews in occupied Poland from urban ghettos to death camps.

June 11–12: The RAF stages a massive air raid against Düsseldorf, Germany, bombing the city from some 800 planes.

June 13: Soviet director Mikhail Slutsky and 240 camera operators shoot *Day of War*, a documentary record of a day on the Russian front. • Seventy-four die when the Germans drop antipersonnel bombs on Allied troops in a raid over Britain.

June 15: Germany conducts a test-flight of the first jet-powered bomber, the Arado Ar 234.

June 16: The U.S. enjoys a dramatic victory in the skies over Guadalcanal. An attacking Japanese force is mauled, losing 107 of 120 planes.

June 17: In an effort to reduce the number of collateral air-war casualties, the BBC warns civilians living near Axis factories to evacuate to safer ground.

June 18: The Allies "soften" Sicily with a pre-invasion bombing campaign.

June 20: For the first time, the Allies engage in "shuttle" bombing, hitting more than one target per bombing sortie and resting and refueling at remote bases between stops.

June 21: Heinrich Himmler orders the Jewish ghettos of occupied Russia emptied and their remaining occupants deported to the death camps.

June 22: The USAAF attacks the German Ruhr region in daylight for the first time, temporarily decommissioning a critical rubber factory.

Soviet Fighting Women

Women served in the forces of other Allied belligerents, but Soviet women were unique in their role as combatants. Between a half-million and one million Soviet women served in the armed forces or as partisans.

Soviet soldiers with snow gear and skis

air and ground crews for three regiments—the 586th Fighter, 587th Bomber, and 588th Night Bomber. Among them, these units flew 30,000 combat missions and produced at least two aces, including Lilia Litviak. The 587th and 588th received the coveted "Guards" appellation as elite units.

In 1943 women comprised eight percent of the Soviet armed forces. Although many female recruits served behind the front, up to half were at the front. One source puts the total there in 1945 at 246,000. Women soldiers fought as snipers, mortar crew members, tank drivers, artillery crew, and medics. They were given few if any sanitary and medical amenities.

Female aviators won particular acclaim. Marina Raskova, a celebrated prewar aviator, took the initiative in the creation of the all-female Aviation Group 122 in October 1941. It trained

Other women served in mixed aviation regiments, and 33 Soviet female aviators received the title "Hero of the Soviet Union." So did some 57 other women. More than 100,000 women received one or more Soviet decorations. The nation regarded its use of women combatants as temporary. After the war, the women were rapidly demobilized, passing into historical obscurity.

The reliable, versatile P-38 The P-38 was designed to meet a 1936 U.S. Air Corps specification for a twin-engined interceptor. Lockheed's first military aircraft, the P-38 faced teething problems and went through numerous modifications before and after deliveries began in 1941. Ultimately, its reliability, exceptional range, and versatility compensated for its slightly inferior maneuverability. About 10,000 were built, including versions that carried rockets, lugged up to 4,000 pounds of bombs, and acted as ambulances and photographic aircraft. Lightnings, as the British and then Americans called them, saw action in North Africa, Europe, and the Pacific.

1943

June 24: African American troops and American military police engage in a gun battle in the streets of the village of Bamber Bridge, England, after the MPs attempted to detain the soldiers in a pub.

June 25: The ghettoized Jews of Czestochowa, Poland, are transported to Auschwitz after the SS crushes their resistance.

June 27: Following Jewish resistance, the ghetto at Lvov, Poland, is officially closed. Most of its 20,000 residents are en route to the Belzec or Auschwitz death camps. • The Allies attack the Greek mainland with a bombing raid. They target air facilities near Athens.

June 28: The air war continues in earnest, with Allied planes hitting such targets as Livorno, Italy, and Messina, Sicily.

June 30: The U.S. launches Operation Cartwheel in the Pacific, beginning in the central Solomon Islands. • As Washington closes the books on its fiscal year, it is revealed that a full 93 percent of the federal budget was allocated to national defense spending.

July 4: Prime Minister-in-Exile General Wladyslaw Sikorski and other members of Poland's ruling elite die when their plane crashes immediately after takeoff from the airport at Gibraltar. With the Soviet Union and Axis alike potentially benefiting from Sikorski's demise, there will be no shortage of conspiracy theories in the aftermath.

July 5: A German attack on Red forces at Kursk ends with a decisive Soviet victory. • Boise City, Oklahoma, is inadvertently bombed by a B-17 pilot who mistakes the lights on the town square for his training target.

America's female pilots Shirley Slade, with the Women's Flying Training Detachment (WFTD), appears on the cover of *Life*. In August 1943, the WFTD merged with the Women's Auxiliary Ferrying Squadron (WAFS) to form the Women Air Force Service Pilots (WASP). The WASPs were American civilian pilots who freed male pilots for combat duty. Some, including Slade, were ferry pilots, transporting military aircraft from factories to embarkation ports and training bases. Others served as test pilots, trainers, and combat simulators. Despite their noncombat status, they faced real dangers. Of the 1,074 WASPs active during the war, 38 lost their lives.

Polish kidnappings A Polish girl is chosen for inclusion in the Nazi *Heuaktion* (Hay Action) program. This program involved the kidnapping of "Germanic-looking" children and taking them to *Lebensborn* (source of life) institutions. Even though the Nazis considered Poles inferior, they took selected children with "Aryan" characteristics from their parents and raised them as Germans. Estimates of children kidnapped from Eastern countries run as high as 250,000. Only about 25,000 were returned to their families after the war. Some German families refused to give up the children, and some children refused to believe they were not originally German. Many children who did not adapt well were exterminated in concentration camps.

Navajo code-talkers Navajo Indians radio a message during fighting in the Pacific. The Navajo code-talker teams were used to relay radio and phone messages in their native dialect during combat operations. The method was fast and indecipherable to enemy eavesdroppers. At the time of World War II, the Navajo language was understood by fewer than 30 non-Navajos. The code was never broken by the Japanese, and its security has been credited with contributing significantly to the seizure of Iwo Jima in 1945. Approximately 400 Navajo code-talkers served with the six U.S. Marine divisions during the war.

1943

July 5–6: The light cruiser USS *Helena* is sunk in the overnight Battle of Kula Gulf. More than 150 of its sailors perish in the oil-slicked waters off the Solomon Islands.

July 7: The island of Malta, which suffered hundreds of punishing raids in the early days of the air war, receives word that Britain will grant it independence after the conclusion of hostilities.

July 8: Jean Moulin, the celebrated French Resistance leader, dies after weeks of torture at the hands of Klaus Barbie, the "Butcher of Lyon."

July 9: The USAAF and RAF drop paratroopers on Sicily. However, they are mistakenly dropped in an area too remote from their destination to fulfill their mission of securing airfields for the imminent Allied invasion.

July 10: More than 150,000 Allied soldiers land on Sicily, catching the meager Axis defensive force completely by surprise.

July 12: Some 3,000 tanks clash in the Battle of Kursk, the largest tank battle in world history. Although the Soviets will lose more tanks than the Germans, they can replace them more quickly.

July 13: In a desperate bid to realign his forces, Hitler reallocates troops from the Russian front to reinforce the defense of Italy.

July 14: The Allies stage an intense bombing raid on the Sicilian city of Messina, which serves as the importation point for Axis troops and materiel.

July 15: The Japanese naval air force suffers a stunning defeat, losing 45 of 75 planes while knocking out only three U.S. aircraft in a daylight raid against the Allies in the Solomon Islands.

Kids contribute to war effort American youngsters participated enthusiastically in wartime "victory drives," collecting scrap metal, aluminum foil, rubber, and other materials that could be reused. Some pulled their wagons from door to door collecting old tools and appliances from their neighbors. Here, boys pose on a scrap metal heap, displaying their finds along with a poster of the American flag. Kids also helped cultivate homegrown vegetables in community or family "victory gardens," and they took over jobs such as mixing yellow dye into the white butter substitute called oleomargarine.

1943

July 16: In an Allied leaflet drop over Italy, President Roosevelt and Prime Minister Churchill ask the Italian people if they would like to "die for Mussolini and Hitler...or live for Italy and for civilization."

July 17: Hitler orders reinforcement of German forces to the Balkan States, believing the region will be the site of the Allies' next move.

July 19: Pope Pius XII offers to shelter Italians in Vatican City as the Allies drop more than 500 tons of munitions on strategic targets around Rome.

July 20: Reversing an earlier order, Roosevelt directs his Los Alamos team to share advances in atomic weapons research with America's British allies.

July 22: The Allies capture Palermo, the administrative seat of Sicily and the provincial capital.

July 25: Having lost the support of fellow politicians, his own military, and a majority of the Fascist Grand Council, Mussolini is ousted in a bloodless coup. • Naunita Harmon Carroll christens the destroyer escort *Harmon*, which is named for her late son. Leonard Roy Harmon, a hero of the Battle of Guadalcanal, is the first African American to be honored with a U.S. Navy ship. • Still thoroughly fooled by Operation Mincemeat, Hitler believes that the attack on Sicily is a diversion and sends Erwin Rommel, one of his better generals, to Greece. • Krupp steelworks in Essen, Germany, is put out of commission by a punishing air raid executed by more than 600 RAF bombers.

July 26: Pietro Badoglio, appointed by King Victor Emmanuel III to head the Italian government following the deposition of Mussolini, abolishes the Fascist political party.

The Marauder exceeds its reputation An engine of a B-26 Marauder is blown off by ground fire over the French city of Toulon. The American-made medium bomber was dubbed the "Widowmaker" after a number of disastrous early tests. Indeed, the plane was never popular with pilots, who jokingly claimed that it required half the state of Texas for takeoff and glided like a flatiron. Nevertheless, it had the lowest loss record of any combat plane flown during WWII. In mid-1943, when the U.S. Ninth Air Force began serving a key tactical role in the European Theater, the Marauder was its primary bomber.

Raid on Ploesti By summer 1943, refineries in Ploesti, Romania (*pictured*), produced 60 percent of Germany's crude oil supply. The location was too far for bombers to reach from England, but the capture of Libya made such a raid possible. At dawn on August 1, 1943, 177 U.S. B-24 bombers flew out of Libya for a raid on Ploesti, one of the most heavily defended targets in Europe. Confusion after the lead navigators were shot down reduced the effectiveness of the raid. By the end, 54 bombers were lost. About 42 percent of the refineries' production capacity was lost, although they were rebuilt by the Germans within weeks.

1943

July 27–28: Some 20,000 German civilians die when an RAF raid on Hamburg ignites a series of deadly firestorms.

July 28: The U.S. continues to develop plans for an invasion of Kiska, unaware that the Japanese have secretly withdrawn from the Aleutian island.

August 1: The Americans hit Axis fuel supplies with a damaging air raid on the oil refineries in Ploesti, Romania. • German troops begin to execute a plan to seize control of Italy in the wake of Mussolini's fall from power. The Germans infiltrate northern Italy and disarm Italian forces on Crete. • With the occupation of Burma complete, the Japanese announce that Burma is henceforth independent, no longer a colony of Britain. • Nazi propaganda minister Joseph Goebbels broadcasts an announcement on Berlin radio recommending the evacuation of all nonessential personnel. For many Germans in the capital city, this is the first admission that Berlin could be in jeopardy from heavy air raids.

August 2: An uprising at the Treblinka death camp leads to the deaths of 16 SS guards, while about 150 of the approximately 700 prisoners manage to escape in the melee. • The Japanese destroyer *Amagiri* rams and sinks USS *PT-109*. Lieutenant John F. Kennedy and 10 of the 12 men under his command will survive the incident. Though Kennedy will be hailed by most for saving the crew, General MacArthur will be unimpressed with Kennedy and will question why the highly maneuverable PT boat was unable to evade the *Amagiri*.

August 4: About 150 Italian civilians die when the USAAF bombs the southern port of Naples.

Das Geschäft mit dem Tode

„Haben wir schon viel Dollars verloren, Delano?"
„Unbesorgt, Eleanor, wir bezahlen ja nur mit Menschenleben."

Japanese demolish Kennedy's PT boat Naval lieutenant and future U.S. president John F. Kennedy rides aboard *PT-109* in the Southwest Pacific. Kennedy was at the helm in the early morning hours of August 2, 1943, when his PT boat (a motor torpedo boat) was rammed by the Japanese destroyer *Amagiri*. *PT-109* was sliced in half, and two crewmen were killed. Though Kennedy was later awarded the Navy and Marine Corps Medal for his actions following the sinking, some officers felt he should have been court-martialed for negligence. *PT-109* was the only PT boat in the war to be surprised and rammed by an enemy ship.

The Nazis' portrayal of the Roosevelts In this 1943 German cartoon, President Franklin Roosevelt holds the war casualty list as Eleanor Roosevelt asks, "Have we lost many dollars, Delano?" The president replies, "Don't worry, Eleanor, we are paying only in human lives." Note the Star of David that Eleanor Roosevelt wears and her exaggerated lips. Nazi propaganda frequently presented the Roosevelts as puppets of the Jews, and also made fun of the first lady's support of African American singer Marian Anderson.

FDR's vice president Henry Wallace was President Roosevelt's secretary of agriculture from 1933 to '40 and vice president from 1941 to '44. A committed anti-segregationist, he declared in a 1943 speech that America could not fight the Nazis abroad and condone racism at home. Wallace's vision of a postwar America included close relations with the Soviet Union. This position put him at odds with Roosevelt's successor to the presidency, the staunch Cold Warrior Harry Truman, who fired him from his cabinet post as secretary of commerce in 1946. Wallace made an unsuccessful run as the Progressive Party's presidential candidate in 1948.

Operation Strangle in Italy British general Bernard Montgomery (*left*) and American general Dwight Eisenhower study the Italian mainland. The lack of coordination between Allied commands in Sicily not only prolonged the fighting but also contributed to the escape of more than 100,000 Axis troops and thousands of vehicles across the Strait of Messina to the mainland. For several months, the Allied air force had been active in its own operation over Italy, Operation Strangle. The objective was to shut down the Axis supply lines throughout Italy. Rail facilities, railroads, and bridges were pounded from spring 1943 to 1944.

1943

August 5: The Soviets recapture the city of Orel, Russia, from the Germans. • Sweden revokes the right of troop transit it had granted to the Germans at the beginning of the war. • A series of fierce battles concludes in the Pacific island chain of New Georgia, where the Japanese fled following their defeat on Guadalcanal. The Allies emerge victorious, capturing the airfield at Munda on New Georgia.

August 6–7: A small Japanese fleet attempting to resupply Japan's Solomon Islands base at Kolom-bangara is intercepted and badly damaged by a fleet of American destroyers.

August 9: In one of the first viable challenges to National Socialism in years, several German leaders form the Kreisau Circle, a resistance group calling for, among other things, the "acknowledgement of the inviolability of human dignity as the foundation for an order of peace and justice."

August 12: With Sicily all but lost to the Allies, Germany begins the successful withdrawal of a substantial portion of its reeling defensive force. Casualties include 32,000 Germans and 132,000 Italians. • More than 600 RAF bombers pummel Milan, Italy.

August 14: On orders from General Eisenhower, foul-tempered General George Patton apologizes to the two American soldiers he slapped in field hospitals after accusing them of malingering.

August 14–24: Allied leaders meet in Quebec for the Quadrant Conference, at which they hammer out details for the next phase of the war. It is decided that both the invasion of France and the occupation of Italy remain on the table. The invasion of France will take precedence.

Soviet Casualties

For those who doubt that the principal scene of conflict of World War II was other than the Eastern Front, the Russian casualty figures settle the issue. During almost four years of total war fought across the unending vastness of the Russian Steppes, among the ruins of the Soviet Union's towns and cities, and through the devastation of Eastern Europe to the very heart of the Third Reich in Berlin, nearly nine million Red Army soldiers were killed and 18 million were wounded.

From October 1944 to May 1945 alone, the Red Army sustained 319,000 fatal casualties. Also, of more than 4.5 million Red Army prisoners captured by the *Wehrmacht*, only 1.8 million ultimately survived. Many of them were then persecuted by an unforgiving and suspicious Soviet regime. The wholesale destruction of Russian towns and villages during combat, and the reprisal operations and executions carried out by the SS and the *Wehrmacht* during an uncompromising counter-partisan campaign, resulted in at least 18 million Soviet civilian war dead. Altogether, some 26 million to 27 million Soviets died. In contrast, this was more than five times greater than the total German war dead incurred from 1939 to 1945.

Dead Soviet POWs

1943

August 15: A 34,300-man Allied invasion force lands on Kiska, the last Japanese-occupied island in Alaska's Aleutians, only to discover it was abandoned weeks earlier.

August 16: The Nazis purge the Jewish ghetto at Bialystok, Poland, sending most of the remaining 25,000 inhabitants to the death camps at Majdanek and Treblinka.

August 17–18: Nearly 600 RAF bombers target the Nazis' rocket factories in Peenemünde on the German island of Usedom. • The Americans score a major victory over the Japanese on New Guinea when they ambush the airfield at Wewak and destroy an entire bombing formation of 150 planes.

August 18: *Luftwaffe* chief Hans Jeschonnek kills himself in despair over the failure of the *Luftwaffe* to defend Germany against the Allies. The Nazi command will lie about his cause of death to conceal their concerns about the status of the Reich.

August 22: Allied forces declare Kiska secure (and uninhabited) after a weeklong sweep of the island and a few friendly-fire casualties.

August 27: Germans and Italians clash in Ljubljana, Slovenia.

August 28: Bulgaria's King Boris III dies following an audience with Hitler, leading to rampant, though un-proven, speculation that he was assassinated.

August 29: Washington puts Berlin on notice, saying it has become aware of German atrocities against Poles and that the perpetrators will pay for any war crimes when the day of reckoning arrives. • Following Nazi suppression of Danish civil rights and the arrest of King Christian X, the Danes sink most of their naval fleet to prevent it from falling into Nazi hands.

The Hellcats Despite its inelegant appearance and hasty development, the Grumman F6F Hellcat naval fighter contributed hugely to Allied victory. An improvement on the Wildcat, it proved superbly reliable and potent. Production figures reflected its effectiveness: 12,272 built from 1942, mainly in 1944 and 1945. Altogether, Hellcats destroyed some 6,000 enemy aircraft, most of which were Japanese. First sent into action in August 1943, Hellcats were usually carrier-borne and armed with six .5-inch machine guns. They

could carry bombs, and ground-attack Hellcat aircraft employed rockets, notably at Iwo Jima and Okinawa. Night-fighter and reconnaissance versions also were made.

Skorzeny's daring feats After Italian king Victor Emmanuel stripped away Mussolini's power on July 25, 1943, he placed *Il Duce* under arrest and imprisoned him on the island of Ponza. After Mussolini was transferred to the mountain resort of Abruzzi a few months later, Hitler sent his best agent, Colonel Otto Skorzeny (*pictured*), and a commando unit to Italy in September 1943 to free Mussolini. Skorzeny's exploits later in the war included kidnapping Hungarian leader Miklos Horthy to prevent him from signing an armistice with the Soviets. Skorzeny also placed German agents in American uniforms behind Allied lines during the Battle of the Bulge.

The Hitler, Mussolini relationship As he reshaped Germany's government and society in the 1930s, Hitler turned to Benito Mussolini as a mentor for implementing his Fascist reforms. The war was not very old when Hitler realized that the Italian army could not be depended on to stop the Allied advances in the Mediterranean, but that did not affect his relationship with Mussolini. The situation changed, however, when *Il Duce* was deposed and imprisoned in July 1943. Hitler arranged for Mussolini's rescue and installed him as head of a puppet Fascist government. However, he no longer considered Mussolini a mentor or an equal.

Polish women led to their deaths German security forces lead Polish women to their execution in the Palmiry Forest. The Nazis spread their plans for genocide throughout each occupied country, killing Jews, political opponents, and anyone else they believed was a threat or an inferior to the Aryan race. They often took pictures like this to denigrate victims as they were led to their deaths. German officers showed these to their troops in order to dehumanize the victims, making it easier for them to perform their gruesome assignments.

Gruesome experiments at Ravensbrück During the course of the war, the Nazis built concentration camps throughout Europe. Ravensbrück, a camp primarily for women from many different nationalities, religions, and lifestyles, was located about 60 miles north of Berlin. As in most of the other camps, the Ravensbrück prisoners were required to do heavy labor or work in sweatshops making military supplies. Medical experiments were also conducted on helpless inmates. Two types were performed at Ravensbrück: testing the effects of sulfanilamide drugs on infected wounds, and studying the regeneration of bones, nerves, and muscles. This picture of Polish inmate Bogumila Babinska, smuggled out of the camp, shows the effect of four deep cuts on her thigh muscles.

Frick's fall from power Nazi Wilhelm Frick became Reich minister of the interior in 1933. He drafted anti-Jewish laws and other legislation that sent political foes to concentration camps. In 1943, after losing a power struggle with Heinrich Himmler, Frick was demoted to the ceremonial post of protector of Bohemia and Moravia. He refused to defend himself at the 1946 Nuremberg Trials, where he was found guilty and hanged. Frick's final words were "long live eternal Germany."

1943

September: The efficacy of Allied forces in India is jeopardized by a devastating famine in the Bengal province.

September 1: The U.S. military introduces its F6F Hellcat fighter during an attack on the Japanese base on Marcus Island.

September 2: The Polish government-in-exile publishes a report detailing atrocities against concentration camp inmates. The atrocities include bizarre medical experiments on healthy inmates at Ravensbrück and human skin "tanneries" at Dachau and Buchenwald.

September 3: A substantial Allied force lands in southern Italy and captures the town of Reggio in the province of Calabria. • Italy signs a treaty with American officials in Sicily, effectively surrendering to the Allies. The treaty will be kept secret for a time, both to aid Allied operations in Italy and prevent immediate Nazi reprisals against the Italian people.

September 6: For the first time in this war, Allied merchant ships are able to safely operate in Italy's Strait of Messina. • U.S. general Stilwell, Chiang Kai-shek's chief of staff, suggests that the Chinese Nationalists join forces with the Communists to defeat the Japanese. Chiang is disgusted by the suggestion and will ask the U.S. high command to recall Stilwell.

September 7: Corsicans take up arms against the Axis troops that have been occupying their French Mediterranean island. • Hitler permits his German troops, badly battered by the Red Army as they attempted to hold the Ukraine, to retreat to the Dnieper River.

British Defeat in the Aegean Sea

In 1912 Italy seized the 12 Dodecanese islands, located in the Aegean Sea, from Turkey. By 1940 Italian and German troops garrisoned the islands, just off the Turkish coast. Italy's surrender on September 8, 1943, prompted Winston Churchill to try to seize the islands so the Allies could strike at Germany's Balkan flank.

RAF fighter striking a German flak vessel near Kalimnos, Dodecanese

After British officers failed to incite the Italians to disarm the smaller German garrisons, Churchill ordered British infantry brigades and special-forces units to eight of the islands and the Greek Aegean Sea island of Samos. The Germans reacted swiftly. With naval and air forces already in the Aegean, they added reinforcements from Greece and Crete. These included *Luftwaffe* paratroops and a coastal raiding unit of the elite Brandenburg Division.

Airpower was crucial to the defeat of the scattered British garrisons. British (and South African) planes fought a losing fight against the *Luftwaffe* over the islands. By early October, the Germans had recaptured Cos. They seized Leros a month later and took Samos by late November.

German losses were minimal, while British casualties included more than 4,000 troops captured and the loss of more than a hundred aircraft. Losses also included four cruisers and seven destroyers sunk or damaged (including several Greek ships). The hapless Italians and the islands' people (who had welcomed the British landings) suffered from German reprisals.

The venture exposed Allied tensions over a Mediterranean strategy. Churchill persisted in his aim, ignoring his generals' arguments against a campaign far from the nearest Allied bases (in Cyprus and Egypt). Eisenhower and other U.S. and British commanders saw the diversion from the Italian campaign as unjustified. The two-month campaign was the Allies' last defeat of the war.

B-17s pound factories Beginning in January 1943, Allied bombing runs focused on German wartime industries. The first mass-produced, four-engine heavy bombers were Boeing B-17s, known as Flying Fortresses. These heavily armed bombers were designed to be able to protect themselves, but a loss of one plane in every 10 was standard. This B-17, called *Virgin's Delight*, flies over the Focke-Wulf aircraft factory it has just hit at Marienburg, Germany. Although the Allies destroyed many German factories during 1943, the Nazis quickly compensated by stepping up production in others.

1943

September 8: General Eisenhower announces Italy's surrender under Marshal Badoglio. Nazi officials characterize the act, undertaken by the new government under Badoglio, as treason.

September 9: The Allies land in Italy in full force, with the Americans establishing a beachhead near Salerno and the British landing on Italy's "heel." The city of Brindisi will fall to the British within two days, securing the region for the Allies. • Germany attacks the Allied base on the Arctic whaling island of Spitsbergen, causing considerable damage.

September 10: In answer to Italy's surrender, the German army captures Rome, taking control of the Eternal City from its former Axis partner.

September 12: Mussolini, under arrest at Abruzzi's Hotel Campo Imperatore, is freed in a dramatic raid by German troops, on Hitler's order.

September 13: The Allies' position at Salerno is in serious jeopardy, as several German divisions come within a few miles of completely repelling the Americans and British from their beachhead. • More than a month after the death of his predecessor, Lin Sen, Chiang Kai-shek is appointed president of Nationalist China.

September 15: Mussolini reorganizes Italy's National Fascist Party in an effort to regain power and restore ties to Hitler.

September 17: A depleted and heavily bombarded German force begins to withdraw from the Salerno beachhead as the Americans push inland to rendezvous with the British.

September 20: U.S. forces pushing in from Salerno in the west and British troops marching from Calabria in the southeast link up at Eboli, bisecting Italy with a solid Allied force.

Beheadings Naval civil service officer Chikao Yasuno prepares to decapitate Sergeant Leonard George Siffleet, an Australian Army radioman caught operating behind Japanese lines in New Guinea. Siffleet and two comrades were beheaded on October 24, 1943, at Aitape after natives betrayed them to the Japanese. American troops found this film on the body of a dead Japanese during the invasion of Hollandia in 1944. The photo received wide publicity, reinforcing the perception that the Japanese were savages who gave no mercy and deserved none. Chikao was sentenced to hang after the war, but his sentence was later commuted to 10 years in prison.

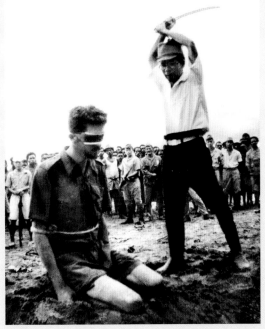

The *Kempeitai* Members of the *Kempeitai* (Japanese military police) pose with British POWs. Though the *Kempeitai*'s authority over Japanese civilians was limited, the organization had free rein in the occupied territories, where harsh military justice prevailed. The *Kempeitai* dealt severely with anti-Japanese efforts in occupied territories. It was also responsible for travel permits, labor recruitment, rear area security, counterintelligence, operating POW camps, and providing "comfort women" to military brothels. Though the *Kempeitai* is sometimes equated with the Gestapo or secret police, that description is more accurately applied to the *Kempeitai*'s civilian counterpart, the *Tokkou keisatsu*, which combined criminal investigation and counterespionage functions.

1943

September 21: Japan leaves the central Solomon Islands to the Allies after losing 600 men in an unsuccessful bid to defend Arundel Island.

September 22: British submarine troops sabotage the *Tirpitz*, Germany's preeminent battleship, as it sits in port at Norway's *Altenfjord*. • Recognizing that a two-front war is straining the Reich's resources, Joseph Goebbels suggests that Hitler agree to a separate peace with the Soviets, but Hitler declines.

September 23: Mussolini announces the creation of the Salò Republic, in the Axis-controlled part of Italy beyond the scope of the Badoglio administration.

September 27: German troops abandon the Italian province of Foggia, with its strategically critical airstrips, to the Allies. • Chiang Kai-shek orders the execution of Chen Tu-hsiu, the founder of China's Communist Party.

October 1: The Allies occupy Naples, southern Italy's largest port city. It will become an important Allied naval and supply base. • The Nazis come up short in their effort to relocate Denmark's Jews, testimony to the character of the Danish people who have enabled their Jewish friends and neighbors to escape to Sweden. Most Danish Jews will survive the war.

October 3: Germany recaptures the British Aegean island of Kos. • Japanese troops complete their retreat from the Solomon island of Kolombangara.

October 4: More than 500 die on the ground when the USAAF and RAF join forces to keep bombs falling on Frankfurt day and night.

October 5: Germany incorporates the Istrian Peninsula, much of the Italian Alps, and the eastern Italian city of Trieste into the Reich.

The Soviets' Yak fighters The Yak series of fighter planes was manufactured by the Soviet Union's Yakovlev company throughout World War II. Beginning with 1940's Yak-1, Yaks were regarded as among the war's finest aircraft. The Yak-3 (*pictured*) first saw service in 1944. Although it was manufactured in fewer numbers than the longer-range Yak-9 (which went into service in 1942, despite its higher designation number), the Yak-3 was widely favored by pilots for its strength, lightness, and maneuverability. At lower altitudes, it was considered superior to any of the *Luftwaffe*'s sophisticated fighters.

Josip Broz Tito

Josip Broz Tito, secretary general of Yugoslavia's Communist Party, released a message to Yugoslavians as German tanks drove through their country. "You who are struggling and dying in this battle for independence," he declared. "Do not lose heart, close your ranks, and do not bow your heads under the heavy blows which you are suffering."

In Yugoslavia, the Communist Party had been persecuted by the government for years. In reaction, the party formed an underground to fight the government. It was, therefore, in the absence of an organized military resistance, ready to wage an underground campaign against the German invaders after the German invasion of the Soviet Union.

Tito, who became military commander of the partisans, called for the support of the Yugoslavian people with the slogan "Death to Fascism, Freedom to the People!" His forces fought a tough campaign against the Germans at the cost of thousands of lives. In the spring of 1943, Germans bombed his position. Tito dove for shelter behind a beech tree. He was saved from the blast of a German bomb by his dog, who had thrown himself across Tito's head.

The Soviet Union supported Tito's partisans throughout the war, and support from the British and Americans came in 1943. The Soviets entered Yugoslavia in April 1945 and backed his election as prime minister. Thus began his autonomous 35-year reign as the leader of Yugoslavia.

Yugoslavian women fight the Axis After the Axis powers seized Yugoslavia in 1941, Marshal Tito's Yugoslav Partisans proved themselves more capable of effective armed resistance than their rivals, the royalist Chechniks. By 1943 the Western Allies supported the Partisans over the Chechniks, despite misgivings about the Communist commitment of Tito's group. Some two million women (12 percent of Yugoslavia's prewar population) joined the Partisans in all capacities. Most of them were under 20 years of age. Many, like those pictured here, served in combat side by side with men.

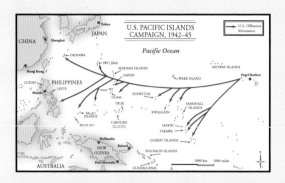

U.S. PACIFIC ISLANDS CAMPAIGN, 1942–45

Pacific Ocean

U.S. Offensive Movement

CHINA — Shanghai — Hong Kong — OKINAWA — IWO JIMA — MARIANA ISLANDS — SAIPAN — GUAM — TRUK — PALAU ISLANDS — PELELIU 1944 — CAROLINE ISLANDS — ENIWETOK — KWAJALEIN — MARSHALL ISLANDS — MAKIN — TARAWA — GILBERT ISLANDS — MIDWAY ISLANDS — WAKE ISLAND — Pearl Harbor — Tokyo — JAPAN — LUZON — PHILIPPINES — Manila — LEYTE — Hollandia — Rabaul — NEW GUINEA — Port Moresby — AUSTRALIA — GUADALCANAL — SOLOMON ISLANDS

1000 km 1000 miles

America's Pacific triumphs The turn of the strategic tide in the Pacific began in 1942 with the decisive U.S. naval victories at the Coral Sea (May) and Midway (June), followed by the successful operations on Guadalcanal from August. The subsequent "island-hopping" campaign concluded with the end of Japanese resistance on Okinawa on June 22, 1945. Other notable Allied successes during a consistently hard-fought series of amphibious landings and battles were Kokoda (1942); Bougainville (1943); Saipan, Guam, and Leyte Gulf (1944); and Iwo Jima and Corregidor (1945). Meanwhile, from November 1944, the capture of the Marianas enabled U.S. bombers to fly strategic missions against Japan—including the atomic bomb missions in August 1945.

1943

October 8: Civil war erupts in Greece when the country's pro- and anti-Communist factions face off.

October 10: A German U-boat lays mines at the eastern end of the Panama Canal. • The U.S. attacks the Axis-held islands of Crete and Rhodes with B-17 Flying Fortress bombers.

October 12: The Allies obtain permission to establish a convoy defense base on the Azores, an important island chain in the Atlantic that belongs to Portugal.

October 13: Italy joins the Allies when Premier Pietro Badoglio declares war on Hitler's Germany. • Yugoslavian partisans sabotage the Krupp steelworks in the city of Zeneca.

October 14: An uprising at the Nazis' Sobibór death camp claims the lives of 11 guards, while more than 100 prisoners manage to escape.

October 18: The Nazis begin the "resettlement" of Italian Jews to death camps in Poland. • The U.S. launches an air raid on the Japanese base on the northern Solomon island of Bougainville.

October 19: Some 5,000 seriously wounded German POWs and about the same number of British captives are heading home after the first British-German prisoner exchange of the war. • A civilian uprising in Jesselton, North Borneo, claims the lives of 40 occupying Japanese soldiers.

October 19–30: Allied foreign ministers meet in Moscow. They confirm the May 1944 date for the invasion of France, and agree that the Soviets will join the fight against the Japanese once the Germans are neutralized. They also announce plans for the postwar trials of war criminals. The Soviet Union promises to join a new international organization to keep the peace.

Americans land on Bougainville U.S. troops clamber into assault boats assembling for the landing on Bougainville, the largest of the Solomon Islands. Part of the effort to neutralize the Japanese base at Rabaul 220 miles away, the landing was spearheaded by the Third Marine Division on November 1, 1943, at Cape Torokina. Though the Japanese had some 17,000 troops on southern Bougainville alone, they had not considered swampy Cape Torokina a likely target, and the landing was lightly opposed. Work began on an airfield, and U.S. Army troops were brought ashore. Futile enemy attacks on the perimeter began immediately, the last occurring in March. Australian forces took over the fighting on the island until the Japanese surrendered in 1945.

Nasty fighting in the jungle American troops operate amid dead bodies on the island of Bougainville. Much of the fighting on Bougainville focused on efforts to dominate valuable high ground and the few trails that traversed the swampy terrain. Roadblocks, ambushes, and terrifying patrol encounters at point-blank range in the thick jungle were routine. Japanese machine gunners sheltered in well-concealed log and earthen bunkers had to be reduced one by one by infantrymen using hand grenades, small arms, and flamethrowers.

1943

October 20: The Allies take one step closer to Nuremberg with the establishment of a commission charged with the investigation of war crimes.

October 23: A brief uprising on the threshold of an Auschwitz gas chamber results in the death of a hated SS guard and the wounding of several others. The mutineers are then shot.

October 24: For the first time, the Allies stage an air raid on Axis targets from bases in the former Axis nation of Italy.

October 29: Dockworkers on England's Thames River go on strike, forcing soldiers to pick up the slack. • The U.S. Navy heavily mines the waters off French territory in Indochina.

October 31: The Red Army has cut the supply line and isolated some 150,000 German and Romanian troops in the Crimea.

November 2: The Battle of Empress Augusta Bay erupts when the U.S. Navy attacks a small Japanese fleet attempting to reinforce Bougainville, where the Marines landed the day before.

November 3: A massive force of 539 U.S. planes bombs the key German port of Wilhelmshaven. • The Red Army launches an offensive across the Dnieper River in a bid to retake Kiev from the Germans. • The Nazis purge the population of the Majdanek death camp, murdering some 17,000 Jews in a single day.

November 4: The United States begins to manufacture plutonium at a facility in Oak Ridge, Tennessee.

November 6: The Red Army recaptures Kiev from the Germans with relative ease. This third-largest Soviet city has been largely reduced to a smoldering ruin.

The dangers of carrier landings A crewman on the USS *Enterprise* scrambles to help the pilot of a burning F6F Hellcat, which crashed on the flight deck during operations off Makin Island. Flying on and off the heaving carrier decks was hazardous under the best of circumstances. One miscalculation could send the plane hurtling into the crash barrier at the end of the deck, or over the side. The process was also dangerous for the deck crews, known as "deck apes," who were exposed to everything from crash landings and spinning props to loose bombs. As one seaman remarked, "every landing was a potential casualty."

The mythical "gremlins" Faced with unexpected and seemingly inexplicable mechanical problems during WWII, RAF pilots added a supernatural, gnome-like creature to world folklore: the "gremlin." Perhaps more than semi-seriously, pilots discussed gremlins, their mischievous expertise, and methods of placating and controlling them. Gremlins were nothing but a myth. But like the one pictured on this book cover, they were said to often ride on wings, sometimes manipulating ailerons to tip the plane.

The coastwatchers Working on remote Pacific island locations, "coastwatchers" reported enemy activity and guided Allied attacks and guerrilla operations. They also rescued hundreds of civilians and Allied servicemen, including future U.S. president John F. Kennedy. White Australian, New Zealander, American, and Solomons Islands civilians provided most personnel, but they relied on natives as spies, guards, messengers, and laborers. Pictured is an islander at a New Georgia coastwatcher station.

The supreme commander General Douglas MacArthur was supreme commander of Allied forces in the South West Pacific Area during World War II. After commanding the futile defense of the Philippines in 1941–42, he escaped to lead the defense of Australia and later the recapture of New Guinea and the Philippines. MacArthur's personal attachment to the Philippines led him to insist on a speedy return to the islands, a course criticized by some strategists. During his southwest Pacific campaigns, MacArthur astutely bypassed heavily defended areas whenever possible, leapfrogging to strike where the enemy was weakest. He was a powerful personality—talented but also vain, imperious, a political machinist, and a shameless publicity seeker. During his career, he gained a reputation in the public mind as a military genius—a stature now in dispute among historians.

The Red Air Force Soviet pilot Victor Radkevich animatedly tells fellow fliers of his triumph over a German plane. On the first day of the 1941 German invasion of Russia, the *Luftwaffe* destroyed more than 1,000 largely outmoded Russian military aircraft—about 800 of them still on the ground. The next year, the Soviets began a huge buildup of air forces. Instead of British- and American-style long-range bombings intended to destroy enemy infrastructure and morale, the Red Air Force focused on supporting ground forces against the German invaders. By late 1943, the Soviets had achieved clear air superiority over the *Luftwaffe*.

1943

November 9: General Charles de Gaulle is named president of the French Committee of National Liberation, the "Free French," in the wake of the resignation of General Henri Giraud.

November 11: Vichy police arrest 450 demonstrators in Grenoble, France, for rallying against the Nazis. • The Nazis running the Theresienstadt death camp torture some 47,000 Jews, forcing them to stand exposed for eight hours in a bitterly cold November rain.

November 12: Unaware of the Enigma breach, German admiral Karl Dönitz claims of the Allies: "He knows all our secrets." • Japanese bases in the Marshall and Gilbert islands come under heavy air assault by Allied planes. The attacks will continue on a daily basis.

November 14: A friendly-fired torpedo narrowly misses striking the battleship USS *Iowa*. President Roosevelt, en route to the Tehran Conference, is on board.

November 15: Effective immediately, all Gypsies in Germany are to be deported to death camps on the order of SS chief Heinrich Himmler. • The Nazis attempt to put a lid on sabotage by the nascent Italian resistance by taking some 2,000 of Milan's industrial workers hostage.

November 16: The Nazis round up another 2,000 Jews in the Netherlands and send them to Auschwitz. • The Germans effectively abandon their atomic bomb-building ambitions when the Allies launch another raid on the Vemork, Norway, heavy-water plant.

November 19: The Fog Investigation Dispersal Operation (FIDO) is employed for the first time by RAF officials hoping to enable landings in heavy British fog.

German POWs in Soviet Hands

German POWs in Stalingrad

Considering Germany's aggression toward the Soviet Union, it is not surprising that the Soviets treated German POWs without mercy. The Germans not only invaded Soviet territory, but the SS and *Wehrmacht* committed a litany of atrocities against those who Nazi leadership called Soviet *Untermenschen* (sub-humans). Despite some isolated instances of Russian compassion, conditions in the POW camps were generally abysmal, with a daily death rate of one percent in the camp hospitals.

German POWs were often forced to build their own camps—but with underground earth bunkers rather than huts for accommodation. The bunkers regularly flooded in the spring and autumn. Suicide, disease, dysentery, summary execution, and death by freezing were all commonplace. Even POWs who were fit when captured often succumbed to a below-starvation diet of unground millet and a punishing program of hard labor. POWs worked on major construction projects, such as the reconstruction of Stalingrad, hydroelectric schemes, and excavation of the Don-Volga canal.

In Soviet philosophy, man was just another material to be used to maximum effect and then discarded. In May 1945, the Soviets held nearly 1.5 million POWs in Germany alone. Several million more had already been transported to the Soviet Union to join the several hundred thousand German POWs captured earlier in the war. Of the POWs, two-thirds survived to return home to Germany. The final 9,626, who were sentenced for war crimes, were not released from the Soviet Union until 1955.

U.S. seizes Kwajalein, Roi-Namur Hit by antiaircraft fire, a Japanese torpedo bomber explodes during an attack off Kwajalein Island. The U.S. assaults on Kwajalein and nearby Roi-Namur, deep in the Marshall Islands chain, in February 1944 surprised the Japanese, who had committed more defensive effort to the outermost islands. The Fourth Marine Division seized Roi-Namur in two days, and the Seventh Infantry Division took Kwajalein in four. U.S. casualties were relatively light. Capture of the island air bases deprived the Japanese of a defensive shield and opened the way to the Carolines and Marianas, which were the true strategic springboards for any assault on Japan.

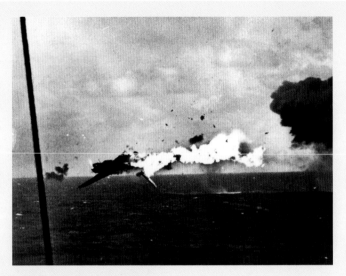

Japan defends Tarawa Draped with hand grenades and ammunition, a Marine pauses to drink from his canteen on December 6, 1943, during the fight for Tarawa. The Second Marine Division had fought in the Solomons, but the amphibious assault on tiny, heavily defended Tarawa was a new experience. Japanese rear admiral Shibasaki Keiji boasted that "a million Americans couldn't take Tarawa in a hundred years." Defenses included barbed wire, mines, tetrahedrons, nearly 500 pillboxes, light tanks, heavy machine guns, and eight-inch naval rifles. Thanks to the stubborn courage of individual Marines, Shibasaki was proven wrong, but the cost was high. More than 1,000 Americans were killed or went missing.

Shot down by the hundreds Dead Marines litter the beach following the 76-hour battle for Betio (at the southwest corner of Tarawa Atoll) and its strategically important airstrip. As the first large-scale test of U.S. amphibious doctrine against a strongly fortified enemy beach, the Tarawa assault was a costly learning experience. Preceded by an inadequate bombardment, hampered by a disastrously low tide, and lacking sufficient tracked vehicles to negotiate Betio's wide reef, Marines were shot down by the hundreds as they waded toward the heavily defended landing beaches. "It was a time of utmost savagery," wrote a witness. "I still don't know how they took the place."

Japanese choose suicide Trapped in their bunker on Tarawa, these two Japanese Special Naval Landing Force troops chose suicide over surrender. U.S. Marines would become accustomed to such tenacity in their march through the central Pacific. Typical of what was to come on Saipan, Guam, and Iwo Jima, the enemy garrison at Tarawa fought almost to the last man. Of the approximately 5,000 enemy personnel on Betio, 4,690 were killed. Of the 146 prisoners taken by U.S. Marines, virtually all were conscripted Korean laborers. Only 17 Japanese—all wounded—were captured.

1943

November 19: Fourteen British sailors, survivors of the mine-sunk freighter *Penolver*, are rescued by the American freighter *DeLisle*. The *DeLisle* promptly strikes another mine, sending the British back into the Atlantic, where they are miraculously rescued for a second time.

November 20: U.S. forces battle fierce Japanese resistance as they land on the Gilbert islands of Makin and Tarawa.

November 21: In one of the most overpowering air raids in the history of warfare, Berlin comes under assault by 775 RAF planes.

November 22–26: At the Cairo Conference, Roosevelt, Churchill, and Chiang Kai-shek discuss strategy for the Burma front. They announce that all areas seized by Japan since 1894 will be returned to their former owners.

November 25: The Allies bomb Japanese positions in Rangoon, Burma.

November 28: Roosevelt, Churchill, and Stalin hold their first face-to-face meeting in Tehran, Iran. They restate their commitment to prepare for Operation Overlord, the invasion of France. • The Allies complete their conquest of the island of Tarawa. Some 4,600 Japanese and 1,100 Americans lose their lives in the battle.

December 2: The U.S. brings 15 noted atomic scientists to New Mexico to help build the bomb. • Facing a sharp decline in the number of miners working on the home front, British labor minister Ernest Bevin decrees that one of every 10 draftees will be sent to the coal mines instead of the front lines. • The southern Italian port of Bari is devastated by a German air raid. Nineteen ships are destroyed when bombs strike two shipboard ammunition stores.

Germans fight on in Italy Since the Casablanca Conference in January 1943, Churchill pushed for the invasion of Italy, the "soft underbelly of Europe." Roosevelt and his military advisers believed such an invasion would be an unwise distraction from preparation for the invasion of France. The third allied partner, Stalin, was also against the Italian campaign. The fighting in Sicily had not yet started when discussions were renewed about Italy. It was finally decided not to stop the offensive momentum. British and Canadian troops invaded Italy on September 3 with little opposition. Before the second landing at Salerno on September 9, the troops learned that Italy had surrendered. German troops, however, stubbornly contested the Salerno landing and every inch of the Allied advance. Here, American troops prepare for an advance in December.

1943

December 3: *Reichsmarshall* Hermann Göring orders an intensification of Germany's bombing campaign over Britain.

December 3–4: Some 1,000 civilian casualties result from an RAF raid on Leipzig, Germany.

December 3–7: Allied leaders return to the conference table at Cairo. They reach additional agreements about the prosecution of the war in the Pacific.

December 4: Josip Broz Tito is named head of a provisional Communist government in Yugoslavia. • The Japanese employ poison gas in an attack on the Chinese city of Changteh.

December 5: Some 350 die in a Japanese raid on the Indian port city of Calcutta.

December 8: Some Italian forces enter combat for the Allies, as the series of battles along Germany's Winter Line in Italy intensifies.

December 11: Germany loses nearly 140 planes in a dogfight in the skies over the Emden U-boat facility.

December 12: The Soviet Union and Czechoslovakia sign a mutual assistance treaty at the Kremlin. • Hitler sends General Rommel to mobilize forces along the French coast to prepare to defend against the anticipated Allied invasion.

December 14: Having experienced success against the Germans in bitterly cold Russian winters, the Red Army kicks off a new winter offensive against Hitler's troops in the western Soviet Union.

December 16: Three German POWs and their Soviet driver are tried in Kharkov for the deaths of tens of thousands of local civilians during the German occupation of Russia. They will hang on the 19th.

BBC and "V for Victory" Tangye Lean, a BBC European Service radio commentator, broadcasts in 1943. During the war, the BBC transmitted information and propaganda in 45 languages, reaching every major European nation, North America, Iran, India, and Japan. Although the Nazis made listening to the BBC punishable by death, even German officials were among the millions of European fans. The BBC "V for Victory" campaign popularized the letter "V," its hand sign, and its Morse code signal (three dots and a dash). The opening bars of Beethoven's Fifth Symphony (replicating the code) became the European Service's call sign.

The logistics of ship loading Crammed with everything from stretchers to jeeps, an LST (landing ship tank) brings in materiel for the invasion of New Britain, a Pacific island. Despite the apparent clutter, Navy and Marine Corps logistics personnel transformed combat loading into an exact science. The least critical items were loaded aboard ship first, stowed deep in the holds. Priority items, such as ammunition, were loaded last so they could be made available more quickly during an assault. Special shore parties under the command of a beachmaster were responsible for unloading the ships, gathering supplies in organized dumps, and ensuring a smooth logistics flow as the battle developed.

1943

December 17: In gratitude for Chinese assistance in the Pacific Theater, President Roosevelt signs the repeal of the 1882 Chinese Exclusion Act and allows limited Chinese immigration to the United States.

December 22: One of the last remnants of the Warsaw Ghetto is wiped out when the SS murders more than 60 Jews discovered hiding in a basement in the Polish city.

December 24: General Eisenhower is promoted, receiving the title of Supreme Commander, Allied Expeditionary Force.

December 25: Having reached a stalemate on the Italian front, the Allies agree to a plan to send an amphibious force onto the beaches south of Rome.

December 26: Only 36 of a 1,900-man crew survive the Royal Navy's sinking of Germany's *Scharnhorst.* This ends the German interception of Allied convoys to Murmansk, a port city in northwest Russia.

December 28: Ortona, Italy, is finally in Allied hands after two weeks of violent clashes in the streets of the small city. The battle earned Ortona the nickname "Little Stalingrad." • Realizing that the Nazi war machine is short on labor and being undone by its own brutality, Heinrich Himmler orders labor camp commandants to reduce the death rate among their inmates.

December 29: The Red Army scores a dramatic victory along the line west of Kiev, forcing some 200,000 German troops back toward Poland.

December 30: The First U.S. Marines capture a strategically key airfield at Cape Gloucester on the South Pacific island of New Britain.

Logistics and Distance

"I want to tell you from the Russian point of view," Soviet leader Joseph Stalin declared at the Tehran Conference in December 1943, "what the President and the United States have done to win the war. The most important things...are machines.... The United States...is a country of machines. Without the use of those machines...we would lose this war."

By 1943 the United States led all other countries in the production of military supplies. The success of the Allies in World War II was due not only to America's production capability, but its ability to place these materials into the hands of those who needed them most—the soldiers on the front lines. In the end, logistics won the war.

Realizing that they would have to fight a war on two fronts thousands of miles from their mainland, America's military leaders were determined to conquer Axis nations by creating and strengthening their supply lines across the Atlantic and Pacific oceans. America's strategy against the Japanese was to gradually push westward across the Pacific, seizing one enemy base after another. The U.S. not only wanted to drive ever closer to the Japanese mainland, but also provide the logistical support (fuel, ammunition, and food) necessary to keep its

Army trucks on flatbed railroad cars in Virginia

ships, aircraft, and infantry moving forward. The same strategy was followed in the European Theater. Ample supplies were assembled in Africa and England before the invasions of Sicily and France, respectively.

While the Allies grew stronger as the war progressed, the Germans and Japanese were steadily weakened. Their war plants were bombed, their number of workers decreased, and their supply lines were gradually strangled shut. The logistical strength of the Allied nations, with America as the chief contributor, was a decisive factor in the war's outcome.

Mortar combat on New Britain
Marines man an 81mm mortar in
the fighting at Cape Gloucester, New
Britain. Swampy terrain and thick rain
forest severely hampered mobility on
the island. Fighting was often at arm's
length in heavy vegetation. Weighing
87 pounds and with a range of 4,000
yards, the 81mm mortar and its smaller
counterpart, the 60mm mortar, provided
close support both in offense and
defense. Crews had to take care that the
high angle shell had a clear upward path
through the heavy jungle canopy.

Krueger the perfectionist As commander of
the Sixth Army during the war, General Walter
Krueger directed 21 successful amphibious
operations in the southwest Pacific, including the
seizures of Leyte and Luzon in the Philippines. A
former enlisted man who rose through the ranks,
Krueger was a hard-driving perfectionist. No detail,
down to the condition of an infantryman's feet,
was too small for his attention. Though sometimes
ridiculed as "Molasses in January" for his cautious
approach to battle, Krueger was the general whom
MacArthur singled out to lead the ground assault
on Kyushu, Japan, before the atomic bomb made
the operation unnecessary.

Germany's *Scharnhorst* wreaks havoc Commissioned on January 7, 1939, the 31,000-ton German battleship *Scharnhorst* prowled the North Sea with its sister ship, *Gneisenau*, through 1939 and 1940. The ships sank the British armed merchant cruiser HMS *Rawalpindi* in late November 1939, covered the German invasion of Norway in spring 1940, and sank the British aircraft carrier HMS *Glorious* and two escorting destroyers on June 8, 1940. Repairs kept the *Scharnhorst* in dock through the rest of 1940, after which the sister ships broke into the Atlantic, where they sank 22 merchant ships.

No sympathy for slackers The U.S. War Production Board flooded manufacturing plants with posters designed to instill a sense of duty in workers. An employee who was slacking off or not on the job every day, six days a week, was accused of aiding the enemy. Although the system could absorb lazy or absent individual workers, the government wanted to head off the contagion of mass absences. On this poster, an idler is said to be "working for Hitler." On others, an idle machine was described as "an empty gun" that "may cost your pal's life."

ALLIES STORM THE BEACHES

JANUARY 1944–JUNE 1944

On January 27, 1944, the besieged Soviet city of Leningrad, where an estimated one million people had died from starvation, disease, and constant shelling, was finally fully freed from encirclement after almost 900 days. It was the end of a terrible epic of suffering in which the old had been sacrificed to save the young on the principle of Soviet doctrine that "he who does not work does not eat." Life in wartime Leningrad represented the idea of "total war" at its most intense. Every citizen was a potential victim. Everyone was obliged to do their utmost to defend the city. "We are all on death row," confided a nurse to her diary, "we just don't know who is next."

The year 1944 saw every combatant nation exert itself to the fullest extent. After three to four years of warfare, populations had become used to ceaseless rationing, travel restrictions, air-defense blackouts, and long hours in fields and factories. In Europe, approximately two-thirds of the countries' national product was diverted to war. Germany and the Soviet Union between them mobilized about 46 million men and

women in the armed forces. These were levels of effort that few populations could sustain for long.

Total war necessitated the mass participation of women, who comprised 35 percent of the British and American workforce and more than 50 percent in Germany and the USSR. Only in the United States, whose geographical immunity freed the population from the more onerous restrictions, did the war produce an economic boom. The American economy alone could afford large armaments while maintaining reasonable living standards.

For the first six months of 1944, the pace of advance on land against the Axis slowed. Both sides knew that at some point Europe would be invaded from the west, and that this blow, if successful, would probably ensure the defeat of Germany and its European allies. But while preparations went ahead for the invasion of France, Allied forces engaged in prolonged and bitter fighting on other fronts.

In Italy, the German redoubt around the ancient monastery of Monte Cassino, perched high in the mountains, proved a firm barrier. On January 22, an Allied task force landed at Anzio, farther up the coast toward Rome, in the hope of outflanking the German line. But the beachhead was contained, and for five more months the front stalled. Only on May 18 did a fierce assault by a Polish unit fighting with the Allies secure Monte Cassino. This victory broke the German line. On June 4, American forces entered Rome. The German army retreated northward to a new defensive position, the Gothic Line, from Pisa to Rimini.

In the Soviet Union, the momentum achieved after the Battle of Kursk (summer 1943) slowed. But in the winter of 1943–44, the Soviets advanced into the Ukraine against isolated counteroffensives from the German army. After six months, Soviet forces reached the Romanian and Hungarian borders. The Crimea was cleared, and on May 9 the Germans surrendered Sevastopol. Farther north, the Red Army reached the edge of the Baltic States and was poised for an assault on Poland.

In the central Pacific, the Americans' island-hopping campaign brought them control of the Gilbert Islands and Marshall Islands by February 1944. Moreover, landings along the coast of northern New Guinea isolated Japanese strongholds and brought the Philippines within striking distance. The Japanese carrier base at Truk in the Caroline Islands was neutralized by superior American airpower, and the advance on the Mariana Islands in June destroyed Japanese land-based airpower there.

When U.S. Marines landed on the Mariana island of Saipan on June 15, the Japanese fleet finally intervened. Admiral Ozawa Jisaburo led nine carriers and 450 aircraft against 15 American carriers and more than 900 aircraft. The Battle of the Philippine Sea was fought from June 19 to 20. By the end of it, the Japanese had lost the majority of their aircraft and withdrew. The 30,000-strong Japanese garrison on Saipan fought to the death, and by early July the island was in American hands. From the Marianas, it was possible to begin long-distance bombing of the Japanese homeland with the new B-29 Superfortress.

Throughout these months, the Allies' western strategy was dominated by preparation for Operation Overlord, the invasion of northwestern France by a combined American and British Commonwealth force. The planning and administration alone absorbed 300,000 people. A combined arms assault on a heavily defended coastline was an operation fraught with risk. The deadlock at Anzio and the cost of assaults in the Pacific against small but determined garrisons made it clear that a frontal attack on continental Europe across

Russian soldiers celebrate the end of the 872-day siege of Leningrad in January 1944. Beyond this hard-fought victory, the siege of Russia itself was coming to an end in 1944. German forces went on the defensive, and the Soviets commenced their own inexorable advance toward the enemy homeland and Berlin.

the Atlantic Wall defenses would be a costly and uncertain enterprise.

The attackers did have some clear advantages. Britain and the United States now had overwhelming naval power, and after their victories in the Atlantic in 1943, they could maintain seaborne supply chain logistics without considerable difficulty. The Allies also had attained air superiority over Western Europe in February and March 1943. During the invasion, 12,000 aircraft would support Allied forces against only 170 serviceable German aircraft. The Allies also could choose the place and time of the invasion, as long as it could be concealed from the enemy.

The greatest success enjoyed by the Allies in the run-up to Overlord was in the field of disinformation. The extensive use of double agents, careful camouflage, and the strictest secrecy prevented the Germans from guessing the invasion point or the precise day. The German commander of the Atlantic Wall, Field Marshal Erwin Rommel, believed like most of the high command that the Allies would take the short route across the English Channel toward the Pas de Calais. Limited German forces were kept in Normandy, France, but it was always assumed that an attack there would be a feint.

U.S. general Dwight D. Eisenhower would decide the final date. He had been appointed the supreme commander of Allied forces due to his great skills as an organizer and diplomat, qualities he needed to the full in holding together his command team. General Marshall thus could be held in reserve in case the invasion failed and a second one had to be mounted. The Allies had appointed General Bernard Montgomery, who had already defeated Rommel once, as ground forces commander. In late May, the final battle plan was approved. Allied forces would attack in Normandy across five selected beaches. Once established, the bridgehead would be consolidated for a breakout. The Allies would roll up the German front in France and push it back to the Rhine River.

The date for the invasion was fixed as early May, but postponed to June when more landing craft would be available. The weather in early June was so severe that German commanders relaxed. Rommel went back to Germany for his wife's birthday. Eisenhower set D-Day—military shorthand for the first day of any major operation—for June 5. But with no improvement in the weather by June 4, Eisenhower was faced with a difficult choice. At 9:45 p.m. on the 4th, he gathered his commanders to order the invasion for June 6. Though heavy rain continued outside, there was better meteorological news. Eisenhower said quietly, "OK, let's go," launching the largest seaborne invasion in history.

Twenty-seven hundred ships moved to position, and in the early hours of June 6 they approached the French coast. By the time German forces were alerted, the invasion was upon them. A colossal naval barrage and around-the-clock bombing reduced resistance on all but one beach, Omaha. There, U.S. forces faced stiff opposition from defenders who were dug in on high cliffs and had avoided the worst of the bombardment. The American army did not have a foothold on Omaha until the evening. On the other beaches, rapid progress was made and a bridgehead a few miles wide and deep was carved out in the first hours. Within days, more than 300,000 soldiers and 54,000

A welder at the Electric Boat Company in Groton, Connecticut, adjusts her goggles before getting to work in late 1943. This scene would have been unthinkable in the U.S. only two years before. However, total war brought many social changes, including the mass influx of women into jobs once considered the sole domain of men.

vehicles went ashore, using prefabricated harbors known as "Mulberries" that had been towed in sections across the Channel.

Throughout June, the Allies made slow progress. U.S. forces cleared the Cotentin Peninsula further west, but the city of Caen—which was to be the hinge of the whole operation—remained in German hands. Relations between Eisenhower and Montgomery worsened. Historians to this day have argued that the British were too cautious in the face of fierce German resistance. Britain's chief concern was to avoid defeat at all costs. Most of the Anglo-American troops lacked battle experience, and the invasion was a steep learning curve. At no point in June could ultimate victory be taken for granted.

On July 1, Rommel began an assault on the British line with five panzer divisions, provoking the fiercest fighting of the campaign so far. American attempts to accelerate the breakout southward (code-named Operation Cobra) were slowed by the rapid redeployment of German armor.

The situation was made more awkward for the Western Allies by the rapid success of the Red Army in the East. Stalin had promised a renewed summer campaign to coincide with Overlord. The operation, code-named Bagration, was undertaken against the largest concentration of German forces in the East, Army Group Center. Bagration also was meticulously prepared, veiled in secrecy, and covered by a deception operation as successful as that in the West. Soviet forces moved into concealed positions, while partisan attacks disabled German communications and Soviet aircraft pounded German positions. On June 22, the full-scale operation was launched with devastating success. Within a week, Soviet forces broke through the German defensive line, captured tens of thousands of German soldiers, and advanced at a rate of up to 25 miles per day. Farther south, the Ukrainian campaign began again with assaults toward Lvov. Here, too, German defense crumbled. While the Western Allies were facing 15 German divisions, the Red Army engaged 228 German divisions across a 500-mile front.

Farther east, Japan launched a wide offensive across large tracts of central China. This was one of the last major offensives by the Axis powers, and it came at a time when Japanese fortunes in the central Pacific were waning. On April 18, the Japanese army began Operation Ichi-Go to destroy air bases that could be used by American aircraft to attack the Japanese mainland. The operation was also designed to open a continuous overland route (road and rail) between Manchuria and Singapore to facilitate the importation of strategic resources from Japanese conquests in the Southeast without interdiction from American submarines and aircraft.

On May 27, the Japanese launched a separate operation to capture the area of the middle Yangtze River. After six months of fighting, Japanese-held territory was consolidated into a single bloc. The campaign caused a growing rift between Chiang Kai-shek and the Americans, represented in China by General Joseph Stilwell. With the loss of air bases, there was little more that the Americans could achieve. Stilwell was recalled at Chiang's insistence, and the Chinese theater remained a contest between Nationalist, Communist, and Japanese forces over the future of Eastern Asia.

Australian infantrymen engage the Japanese in New Guinea. From 1942 until about January 1944, Australian troops shouldered the brunt of the ground combat against the Japanese in New Guinea. In late 1943, the Australians drove the Japanese from Lae and Salamaua and then from the Huon Peninsula and the Ramu Valley. Defeated and starving, the Japanese 18th Army was sent into full retreat toward Wewak. About 35,000 Japanese died while the Australians lost fewer than 1,300.

1944

January 1: American Louis Jordan and his Tympany Five hit No. 1 on the *Billboard* R&B charts with their song "Ration Blues."

January 3: Thousands of German troops die, and others are captured, as the Red Army invades Nazi-occupied Poland and sends Hitler's army into retreat.

January 4: The United States launches operations behind Axis lines, delivering weapons and supplies to anti-Nazi partisans in France, Italy, and the Low Countries.

January 7: In preparation for the invasion of France, Allied planes drop airborne operatives into the occupied country to help train their partisans in guerrilla tactics to support regular troops.

January 8: Count Ciano, Mussolini's one-time foreign minister, ambassador, and son-in-law, faces a tribunal for his role in the vote to oust *Il Duce*. His wife will escape to Switzerland the next day, but the count will die before a firing squad on January 11.

January 9: Churchill meets with Free French leader Charles de Gaulle to discuss the role the Free French will play in the Allied invasion of France. • The Allies attack Cervaro and Monte Trocchio, Italy, in yet another effort to break through the defenses known as the German Winter Line. • Twenty-two civilians are murdered in Lyons, France, in reprisal for the assassination of two German soldiers by members of the French Resistance.

January 10: The waters off Burma are heavily mined by the RAF. This will ultimately bring a complete, though temporary, halt to Japanese shipping in the area.

"The neutrons emitted from the gadget will diffuse through the air over a distance of 1 to 2 km, nearly independent of the energy release. Over this region, their intensity will be sufficient to kill a person."

—Physicist Hans Bethe, Los Alamos, New Mexico, in a memo entitled "Expected Damage of the Gadget," 1943

Groves leads the Manhattan Project U.S. brigadier general Leslie Groves named the Manhattan Project and was a driving force behind the creation of the first atomic bomb. He chose the sites for research and materials production and put physicist J. Robert Oppenheimer in charge of the scientific laboratory. Groves was intelligent and highly organized, and although his arrogance offended some scientists, he worked well with Oppenheimer. Groves maintained high security at the Los Alamos, New Mexico, facility, having mail censored, long-distance calls monitored, travel restricted to within 100 miles, and contact with those on the outside limited.

Oppenheimer directs Los Alamos team The presence of brilliant American physicist J. Robert Oppenheimer attracted scientists from all over the world to the remote New Mexican desert to work on the Manhattan Project. Oppenheimer directed the scientific team headquartered at Los Alamos. Although he suffered from periods of depression, he personally helped resolve or control conflicts that inevitably rose among the diverse international group. He, like most Los Alamos scientists, was dedicated to ending war for all time. After atomic bombs were used at Hiroshima and Nagasaki, Oppenheimer was appalled at the civilian deaths. Following the war, as chief advisor of the United States Atomic Energy Commission, he lobbied for the international control of atomic energy.

1944

January 29: More than 700 civilians die when U.S. bombers attack Frankfurt, Germany, with about 800 bombers. • The *Luftwaffe* takes another hit in a disastrous raid on Britain, losing 57 aircraft. • The U.S. begins an air campaign over the Marshall Islands to soften Japanese defenses prior to a ground-based assault.

January 30: The U.S. Army suffers a tremendous loss when an offensive against the Italian town of Cisterna turns into an ambush. Nearly two battalions of U.S. Army Rangers lose their lives.

February 1: Relaxed rationing rules in Britain allow for the return of pockets, pleats, buttons, and collars to men's suits.

February 2: The Americans obtain authorization to use Soviet air bases to rest and refuel during shuttle sorties. • One hundred Polish civilians are murdered by the Nazis in reprisal for the partisan killing of Franz Kutschera, the SS chief in charge of the Warsaw district.

February 3: The *Wehrmacht* is forced to divert valuable resources to rescue some 60,000 Eighth Army troops caught in a snare by the advancing Red Army within Soviet territory. • The U.S. Navy attacks Japanese soil for the first time, blasting the northern Japanese island of Paramushiro with ship-based artillery.

February 4: The United States loses nearly 150 troops while capturing the Marshall island of Kwajalein. The defeated Japanese fare far worse, losing nearly 5,000 soldiers.

February 5: Michel Hollard, the French Resistance leader who warned the British about Germany's V-bomb capabilities—enabling the Allies to destroy some related facilities—is captured by the Nazi Gestapo. He will survive the war.

The Los Alamos community In 1943 hundreds of families moved to the highly secret Los Alamos National Laboratory community in New Mexico, where the first atomic bomb was built. Isolated on primitive roads, fenced with barbed wire, and patrolled by mounted guards, the community was shut off from the outside world. Even so, young Princeton scientist Richard Feynman demonstrated security weaknesses by repeatedly sneaking out through holes in the fence and then walking back in through the gate to draw guards' attention to the flaws. Workers lived in simple housing (*pictured*), although those higher in the scientific hierarchy had proportionately better homes. Los Alamos residents worked hard and relaxed at movies, restaurants, and parties within the compound.

U.S. bombards Kwajalein GIs of the Seventh ("Hourglass") Division manhandle a gun forward during fighting on Kwajalein in the Marshall Islands. A model amphibious operation, the landing on February 1 was preceded by a naval, air, and artillery bombardment so intense that "the entire island looked as if it had been picked up to 20,000 feet and then dropped," said a witness. Initial U.S. casualties were light, but resistance stiffened on the third day. The island, with its valuable anchorage and airfield, was secured the following day. GI casualties included 142 killed and 854 wounded. Japanese casualties included 4,938 killed and 206 captured.

1944

February 7: The first U-boat outfitted with a *Schnorkel*, which allows delivery of outside air to the submerged ship, becomes operational.

February 8: The RAF drops the heaviest bomb of the war thus far, six tons, on the *Gnome-et-Rhone* aircraft engine manufacturing facility in Limoges, France.

February 9: Dr. George Bell, Bishop of Chichester, questions the necessity of bombing raids against German targets in a speech before the House of Lords. His concerns are rebuffed.

February 10: The Allies are told that Hungary might offer its unconditional surrender, provided that the Soviet Union is not represented at the ceremony.

February 10–11: Germany's prized battleship *Tirpitz* once again survives an attempt on its life, this time by the Soviet air force.

February 12: Wary of men in his own inner circle who would like to see him dead, Hitler merges the SD (political foreign intelligence organization) and the *Abwehr* (German military intelligence organization).

February 15: The historic monastery at Monte Cassino in Italy is bombed by the Allies in an effort to root the Germans from their strategically superior hilltop post. Though the monastery is destroyed, the Germans tenaciously hold the hill.

February 15–16: In the most intense raid to date, more than 800 Allied bombers rain destruction on Berlin.

February 15–20: New Zealand takes Green Island in the eastern Solomons, winning an important forward air base.

Kleist defies Hitler
After participating in the invasions of Poland in 1939, France in 1940, and Yugoslavia in 1941, General Paul Ludwig Ewald von Kleist led his tanks across the Russian border on June 22, 1941. By September, he had played critical roles in astounding military successes, including the capture of much of the Ukraine. He was promoted to field marshal in 1943. But even Kleist's considerable prowess faltered before inexorable Soviet offensives. Never one of Hitler's yes-men, Kleist in 1944 defied the *Führer*'s orders by retreating across the Ukrainian territory he had earlier conquered. In March, Hitler permanently relieved him of command.

Soviet advances This grim picture of a slain soldier, mashed by military vehicles like "roadkill," hints at the savagery of the fighting on the Eastern Front. By early 1944, when this picture was probably taken, the Soviets had turned the tide against the Germans. On January 4, Axis forces were routed westward across the prewar Polish border. A month later, Soviet troops had advanced 100 miles into Poland. In the Ukraine, the port city of Odessa fell to the Soviets on April 10, and the Germans lost Sevastopol on May 9.

1944

February 16–17: Japan's Imperial Navy is forced to withdraw from Truk, its main base in the central Pacific, when Truk is subjected to a highly destructive assault by American carrier aircraft.

February 17: The Red Army accepts the surrender of nearly 20,000 German Eighth Army troops, who are among those trapped earlier in the month. However, most of the Germans, some 55,000, go down fighting. • The Americans capture another forward base in the Marshall Islands with the occupation of Bikini Atoll. The atoll will become famous in later years as the site of the first hydrogen bomb test.

February 18: Seventy members of the French Resistance, sitting on death row in Amiens Prison in Nazi-occupied France, escape when Allied bombs damage the walls of their cells.

February 20: A ferry laden with tanks of heavy water en route to German atomic research facilities is sunk by a Norwegian saboteur in the very deep waters of Lake Tinnsjö.

February 20–25: During "Big Week," the American air force in Britain forces the Germans to send up their fighters to protect their aircraft factories against a massive assault by bombers. The escorting Mustang fighters decimate German fighter strength.

February 22: Greek partisans sabotage a track used by German troop trains. As a result, a train plunges into a ravine, leading to the deaths of some 400 German soldiers. • Japanese prime minister General Tojo takes over as chief of the Japanese Army General Staff.

U.S. fights on Bougainville American soldiers advance with a Sherman tank during the fighting on Bougainville in the Solomon Islands. After the initial landings on November 1, 1943, construction of an airstrip at Cape Torokina began immediately. Two other airfields were soon constructed to support the air campaign against Japanese-held Rabaul. U.S. Army troops under Major General Oscar Griswold relieved the Third Marine Division in December to expand the beachhead, protect the perimeter, and tend to the logistics of the newly established base. Army troops saw limited fighting until March 9, 1944, when the Japanese attacked in force. The GIs smashed the enemy assault, and the valuable airfields were never again threatened.

Americans seize Eniwetok Marines of the 22nd Regiment stay low during combat on Japanese-held Eniwetok. The U.S. seized the atoll on February 17–23, 1944, almost as an afterthought to the landings on Roi-Namur and Kwajalein. Those operations had gone so well that Admiral Chester Nimitz decided to capitalize on his good fortune and seize Eniwetok more than two months ahead of schedule. The atoll would serve as a base for future operations against Japanese-held Truk and the Caroline Islands. The 22nd Marines and the 106th Infantry quickly overcame the 3,500 Japanese defenders on Eniwetok and adjacent islands. Fewer than 350 Americans were killed in action.

1944

February 23: The Seventh Indian Division of the British 14th Army scores Britain's first military victory over the Japanese, at Sinzweya, Burma. • The Marianas see action for the first time during the war, as the Allies launch a series of air attacks against the Japanese on the islands of Guam, Saipan, Tinian, and Rota.

February 29: Ukrainian Red Army general Nikolai Vatutin is mortally wounded in an attack by Ukrainian nationalists who are fighting for a Ukraine independent of the Soviet Union. • American infantrymen invade the strategically important Admiralty Islands, north of New Guinea.

March 1: Germany announces that it has detained and enslaved some five million foreign nationals to fulfill the Reich's war-related labor needs.

March 2: More than 400 Italian civilians die on a cargo train when it stalls in a tunnel and asphyxiates them with fumes. The freight cars had become the only means of transportation in a country where all available resources are being devoted to the war effort. • Turkey pays for its stubborn neutrality with the loss of American lend-lease assistance.

March 3: The Allies reveal that the U.S., Britain, and Soviet Union will share equally in the war spoils of the Italian navy. • As many as six million workers in northern Italy strike in protest of deportations of Italians to German slave labor camps.

March 4: The Japanese authorities order schoolchildren as young as 12 to mobilize for the war effort.

March 6: Berlin is bombed by a U.S. force of nearly 700 bombers, but the Americans suffer the loss of 69 planes, a one-day record. • Chinese and American tank forces engage the remnants of a Japanese marine division at Burma's Tanai River.

Allies' dual assaults in Italy The Allied landing at Anzio and the initial Allied assault on the Italian town of Cassino (*pictured*) both took place in January 1944. Allied leadership hoped that the Anzio landing would bypass the Germans' formidable Gustav Line and divert and weaken German defenses at Cassino, the key position on the line. The strategy failed, and fighting dragged on in both places. But in May, the Allies finally broke through both at Anzio and Cassino. Bombing raids left Cassino in ruins.

Allies advance in India, Burma U.S. troops cross the Irrawaddy River in Burma. Alarmed by the buildup in Allied strength in late 1943, the Japanese launched an offensive against Imphal and Kohima in northeastern India in order to cut the railway that supplied "The Hump" airlift to China. After hard fighting, the Japanese conceded defeat by early July and retreated, having suffered 55,000 casualties. It was the largest Japanese defeat up to that time. Elsewhere, Chinese divisions commanded by General Joseph Stilwell were on the attack in the Ledo area of Burma, and in mid-April 1944 Chinese divisions mounted an attack on the Yunnan front. Hard-pressed, the Japanese retreated. By the time monsoon season arrived in 1944, the Allies were poised to recapture Burma.

1944

March 7: The British House of Commons debates whether popular singers, singing about the hardships of war on the BBC, damage morale on the front. • The gas chambers at Auschwitz-Birkenau claim more than 3,800 Jewish deportees from the Theresienstadt Ghetto.

March 11: In the first of what will be many trials of French "collaborators" (French men and women who aided and abetted the Nazis), Vichy interior minister Pierre Pucheu receives a guilty verdict and a death sentence.

March 12: Czechoslovakia's government-in-exile sends a message to Czech citizens back home to revolt against the occupying Nazis. • Britain suspends travel between England and Ireland two days after Ireland denies an Allied request to close down Axis consular offices that effectively serve as espionage operations for Axis nations.

March 14: In Germany, Wernher von Braun (a future NASA star) is detained temporarily for spending time and money on projects that have little to do with the imperialist aims of the Reich.

March 15: Responding to Hungary's recent flirtation with the Allies, German troops stage along the border, forewarning an invasion.

March 16: Oswald John Job, at age 59, becomes the oldest person to be executed under the terms of Britain's 1940 Treachery Act. Job had passed secrets to the Nazis in letters using invisible ink.

March 18: The RAF drops 3,000 tons of bombs on Frankfurt, Germany. A separate raid four days later will claim more than 1,000 civilian lives.

March 20: Germany occupies Hungary two days after Hitler gave his troops the order to march.

1944

March 24: The Chindits, a British special army force comprised of Indian nationals, are left rudderless after their leader, Major General Orde Wingate, dies in a plane crash over Burma. • The Nazis murder 336 Italian civilians to avenge a partisan attack that claimed the lives of 33 members of the SS who were marching through a narrow street in Rome.

March 25: Seventy-six Allied pilots escape from the German POW camp *Stalag Luft III*, outside of Berlin, via an expertly engineered underground tunnel.

March 26: Only one sailor survives to tell the story of the sinking of the *Tullibee*, a U.S. Navy submarine whose own torpedo struck the ship after following a circular trajectory after being fired.

March 27: The Nazi SS carries out a mass murder of the Jewish children of Kovno, Lithuania. No child younger than 13 is spared.

March 29: What will eventually become a massive flow of aid to war-torn Europe begins with a relative trickle when Washington allocates $1.35 billion to aid European refugees.

March 30–April 2: The Japanese suffer major equipment and supply losses when U.S. Navy ships bombard Japanese positions in the Caroline Islands.

March 31: In the worst RAF losses of the war, 95 bombers are lost in one night in an unsuccessful raid of Nuremberg, Germany. • Admiral Koga, commander of the Japanese Imperial Navy in succession to Yamamoto, is presumed dead after his plane disappears over the Philippines.

April 1: Neutral Switzerland loses 50 civilians in an accidental USAAF raid over Schaffhausen.

ENSA provides needed entertainment The British Entertainments National Service Association (ENSA) was similar to the American United Service Organizations (USO). ENSA musicians, actors, comedians, and singers performed in hotels, factories, theaters, and—as seen here—at war-effort work sites. ENSA performers also toured war fronts around the world. The organization presented more than 2.5 million shows to some 300 million British and Allied troops and civilian war workers. Although some British citizens liked to poke fun at the performances, ENSA entertainments were popular with their audiences.

1944

April 2: Nazis murder 86 French civilians in reprisal for partisan aggression. • Soviet troops invade Romania, with a plan to recapture the oil-rich nation for the Allies.

April 3: With the Germans in control of Hungary, the Allies revoke their promise to spare the country and attack German positions in the capital of Budapest.

April 4: General Charles de Gaulle assumes leadership of the Free French army.

April 5: Allied aircraft again attack the Axis-controlled oil production and transport facilities of Ploesti, Romania.

April 6: In Britain, the dramatic increase in the number of wage-earning citizens leads the government to introduce pay-as-you-earn taxation, whereby an employer deducts a set amount from an employee's paycheck per pay period.

April 7: The Soviets decline a renewed Japanese offer to negotiate a separate peace between the Nazis and the Russians.

April 10: The Red Army reclaims Odessa, an important Soviet port on the Black Sea, from the retreating German army.

April 11: The RAF destroys the Gestapo's headquarters in The Hague, including files on individual Dutch nationals scheduled to be deported to the Nazi camps.

April 13: A massive Allied bombing raid hits German targets in Hungary and Yugoslavia, as well as in Germany proper.

ITALY, 1943–45

The fight for Italy The Allies' success in North Africa enabled them to invade Sicily in July 1943 and Italy in September. But despite an Italian armistice on September 8, the Germans continued to fight on determinedly. Due to the impending Allied invasion of Northern Europe, the Italian campaign was consistently accorded a lower priority by the Allies, and consequently was often under-resourced. The strategic failure of the landing at Anzio exemplified this and other Allied deficiencies. Meanwhile, the German defense of Cassino was particularly tenacious. Nevertheless, the Allies advanced relentlessly northward, smashing through the Gustav Line and the Gothic Line. The Germans surrendered in Italy on May 2, 1945.

Eaker's plan
American Ira Eaker, an infantryman during World War I, began training as a pilot in 1918. He won the Distinguished Flying Cross in 1929 for helping set a world flight endurance record. In 1942 he was named commander of the Eighth U.S. Army Air Force based in Britain, where he led the first U.S. bomber raid on Europe. A proponent of daylight precision bombing, he helped persuade Winston Churchill to launch the Combined Bomber Offensive (also known as the Eaker Plan), in which the Americans focused on daylight bombing and the Royal Air Force conducted night bombing. He was named commander-in-chief of the Allied Air Force in the Mediterranean in late 1943.

Britain's WAAFs aid the war effort A member of the Women's Auxiliary Air Force (WAAF), the women's branch of the British RAF, tracks aircraft via radar in 1944. Although WAAFs did not fly planes (unlike their civilian female counterparts in the Air Transport Auxiliary), their duties centered around such vital matters as weather, radar, codes, reconnaissance, and intelligence. Beginning in 1944, many WAAFs served beyond the home front, including in Europe after the invasion of Normandy.

Romans hail American liberators Shortly before the June 4, 1944, liberation of Rome (*pictured*), the city had endured a week of Allied bombings that killed some 5,000 civilians. Even so, crowds of Romans grateful for an end to the Nazi occupation joyfully greeted the soldiers of U.S. general Mark Clark's Fifth Army, showering them with flowers. In his fireside chat of June 5, President Roosevelt reminded his listeners that Ancient Rome had once ruled the known world. "That, too, is significant," he said, "for the United Nations are determined that in the future no one city and no one race will be able to control the whole of the world."

Americans capture a German sub Launched and commissioned in 1941, the German submarine *U-505* sank eight ships and survived more damage than any other German submarine during World War II. On June 4, 1944, depth charges from the USS *Chatelain* forced *U-505*'s crew to abandon ship, after which the sub was boarded and saved from sinking by U.S. sailors (*pictured*). Valuable documents and codebooks were taken from the submarine, which was then towed to the United States. This was the first enemy ship captured by the U.S. since 1815.

1944

April 13: The Allies confront Sweden, which—despite increasing pressure from the international community—continues to supply the Nazis with ball bearings for their equipment and weapons. • Less than two months before the planned Allied invasion of France, American and British warplanes soften German defenses on the Normandy coast.

April 14: The Nazis deport the first trainload of Greek Jews from Athens. They are destined for the Auschwitz-Birkenau gas chambers. • At a Bombay port, nearly 1,000 people die, 20 ships are lost, and tens of thousands of tons of supplies are destroyed in a massive series of explosions that are triggered when a TNT-laden ship catches fire.

April 17: The Japanese initiate a major offensive against American and Chinese positions in China's Honan Province.

April 18–19: Nearly 1,400 French civilians die in Allied air raids over the province of Normandy.

April 19: The U.S. House of Representatives approves a one-year extension of the Lend-Lease Act.

April 20: The Allies are finally able to convince "neutral" Turkey to stop supplying the Axis with chrome for weapons and transport production.

April 24: The U.S. Department of War concludes that only through a ground invasion of the Japanese homeland will the Allies succeed in winning the war in the Pacific Theater.

April 25: U.S. general George Patton creates a buzz when he implies that the Allies have plans for world domination.

Sauckel heads forced labor program In March 1942, Hitler put Nazi politician Fritz Sauckel in charge of acquiring manpower for the war effort. Sauckel pursued his duties with extraordinary cruelty, forcing war prisoners and citizens of occupied Eastern territories into brutal slave labor. In a memo, Sauckel ordered, "All the men must be fed, sheltered and treated in such a way as to exploit them to the highest possible extent at the lowest conceivable degree of expenditure." Sauckel's policies brought some five million workers to Germany, only about 200,000 of them voluntarily. After the war, he was convicted of crimes against humanity and hanged.

Tedder's bombers British air chief marshal Sir Arthur Tedder was appointed Eisenhower's deputy supreme commander for the invasion of Normandy. Tedder successfully carried out the Allies' "Transportation Plan," which involved bombing French railways to slow down Axis reinforcements during the Allied landing at Normandy on June 6, 1944. His tactic of using bombers to clear the way for advancing troops ("Tedder's Carpet") also proved effective at Normandy and elsewhere. In May 1945, he signed Germany's unconditional surrender on Eisenhower's behalf.

Sevastopol falls to the Soviets German soldiers go into captivity in the Crimean city of Sevastopol. On April 8, 1944, the Soviets launched a major offensive (500,000 troops) against the German 17th Army, which had been isolated in the Crimea since November. Outnumbered two to one and with their backs to the Black Sea, the Germans attempted to make a stand at Sevastopol. However, after being shattered by massive artillery barrages and relentless infantry attacks, the city fell on May 9. Of the 230,000 Axis troops originally trapped on the peninsula, about 150,000 escaped by sea. The rest were killed or captured.

1944

April 27: In the run-up to D-Day, British authorities ban all travel outside the country in an effort to put a stop to intelligence leaks about the invasion.

April 29: Disaster strikes a D-Day practice run when German naval forces attack an American training exercise, killing more than 600 troops. • Some 120 Japanese planes are destroyed as the Allies return to the key Japanese base of Truk to inflict further damage.

April 30: The first prefabricated, $2,200 home goes on display in London, in advance of Churchill's plan to use hundreds of thousands of these structures to house those left homeless by the war.

May 1944: The Soviets prevail in the Battle of the Crimea. The area is emptied of German and Romanian forces, tens of thousands of whom have been killed. • This month, for the first time since 1940, no British civilians will die in Axis air raids. • Japanese shipping is severely curtailed following Allied mining of the waters off Thailand and Burma.

May 2: Schoolteacher and crossword puzzle creator Leonard Dawe attracts the attention of the Allies when one of his puzzles, published in the London *Daily Telegraph*, contains the word *Utah*. Subsequent puzzles will include the words *Omaha* and *Overlord*, leading Allied security to suspect Dawe is leaking intelligence about the D-Day invasion. He is not doing so.

May 3: Spain's Fascist government under General Francisco Franco agrees to curtail supply shipments to Germany in exchange for an increase in oil shipments from the Allies.

May 4: The United States suspends the rationing program for most types and cuts of meat.

Disputes over area bombing Along with Arthur "Bomber" Harris, RAF chief of the air staff Sir Charles Portal (*pictured*) was a vigorous advocate of area bombing— destroying civilian populations instead of military targets. But Portal's thinking changed, putting him increasingly at odds with Harris. Over Harris's strong objections, Portal sided with Eisenhower's commitment to the "Transportation Plan" of bombing French railroads instead of German cities in preparation for D-Day. Portal grew increasingly skeptical of area bombing's military effectiveness, but was unable to restrain Harris from bombing city after city late in the war.

Ike greets troops before D-Day On June 5, 1944, General Dwight Eisenhower wrote a short note. "If any blame or fault attaches to the attempt," he wrote, "it is mine alone." Success was not guaranteed, and Eisenhower probably composed this message in advance of D-Day for fear that the proper words would not come to him if the invasion failed. Here, "Ike" visits the men of the 101st Airborne as they prepare for their drop. He asked their names and where they were from. Not long after, he watched as the planes carried his airborne troops into the night.

D-Day

Operation Overlord, the Allied invasion of mainland Europe and the establishment of the second front was the greatest amphibious landing operation in history. The invasion at Normandy, France, represented the culmination and fruition of an Allied planning process that had lasted more than two years.

The seaborne operation—Operation Neptune—was preceded by a large-scale airborne assault during the night of June 5–6 into the inland areas beyond and on the flanks of the landing beaches. This assault was carried out by 20,000 paratroopers and glider-borne infantry.

With Allied airborne forces already in place (despite many paratroopers having landed far from their intended objectives during the night), the main seaborne landings began at 6:30 a.m. on D-Day. They were preceded by heavy air bombing and more than two hours of naval bombardment. Some 1,200 warships, 4,200 landing ships and landing craft, and 1,200 merchant ships were engaged off Normandy. Together they transported 185,000 men and 20,000 vehicles in the initial assault lift.

By last light on D-Day, from Varreville in the west to Ouistreham in the east, the U.S. First Army (under General Bradley) and British Second Army (General Dempsey), which together comprised General Montgomery's 21st Army Group, had gained a foothold at the five main landing beaches. These beaches were code-named "Utah" (U.S.), "Omaha" (U.S.), "Juno" (Canada), "Gold" (Britain), and "Sword" (Britain). At Omaha, however, this foothold proved somewhat tenuous for the first 24 hours.

Once safely ashore, the five U.S., British, and Canadian divisions—together with various independent brigades, U.S. Rangers, British Commandos, Free French, and other specialist units—quickly set about consolidating and exploiting the bridgeheads. Meanwhile, Hitler and the German high command believed that the main invasion was still to come at the Pas de Calais, with Normandy merely a diversion. The resultant uncertainty and delay in deploying the reserve panzer divisions held in readiness for this very task meant that by dawn on June 7 the only chance the Germans had possessed to repel the invasion was lost irretrievably. Hitler's "Atlantic Wall" had been breached.

About 4,500 Allied troops died on D-Day, 1,000 of whom were killed on "Bloody Omaha." The Allies were at last ashore in mainland Western Europe in strength, and the principal strategic aspiration of Roosevelt, Churchill, and Stalin had been realized. As a huge fleet of cargo- and troop-carrying vessels plied steadily from ports in England to the newly established beachheads and artificial "Mulberry" harbors, Allied strength in Normandy increased with each week that passed, and was soon unstoppable.

The five beaches Sword and Gold were code names for the beaches attacked by the British Second Army. Americans landed on Utah and Omaha. British troops landing at Sword met with very little resistance, sustaining 600 casualties. The Canadians attempting to land on Juno (*pictured*) met with greater resistance, suffering about 50 percent casualties in the first hour. But once over the sea wall, they faced less opposition. The British who attacked Gold faced some resistance, which decreased as they moved inland. Americans landing at Utah faced the least resistance, suffering only 200 casualties on D-Day. Omaha proved the toughest, as the terrain was best suited for defense. By the time the Americans advanced off the beach, they had left about 3,000 casualties behind.

Perilous advance Americans advance over a sea wall after landing on Utah beach. Allies met with the stiffest resistance on Juno and Omaha beaches. U.S. colonel George Taylor of the First Infantry Division tried to motivate his shell-shocked and fatigued men to advance off Omaha. "Two kinds of people are staying on this beach," he said, "the dead and those who are going to die." Once beyond the obstructions, troops advanced up the slopes to destroy pillboxes, from which machine gun and artillery fire rained down.

1944

May 5: Ailing Indian Congress Party leader Mohandas Gandhi leaves prison nearly two years after his incarceration for impeding Britain's war effort.

May 6: Germany orders an additional 1,800 laborers from France to help staff the Mittelbau-Dora slave labor camp near Nordhausen, Germany. The workers are needed to step up production of the V-2 bombs that will terrorize Britain for much of the year.

May 8: Supreme Allied Commander Eisenhower confirms June 5 as the date for Operation Overlord, the invasion of France.

May 9: *Luftwaffe* installations on French soil are pounded by Allied aircraft in an attempt to render them harmless prior to D-Day. • On the Eastern Front, the Soviets recapture the Ukrainian city of Sevastopol.

May 10: President Roosevelt appoints James Forrestal secretary of the Navy following the death of Forrestal's predecessor, W. Franklin Knox.

May 12: The Allies engage in heated battles with German troops across much of Italy, and manage to make steady gains. • The Allies warn secondary Axis powers Romania, Hungary, and Bulgaria that they will suffer if they continue to stand with Germany. • A Free French tribunal finds Vichy Admiral Edmond Darian guilty of collaborating with the Nazis and sentences him to life imprisonment. • A joint U.S.-RAF aerial assault over Germany inflicts heavy damage on the *Luftwaffe* while wreaking havoc on several synthetic-oil production facilities.

May 13: The Allies finally break through the German Gustav Line, the western segment of the Winter Line, and begin their march northward through Italy.

News of the invasion At about 3:30 a.m. Eastern time in the U.S. on June 6, 1944, the following news was released: "Allied naval forces...began landing Allied armies this morning on the northern coast of France." This landing had been much anticipated in the Allied and Axis nations. Most Americans were anxious for news, as seen in this scene from New York City. President Roosevelt emphasized in a news conference that the invasion did not mean the fighting was almost over. "You don't just walk to Berlin," he said, "and the sooner this country realizes that, the better." The Japanese ambassador in Berlin notified Tokyo that German headquarters told him there would be no counterattack in Normandy because the German army still awaited (erroneously) the invasion of "the main body, which the Allies [have] not yet landed."

Hedgerows impede progress "Too many hedges," an Allied unit reported. "Must go forward slowly... take one hedgerow at a time and clean it up." *Bocage* is French for mixed woodland and pasture separated by thick, high hedgerows, as shown in this photo. Cherbourg Peninsula's terrain proved excellent for defense, undermining America's advantage in air support, armor, and artillery. The hedgerows did not stop a tank, but the machine's underbelly—the weakest part of a tank's armor—was exposed to enemy antitank and bazooka fire as it reached the top of a hedgerow. Units from the U.S. First Army needed 17 days to travel seven miles toward Saint-Lô.

Americans break through at Saint-Lô In mid-June 1944, the Germans' defense stiffened in the hedgerows of Normandy. The British advance stalled at Caen, which was defended by much of Germany's armor. However, the Germans had few tanks in the American sector at Saint-Lô, allowing U.S. forces to breach the German line there in early August. U.S. general George Patton's newly formed Third Army threatened to encircle the German force still deployed across Normandy. Hitler called for a retreat from Normandy on August 16, leaving 50,000 dead and about 200,000 captured. The Germans in this picture surrendered on June 9.

1944

May 13: Klaus Dönitz, son of the German *Kriegsmarine* commander, dies when the Allies sink the ship he is on.

May 15: The Nazis begin the process of deporting Hungarian Jews to labor and death camps with the assistance of the local Hungarian police. Ultimately, close to 440,000 will be deported, with about two-thirds ending their journey in the gas chambers of Auschwitz-Birkenau.

May 18: After four months of bloody battle and at a cost of some 20,000 lives, the Allies finally capture the ruined hilltop of the Monte Cassino monastery in Italy.

May 19: About 50 of the Allied POWs who escaped *Stalag Luft III* via an underground tunnel are executed after almost all who escaped were recaptured. About 20 are returned to the camp to serve as a warning to other inmates.

May 21: The Americans capture Wakde Island, off the north coast of Dutch New Guinea, two days after their initial landing. The conquest gives them an important forward base for their planned invasion of western New Guinea.

May 22: The North Atlantic island nation of Iceland declares itself independent of Denmark.

May 25: Josip Broz Tito, leader of the Communist Yugoslavian partisans, narrowly evades capture in a surprise German raid on his headquarters.

May 26: Nearly 5,500 French civilians die in Allied air raids over the southern part of the country.

May 29: *Luftwaffe* commander Hermann Göring admits that his fleet has yielded the skies over Europe to the Allies, telling Hitler "not a single *Luftwaffe* aircraft dares show itself."

Overlord a resounding success The Allies' successful invasion and subsequent landing of supplies surpassed everyone's expectations. Once the beaches were under Allied control, two prefabricated harbors, made of six miles of flexible steel roadway, were towed from England and constructed at Omaha (*pictured*) and Gold beaches. By the end of June, approximately 850,000 troops, 150,000 vehicles, and 570,000 tons of supplies had crossed the English Channel. Prime Minister Winston Churchill stated that Operation Overlord, the Normandy invasion, was "the most difficult and complicated operation ever to take place."

1944

May 29: Tanks clash in the Pacific Theater for the first time when U.S. forces attempt to evict the Japanese from their strategically important airfield on the island of Biak. • The USS *Block Island*, a Bogue Class escort carrier, becomes the only American carrier to go down in the Atlantic when it is torpedoed by *U-549* in waters northeast of the Canary Islands.

May 30: The Nazis order all Germans to kill downed Allied airmen on sight.

June 1: The French Resistance is given its marching orders and alerted to the timing of the D-Day invasion when the BBC broadcasts Verlaine's poem "*Chanson d'Automne.*" • The Ultra code-breakers at Britain's Bletchley Park press "Colossus"—a speedy, fully electronic Enigma deciphering machine—into service.

June 2: As the Allies approach Rome, appeals come in from all quarters to spare the ancient city the destruction wrought on much of the rest of Europe.

June 4: The Allies march on Rome, one day after Hitler orders his armies withdrawn. Though sporadic fighting occurs in the outskirts, the city center is spared. • A forecast of high winds and excessive cloud cover forces the postponement of D-Day by one day, to June 6. • The U.S. Navy captures *U-505*, an intact U-boat, off the coast of Africa.

June 5: Field Marshal Erwin Rommel leaves his post on the coast of France to travel to Germany to celebrate his wife's birthday. He will spend most of D-Day speeding back to the Normandy front. • Allied paratroopers land in France late in the evening as a prelude to the D-Day invasion.

Rockets constructed in Peenemünde On June 13, 1944, Germany launched the V-1 flying bomb at London for the first time. The "buzz bomb" was an unmanned, pulse-jet aircraft developed in Peenemünde (*pictured*), a town on a small German peninsula in the Baltic Sea. German scientists, under the direction of Wernher von Braun (later the father of the U.S. space program), also developed the V-2 ballistic missile, a pilotless aircraft that traveled at four times the speed of sound, making it invulnerable to antiaircraft and fighter fire. RAF bombers attacked Peenemünde on August 17–18, 1943, destroying much of the missile development site. However, production of these weapons continued there and at other locations.

Marines land on Saipan Invading the Mariana Islands, from which U.S. bombers could bomb Japan, was an immense logistical challenge. Some 535 combat ships and auxiliaries transported 127,571 troops to islands more than a thousand miles from the nearest U.S. base, Eniwetok. The Marianas were 3,500 miles from the troops' departure point, Pearl Harbor. Early on June 15, 1944, after Admiral Turner gave the go-ahead to the landing force, vessels such as this landing craft carried Marines to the key Mariana island, Saipan. More than 600 amphibious craft debarked two divisions on eight beaches on a four-mile front with no serious collisions. Some 8,000 Marines were landed in the first 20 minutes. Once the troops were ashore, they met fierce resistance.

U.S. troops face troublesome obstacles Saipan's terrain was much more diverse than the small, low-lying atolls of the Marines' and Army's recent campaigns. Mountains, tangled vegetation, cane fields, ravines, and caves (such as the one at left) all presented obstacles. The enemy usually proved difficult to locate, and fighting everywhere was at close quarters. Grenades, such as those being thrown here by Marines, proved invaluable. So did satchel charges and flamethrowers. U.S. naval dominance had prevented the Japanese from receiving the reinforcements and supplies needed to strengthen their defenses before the invasion. But the 30,000 Japanese defenders fought with characteristic determination for land that they considered strategically vital home territory.

Japanese choose death over surrender The corpse of one of the 23,811 Japanese known to have died on Saipan leans back on a tree as if asleep. How he died is unknown, but he evaded the fate of thousands sealed in caves or charred beyond recognition. Perhaps he died in a night raid or a *banzai* charge. The last charge, on July 7, cost more than 3,000 Japanese lives. Perhaps this soldier committed suicide rather than surrender. Only 736 of the 30,000 defenders, including 438 Koreans, allowed themselves to be captured. As the garrison commander, General Saito, concluded before committing *hara-kiri*, "Whether we attack, or whether we stay where we are, there is only death."

Marines seek spiritual strength During the initial landings on Saipan, Marines listened as chaplains gave them a prayer and blessing over the ships' loudspeakers. Here, with the campaign in progress, an American pauses before a crucifix in a small cemetery. Of 71,034 officers and men committed to the invasion of the island, casualties amounted to 14,111, or about 20 percent. Nearly four times as many Marines became casualties on Saipan as on Tarawa. Navy chaplains, who supported the Marine Corps, moved between units from dawn till dusk, providing up to 14 services a day. They also performed burial services.

1944

June 14: Free French leader General Charles de Gaulle returns to France some four years after the Nazi occupation sent him into exile.

June 15: Operating out of Chinese bases, American B-29 long-range bombers attack the Japanese island of Kyushu, damaging a steel plant that is a key supplier for the imperial war effort.

June 19–20: The U.S. Navy deals a heavy blow to the Japanese, and their naval air fleet in particular, in the Battle of the Philippine Sea. U.S. losses are relatively small, while the incapacitated Japanese fleet is forced to retreat to Okinawa.

June 22: The Allies bomb the French city of Cherbourg after a warning, delivered a day prior to the occupying German force, is met with silence. • President Roosevelt signs the GI Bill of Rights, a wide-ranging veterans benefits package that will become the catalyst for the "American dream" ideal of the 1950s. • Keeping an eye on the postwar prize, the Soviets establish a puppet Communist government in Chelm, Poland. The new body is called the Polish Committee of National Liberation.

June 27: The U.S. Army occupies the French city of Cherbourg two days after naval bombardments and street fighting began to engulf the city.

June 28: Philippe Henriot, the Vichy minister of information who was known as "the French Goebbels," is murdered in his bed by members of the French Resistance.

June 29: In a meeting with his top commanders at Berchtesgaden, Hitler refuses to listen to their bleak reports on the state of the war. They leave enthused by his comments.

Americans cripple Japanese carrier forces U.S. airman Ronald "Rip" Gift celebrates his survival following a night landing on the USS *Monterey* during the two-day Battle of the Philippine Sea (June 19–20, 1944). The "Get the carriers" exhortation on the ready room blackboard reflects the emphasis placed on aircraft carriers as priority targets. By mid-1944, U.S. carrier task forces were prowling the seas, striking enemy targets at will. By contrast, the Japanese navy was steadily weakening. Losses of Japanese carriers, aircraft, and pilots during the Battle of the Philippine Sea were the final blows to Japanese hopes for naval dominance.

Battle of the Philippine Sea

Thrown on the defensive in the Pacific by 1944, the Japanese navy pinned its hopes on a decisive fleet engagement to revive Japan's fading fortunes. Planners hoped to fight this decisive battle around the Palaus Islands and the Western Carolines, but the U.S. landings on Saipan on June 15 dictated otherwise. Combined Fleet commander Admiral Toyoda Soemu ordered the First Mobile Fleet to the Marianas.

Contrails in the sky during the Battle of the Philippine Sea

Led by Vice Admiral Ozawa Jisaburo, the Japanese force was built around nine carriers. They would face 15 U.S. carriers, but Ozawa expected land-based aircraft from Guam and other island bases to reduce those odds before the naval engagement began. In fact, unbeknownst to Ozawa, U.S. carrier planes were neutralizing these land-based forces even as his fleet steamed into battle.

Believing erroneous Japanese claims that the U.S. fleet had already suffered serious losses from land-based air forces, Ozawa launched his carrier attack on June 19. More than 450 aircraft went after the U.S. Fifth Fleet, only to run into a buzz saw. Because the Japanese pilots were inexperienced, U.S. Grumman Hellcat fighters and massed antiaircraft fire wreaked havoc on the enemy. The Japanese lost 330 planes in the lopsided five-hour exchange, derisively dubbed the "Great Marianas Turkey Shoot" by American pilots. Also lost were the carriers *Taiho* and *Shokaku*, sunk by American submarines *Albacore* and *Cavalla*. The U.S. task force lost a total of 31 planes to all causes.

Left with about 100 aircraft, Ozawa withdrew. The next afternoon, operating at the far extent of their range, U.S. aircraft shot down 65 more Japanese planes, sank the carrier *Hiyo* and two oilers, and damaged two carriers and a battleship. About 80 U.S. planes were lost on the return when they ran out of gas and ditched or crashed, but more than half of the crew members were rescued.

The Battle of the Philippine Sea cost the Japanese 476 planes and about 450 pilots. The Japanese carrier air arm never recovered from this mortal blow.

HITLER'S FINAL GAMBLE

JULY 1944–JANUARY 1945

On July 20, 1944, young German colonel Claus Schenk von Stauffenberg, a wounded veteran of the Tunisian campaign, attended Hitler's morning briefing at the Rastenberg headquarters in East Prussia while carrying a time bomb in a briefcase. He left the case under the heavy oak table at which Hitler was standing and found an excuse to leave. A few minutes later, the bomb exploded—but not before another officer, finding it in his way, had kicked the case farther under the table. The blast killed four of those present, but Hitler was shielded by the heavy table. He emerged alive and vengeful. Stauffenberg was executed that night in Berlin. Several thousand suspects were arrested and about 200 were executed in the weeks that followed.

The assassination attempt coincided with a sudden crisis in the German war effort. Until late July, the front in Normandy had held, though at high cost. Again and again, the Germans struggled to repulse the British effort to capture the French city of Caen. The effort denuded German troops and tanks from other parts of the front, which allowed American commanders to plan a breakout through the German line. After weeks of preparation and with overwhelming air support, U.S. general Omar Bradley launched Operation Cobra on July 25. For the first time, Western forces were able to develop real mobility. The line was broken open, and Bradley—supported by notoriously belligerent general George Patton—drove the German army back toward Paris in a matter of weeks. On August 25, Paris was liberated, partly by the approaching armies and partly by the French Resistance, which staged a final revolt against German occupation.

A second landing in southern France began on August 15, and within two weeks the enemy was cleared from the rest of France, meaning the Allies stood on the frontiers of Germany. The Western Allies grew hopeful that Germany might be defeated before the onset of winter. But General Montgomery's airborne assault on the Dutch city of Arnhem in the middle of September (to make it possible to cross the Rhine River) was bloodily repulsed. German resistance stiffened in immediate defense of the home territory.

A French resistance fighter and an American officer engage German troops in a street battle in an unidentified French city. Resistance movements rose up against the German occupiers throughout Europe as Allied forces advanced from both the west and the east. Resistance fighters harassed German forces, aided Allied soldiers, and prepared for a new postwar political order.

The dramatic collapse of Axis resistance owed something to popular resistance both in the West and the East. In Yugoslavia, a large Communist army under the leadership of Joseph Tito played the major role in liberating Yugoslav territory. In Italy, partisans harried the retreating Germans and prepared for a new postwar order. In some cases, resistance was clearly anti-Soviet. In the Ukraine, a guerrilla war—fought by nationalists—tied down thousands of Soviet soldiers and security forces during 1944 and 1945 and slowed the move westward.

In Poland, the Home Army hoped to liberate its country before Soviet forces had time to construct a Communist state. On August 1, as the Red Army stood on the far side of the Vistula River, Polish nationalist forces in Warsaw staged an uprising against the German occupiers. The result was a savage response from the embattled German forces, which destroyed much of what remained of the city. The Red Army stayed where it was, and would not capture Warsaw until the start of the renewed campaign in January 1945.

In the Pacific, the Allies made rapid progress. Following the capture of Saipan, American forces retook Guam and opened the whole of the western Pacific to Allied forces. The Japanese once again sought a decisive big battle as a key to saving what was left of their new empire. However,

In the East, Soviet troops reached the German border on August 17. Finland sued for peace on September 2, and during the following month the Baltic States were occupied and reabsorbed into the Soviet bloc. Farther south, the Red Army made rapid progress after the destruction of German Army Group Center. Romania was occupied in August and switched to the Allied side. Bulgaria was occupied next, and by the end of October parts of Slovakia were also in Soviet hands. The Red Army stood on the boundaries of Hungary and Yugoslavia.

the American decision to reoccupy the Philippines exposed Japan's air forces to severe attack. When the Japanese main fleet was deployed to oppose the American landings on the Philippine island of Leyte, the force lacked adequate air cover. The encounter was the largest naval battle ever fought, involving 282 ships. In late October, three separate Japanese task forces were deployed to try to defeat the invasion. The result was a decisive victory for the U.S. Navy, as Japan lost 26 front-line warships. The invasion force landed on Leyte and cleared the island by the end of the year. The defeat of Japan was now only a matter of time.

The same could be said of Hitler's Germany, which was now surrounded on all sides by heavily armed enemies and subject to constant aerial bombardment. Yet Hitler still hoped for victory. From June, new "weapons of revenge"—the V-1 flying bomb and the V-2 ballistic missile—were launched against London. Hitler hoped that by holding or destroying ports in the West, combined with a renewed U-boat campaign with new types of submarines, Germany would deprive U.S. and British forces of replacements and supplies.

In December 1944, Hitler ordered the German army and air force to use its scarce reserves for a daring counteroffensive in the West against American forces. The goal was to divide the Western Allies, seize the port

An American soldier guides B-29 bombers to their parking areas on the airfield at Eniwetok in the Marshall Islands in 1944. Though the air campaign against Japan was initially plagued with a multitude of tactical problems, U.S. bombers went on to lay waste to the enemy homeland and play a key role in the Allied victory.

of Antwerp, and force them to rethink their strategy. His commanders preferred a more limited offensive, but on December 16 Hitler unleashed Operation Autumn Mist.

In poor weather, which shielded the panzer armies from air attack, the Germans made rapid progress and carved out a salient 50 miles deep in the Ardennes. The Allies regrouped and counterattacked in what became known as the Battle of the Bulge. American resistance at St. Vith and Bastogne, Belgium, held up the German advance, and heavy counterstrikes drove German forces back to the German frontier. On January 8, Hitler pulled his battered army back. The loss of 600 tanks and 1,600 aircraft marked the defeat of the Ardennes offensive. Germany was now exposed to the grim finale of the European war that Hitler had launched six years before.

Red Army overwhelming on Eastern Front At 5:00 a.m. on June 22, 1944, in Operation Bagration, roughly two million Soviet troops waited—to the east and south of Belorussia—as the Red Army fired thousands of guns for two hours. The main assault (*pictured*) of this Soviet offensive began the following day. The German army, with fewer than a million soldiers, was no match for the Soviets and their firepower. By the end of July, the Red Army reached the outskirts of Warsaw. In a little more than a month, the German army lost approximately 350,000 men, including 31 generals.

1944

July 3: The Red Army liberates Minsk, site of one of the largest wartime Jewish ghettos and the center of the Soviet resistance movement. • After nearly four months, the Battle of Imphal and Kohima in northeast India comes to an end. The Japanese have suffered nearly 55,000 casualties, including more than 30,000 deaths, in this campaign against the Allies.

July 6: German field marshal Gerd von Rundstedt, one of Hitler's top military officers, is replaced after painting a pessimistic picture of Germany's chance of success on the Western Front. • With the battle for Saipan all but lost to the Allies, Lieutenant General Saito Yoshitsugu and Vice Admiral Nagumo Chuichi commit suicide rather than face the shame of surrender.

July 8: Admiral Miklos Horthy, the Hungarian regent, orders an end to the deportations of Hungarian Jews to Auschwitz-Birkenau. His order will come too late for more than 400,000 men, women, and children.

July 9: American bandleader Glenn Miller performs the first of a series of concerts for troops in the European Theater. • The U.S. declares the island of Saipan secured after about 3,000 Japanese troops had died in a suicidal charge against a large contingent of American soldiers on July 7.

July 11: Tens of thousands of women and children evacuate London as the terrifying and destructive German V bombs continue to fall. • Washington formally recognizes the Free French government of General Charles de Gaulle.

July 12: The Nazis empty the so-called Jewish "family camp" at Auschwitz-Birkenau, sending 4,000 to the gas chambers.

1944

July 14: In France, Bastille Day observances feature the public humiliation of French nationals who collaborated with the Nazis.

July 17: German troops are ordered to stand firm as the Red Army crosses into Poland. • German general Erwin Rommel is seriously injured in Normandy when an RAF plane strafes his car, fracturing his skull. • Port Chicago, California, suffers the worst homefront disaster of the war when 320 men die in a massive explosion involving two ammunition-laden ships. • Napalm, the incendiary weapon that will become infamous during the Vietnam War, is used by the U.S. in combat for the first time when Allied planes attack German positions on the ground near St.-Lô.

July 18: The disheartening, bloody Battle of the Hedgerows ends with the U.S. capture of the French town of St.-Lô. • On the heels of a string of military defeats, most recently the fall of Saipan, Tojo Hideki—the political and military leader of Japan—is forced to resign.

July 20: Hitler survives an assassination attempt by a member of his own inner circle, Colonel Claus von Stauffenberg. In retaliation, Stauffenberg and many other senior soldiers and officials will be executed.

July 21: U.S. Marine and Army divisions retake the island of Guam. Originally ceded to the U.S. by Spain in 1898, Guam was captured by the Japanese in 1941.

July 23: A Red Cross visit to the Nazis' Theresienstadt labor camp results in a favorable report due to a beautification program and a tightly controlled tour. The deportations to Auschwitz-Birkenau will resume shortly after the conclusion of the Red Cross visit.

The Port Chicago explosion At 10:18 p.m. on July 17, 1944, an explosion rocked the Port Chicago Naval Magazine in Concord, California. Black naval workers, untrained on how to handle munitions, had just finished loading more than 4,000 tons of explosives on the merchant ship *E. A. Bryan*. The blast killed 320 men and injured about 400. Three weeks after the explosion, 258 African Americans refused to return to work, protesting the dangerous conditions and the Navy's segregation policy. Two hundred and eight received bad-conduct discharges, and 50 were found guilty of mutiny and sentenced to prison. Those 50 received clemency in 1946.

German Opposition Groups

Once in power, the Nazis encountered some continuing levels of opposition within Germany. This opposition developed into a resistance movement in 1938 and eventually evolved into a sophisticated conspiracy.

One such resistance group was *Weisse Rose* (White Rose)—an organization of students at the University of Munich. It was discovered and crushed in 1943, with about 80 arrests and the execution of three of its leaders, Christoph Probst and Hans and Sophie Scholl. Although two attempts on Hitler's life were carried out by army officers in 1943, the most significant attack occurred on July 20, 1944.

That morning, Colonel Claus Schenk von Stauffenberg secreted a powerful time bomb in the conference room of the *Führer*'s headquarters at Rastenburg, East Prussia. This plot involved

German resister Harro Schulze-Boysen

many senior *Wehrmacht* officers, diplomats, and former political leaders, who had planned not only Hitler's death but also to remove the Nazi government. Although the bomb exploded with devastating effect, killing four and wounding many, Hitler avoided serious injury. Hitler's rage and the retribution subsequently inflicted by the Gestapo upon the conspirators, their associates, and many others were ferocious. The key conspirators were tortured and later savagely executed at Plötzensee Prison in Berlin.

About 200 people were executed as a direct result of the July 1944 bomb plot, with many hundreds more consigned to concentration camps. The failure of the July Plot effectively ended any remaining resistance to Hitler, and strengthened the authority of the SS within Germany.

The fate of the conspirators
Some German leaders realized early on that Hitler would destroy their country, but a series of assassination plans either failed or were abandoned. The July Plot was a desperate attempt that resulted in the destruction of the German resistance. General Erich Hoepner (*left*), an early opponent of Hitler, was arrested and tortured by the Gestapo, then executed by hanging. Colonel General Franz Halder (*center*)—not involved in the July Plot—was arrested when searches turned up letters and diaries that implicated him in earlier conspiracies. Halder was sent to a concentration camp but survived the war. Field Marshal Erwin von Witzleben (*right*) had been expected to take over command of the *Wehrmacht* after the coup, but was caught and hanged by piano wire.

1944

July 24: The Red Army liberates the Majdanek death/concentration camp near Lublin, Poland. For much of the world, it is their first look at the horror of the Nazis' "Final Solution" for the Jews. • The Nazis introduce their distinctive "Heil Hitler" salute into German military protocol.

July 26: President Roosevelt meets with Admiral Nimitz and General MacArthur in Honolulu. They decide that the next course of action in the Pacific Theater will be an invasion of the Philippines.

July 29: Germany's Messerschmitt 163 fighter plane becomes the first jet plane to engage in combat operations.

July 30: Major General Mizukami Genzu performs *hara-kiri*, a form of ritualized suicide, after losing Myitkyina, Burma, to General Joseph Stilwell's Allied force.

July 31: Hitler promotes a last-ditch, total-war policy that will call on German troops and civilians to destroy everything in their wake as they retreat. • Heavy fighting develops between German and Soviet troops as the Red Army approaches the Polish capital of Warsaw.

August: In this month alone, some 67,000 Jews from Poland's Łódź Ghetto will die at Auschwitz-Birkenau.

August 1: With the Red Army on the outskirts of Warsaw, Polish resistance activity moves into high gear. • U.S. general George Patton leads his army on a charge to take the French province of Brittany. • Japanese resistance ends on the island of Tinian.

August 2: The *Kriegsmarine* attacks Allied shipping in the English Channel with manned torpedoes operated by frogmen.

Marines face resistance at Guam
Marines jump from an amphibious tractor on the island of Guam. The U.S. seized the island in July 1944 to secure additional airfields for the bombing campaign against Japan. With only 15 miles of potential landing beaches along Guam's west coast, the 18,500-man Japanese garrison knew where to concentrate its defenses and gave the attacking Marines a hot reception. The Third Marine Division landed on beaches swept by fire from the enemy-held high ground. To their right, the First Marine Provisional Brigade encountered easier terrain. However, it also ran into fierce resistance, including an enemy gun position that knocked out two dozen Marine AmTracs.

Fierce fighting on Guam
Marine engineers blow up a series of Japanese dugouts during the fighting on Guam. Fierce Japanese resistance to the landings included a series of well-executed counterattacks intended to push the Americans back into the sea. In the Third Marine Division's zone, the struggle for the high ground behind the landing beaches lasted for days. The terrain included 100-foot precipices "that a trained cliff climber with line and spikes would have a hard time getting up," said one Marine.

1944

August 2: Despite relentless pressure from the Allies, Turkey refuses to join the battle against Nazi Germany.

August 4: After years of hiding in an Amsterdam attic, diarist Anne Frank and her family are betrayed to the German police. • The Germans retreat from Florence, the hub of the Italian Renaissance. Though the Germans destroy most of the bridges over the Arno River, which bisects the city, they spare the *Ponte Vecchio*, which dates to the 14th century.

August 9: With much of France under secure Allied control, General Eisenhower relocates his strategic headquarters to a Reims schoolhouse. • Officials with the Free French headquarters in Algiers, Algeria, announce the demise of Vichy France.

August 10: Hitler moves the entire 2,000-plane *Luftwaffe* force to Western Europe in a bid to challenge the power of the Allies' collective air strength. • The Japanese are crushed by American forces on Guam, leaving the U.S. with an additional solid forward base in the Marianas from which to bomb the Japanese mainland.

August 12: The Allies open an oil pipeline from Britain to France, greatly alleviating the crippling fuel shortages that had recently stalled offensive operations. It is nicknamed PLUTO, an acronym for Pipe Line Under the Ocean.

August 15: The Allies storm ashore in southern France in Operation Dragoon. • Audie Murphy, an American sharecropper's son who will be credited with 240 German kills and will become the most decorated soldier in American history, wipes out a force of Germans occupying a hill.

Dry docks The battleship *Idaho* is lifted out of the water in a floating dry dock at Guam. These repair platforms were constructed in sections in U.S. shipyards, towed to bases, and welded together on the spot. The dry dock was partially submerged to allow a damaged vessel to be towed into place. When water was pumped out of the dry dock's tanks, the whole structure rose, bringing its big passenger up with it. Dry docks carried their own power plants, storage areas, officer and crew quarters, and antiaircraft guns.

Battle of the Falaise Pocket As the Battle of Normandy neared its end, the German Seventh Army and Fifth Panzer Army found themselves encircled by advancing British, French, Canadian, and American forces. The Germans' only escape route was the Falaise Pocket, an area in northern France. The pocket was held by the Polish First Armored Division, which fiercely fought the retreating Germans. The Battle of the Falaise Pocket raged from August 12 to 21, 1944, with many thousands of German soldiers killed and taken prisoner. Vast amounts of German materiel were destroyed, as this photograph shows. However, tens of thousands of Germans escaped to the Seine, partly because the Allies' fear of friendly fire among their converging forces prevented them from fully tightening their stranglehold.

1944

August 18: President Roosevelt announces that he intends to send former war secretary Patrick Hurley to China in an effort to broker cooperation between the Nationalists and the Communists.

August 19: German field marshal Gunther von Kluge, wrongly suspected of involvement with the July 20 Hitler assassination attempt, kills himself. He was on his way home to Berlin two days after being replaced by Field Marshal Model as commander of the German army in the West.

August 20: Disaster befalls the German army in Romania, as the Romanians effectively switch sides at the same time that nearly a million Red Army soldiers march on the Axis satellite state.

August 21: The Dumbarton Oaks Conference is convened in a Washington, D.C., mansion of the same name. During the six-week international meeting, the framework of the United Nations will be largely agreed upon.

August 23: Romanian dictator Ion Antonescu is detained, as Romania's King Michael agrees to make peace with the Soviets.

August 24: The Nazis' sense of desperation is growing more apparent as Joseph Goebbels abolishes holidays, closes schools, and extends the work week, all in an effort to increase production for the war effort.

August 25: The Allies roll down the *Champs Elysées*, as Paris is liberated from the Nazis. • The SS murders more than 120 civilians in the French town of Maille as the Germans continue the practice of committing atrocities as they retreat.

August 26: The Axis satellite of Bulgaria announces that it is pulling out of the war and will no longer tolerate the staging of German offensive maneuvers from its soil.

The liberation of Paris Parisians cheer as Allied tanks roll past the *Arc de Triomphe*. On August 25, refusing to destroy the city as Hitler had ordered, German general Dietrich von Choltitz surrendered Paris to General Jacques-Philippe Leclerc and the Free French forces. French Communist Resistance fighters sought to take power, but Gaullist groups jockeyed into that position. French citizens hoped that Americans were bringing food, clothes, and gasoline, which had been in short supply during Nazi rule, but such items were also in short supply among the liberators.

1944

August 26: On the *Führer*'s orders, German forces begin their withdrawal from Greece. • Operating under the influence of the recently issued "lynch law" order, local residents in the German village of Russelsheim assault and murder the crew of a USAAF plane that crashed nearby.

August 30: The Red Army occupies the Romanian capital of Bucharest as well as the valuable oil fields of Ploesti.

September 2: General Eisenhower is forced to order his armies to stop for lack of fuel, giving Germany an opportunity to fortify its defenses. • The Soviet-Finnish War ends with the cessation of hostilities. A formal armistice will be signed on the 19th.

September 3: The British free the Belgian capital of Brussels from Nazi occupation.

September 5: In one of the quickest capitulations in the history of modern warfare, Bulgaria surrenders less than one day after a Soviet declaration of war. Bulgaria will declare war on Germany on the 7th.

September 6: The decline of the *Luftwaffe* enables Britain to stop enforcing a blackout for the first time in three years.

September 8: The next generation of V-weapons, the V-2, begin falling on London.

September 10: The mayor of Warsaw asks for Allied assistance as the city's partisans rise up against the Nazis. • Heinrich Himmler issues an order calling for the murders of the families of any deserting German military personnel.

September 11: More than 1,200 die when U.S. forces sink two Japanese prison ships containing thousands of Allied captives.

Charles de Gaulle

Born in Lille, France, in 1890, Charles de Gaulle excelled at Saint-Cyr Military Academy and served as an infantry officer from 1914 to '18. He not only was wounded three times, but he was held prisoner by the Germans from 1916 to '18. His interwar military career included fighting the Bolsheviks in Poland. He became an outspoken military theorist, supporting the unpopular position that France's army should be a professional, mobile, and mechanized elite, not a citizen force dependent on fixed defenses.

When Germany invaded France in May 1940, Colonel de Gaulle commanded France's new Fourth Armored Division, which he led in actions at Montcornet, Laon, and Abbeville. Reynaud appointed de Gaulle undersecretary of war on June 6. When Pétain took power 10 days later, de Gaulle escaped to England.

In a broadcast from London on June 18, 1940, de Gaulle urged his countrymen to continue fighting. Though later dubbed "the man of June 18," the new French leader was then little known. The forces at his disposal, ultimately called the Free French, were small. As a Catholic professional soldier, he was not a logical figurehead for the Left-dominated French Resistance. His natural constituency, the Right, was committed to Pétain.

De Gaulle also lacked political skill, but he had immense self-confidence and patriotic fervor. His diplomatic and martial efforts eventually brought recognition at home and alliance with the Resistance. De Gaulle depended on British backing, but he remained eternally suspicious of British intentions. His relations with Churchill and especially Roosevelt were difficult.

In 1943 de Gaulle became joint president of the French Committee of National Liberation (CFLN). He gradually dislodged his American-backed co-president, General Henri Giraud. He engineered the amalgamation of the Free French army and parts of the Vichy army of North Africa, thus enabling substantial French forces to contribute to France's liberation. On June 3, 1944, the CFLN was renamed the Provisional Government of the French Republic, which won recognition from the French population and later the Allies. On August 26, de Gaulle entered Paris to a rapturous welcome. The French hero would serve as president of the provisional government from September 1944 to January 1946.

1944

September 12: The RAF firebombs the central German city of Frankfurt. • Romania formally surrenders to the Allies. It agrees to take up arms against its former Axis partners in exchange for the postwar return of Transylvania to Romanian authority.

September 12–16: Churchill and Roosevelt meet in Quebec to discuss strategy in the Pacific Theater. They agree that a ground invasion of Japan will be necessary for victory.

September 15: One of the most laborious, hard-won battles of the Pacific war begins when the U.S. Marines land on the island of Peleliu. The Japanese will fiercely resist the American invaders for a month.

September 18: The United States and Britain airlift supplies to the Polish resistance in Warsaw. The Soviets, protective of their expansionist aims, are reluctant to prop up any Polish independence movement. The Soviets also refuse landing rights to U.S. and British planes in spite of appeals from Roosevelt and Churchill.

September 19: Female Nazi collaborators in the Dutch town of Nijmegen have their heads shaved and are publicly humiliated. • Churchill returns to Britain following a visit to Roosevelt's home in Hyde Park, New York. In their discussions, the two leaders agreed to fully share atomic research and to use the bomb only by mutual agreement.

September 21: A general strike called in Denmark to protest the deportation of nearly 200 Danes to Nazi concentration camps is violently suppressed by the Germans. • Japanese positions on Luzon, Philippines, come under intense aerial assault by a massive fleet of carrier-based U.S. warplanes.

September 22: Patton's Third Army is halted as supply lines are stretched to the breaking point.

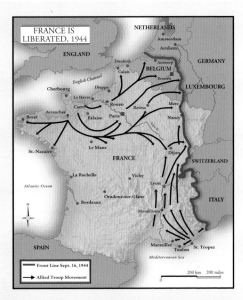

FRANCE IS LIBERATED, 1944

The liberation of France After several weeks of hard fighting among the hedgerows, woodland, and sunken lanes that dominated the post-D-Day Normandy battlefield, the Allied armor at last broke out of the beachheads and drove into France. Allied airpower was a major contributor to this. From July 25, U.S. forces (spearheaded by General Patton's Third Army) launched Operation Cobra, first striking west into Brittany, then south and east toward Paris. Simultaneously, the British Second Army and Canadian First Army struck east, across the Seine and into Belgium. Another Allied army landed in southern France in August. It drove quickly north to achieve a link-up and complete France's liberation.

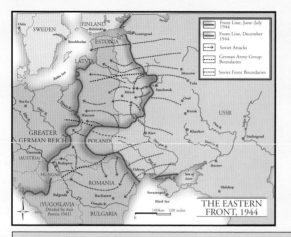

THE EASTERN
FRONT, 1944

The Soviets' westward push Despite the disaster at Stalingrad in January 1943, the Germans subsequently halted a number of Soviet offensives, and even retook Kharkov in March. In July, however, their *Blitzkrieg*-style attacks at Kursk were effectively absorbed and defeated by the Red Army during the greatest tank battle of the war. The Russians then launched successful counteroffensives at Orel and Kharkov. These advances eventually paved the way for a devastating series of Soviet offensives across the whole Eastern Front beginning in June 1944. These included the destruction of Army Group Center in Belorussia and successes in the Ukraine, Poland, the Balkans, and Romania. By December, the Eastern Front no longer lay within the Russian homeland.

1944

September 24: The U.S. releases the Morgenthau Plan, a postwar plan that proposes a total restructuring of the German economy to an agrarian footing.

September 25: Germany organizes the *Volkssturm*, a militia that drafts men as old as 60 and as young as 16.

September 26: Allied planes drop American paratroopers behind German lines in Italy to establish the same sort of resistance network that had been so successful in helping the Allies capture France.

September 27: The British suffer 1,200 deaths and lose some 6,600 more to German POW camps as they fail in their nine-day bid to secure a bridge over the Rhine in the Dutch town of Arnhem.

September 29: The Soviets fly their last sortie in support of the Warsaw resistance.

October 2: After two months of fierce urban warfare, the Germans crush the Polish resistance in Warsaw. As many as 250,000 Poles have died during the struggle. • The Allies break into the Siegfried Line, a defensive line running along Germany's western border. The breach is in the north, near Aachen, and it is there that U.S. troops will penetrate western Germany.

October 7: A group of *Sonderkommandos*, captive Jews whose lives are prolonged while they assist the Nazis with gas chamber and crematorium operations, attacks SS guards at Auschwitz. Though the revolt is quickly and violently quelled, they do kill several SS men and destroy their barracks, as well as Crematorium IV.

October 9–18: Churchill, Stalin, and U.S. ambassador William Averell Harriman meet in Moscow to discuss the postwar status of Poland and the Balkan States.

1944

October 10: Japan's air forces are depleted further as 17 U.S. aircraft carriers launch a massive attack on Japanese installations on Okinawa.

October 13: Stalin once again assures his Allied partners that the Soviets will declare war on Japan, but he insists that he cannot spare the resources until the Allies gain Germany's unconditional surrender.

October 14: German general Erwin Rommel, suspected of having collaborated with the July 20 conspirators, swallows poison after being told by Hitler's chief of army personnel that unless he commits suicide, the Nazis will put him on trial and his family will lose its pension and an estate that had been given to him. The official party line will be that Rommel died of the wounds he suffered in the July RAF attack.

October 15: More than 2,200 Allied bombers pummel industrial cities in the Ruhr. • The Nazis detain Hungarian regent Admiral Horthy hours after he publicly requests peace terms from the Allies. Hungarian Nazi leader Major Ferenc Szálasi will take over the government.

October 18: Premier George Papandreou of Greece is restored to power four days after the last German soldier leaves the ancient capital of Athens. The Germans were driven out by Greek partisans and Allied forces. • Churchill rebuffs a request from Spanish dictator General Francisco Franco to align England and Spain against Communist Russia. • Reeling from losses at Leyte Gulf and elsewhere, the Japanese launch Operation Sho-Go (Victory) in a desperate bid to regain lost territory and protect the Japanese home islands.

October 20: In conjunction with Josip Broz Tito's Army of National Liberation, the Soviets liberate Belgrade, Yugoslavia, from the Germans.

Allies liberate concentration camp Two Allied soldiers examine an oven used to cremate victims at Herzogenbusch, a German concentration camp built outside the Dutch town of Vught. Jews began to be deported to Herzogenbosch in January 1943. While some were forced to work in local factories, others were temporarily held there before being sent to extermination camps in Germany. The camp eventually held more than 30,000 inmates, including Jews, political prisoners, and captured resistance fighters. By the time the camp was liberated in September 1944, about 13,000 had died there.

Casualties high at Aachen Two German prisoners of war, guarded by an American soldier, wait to be taken to a POW camp after the U.S. victory at Aachen. For seven days, fighting had raged from building to building and room to room, with enemy snipers on rooftops picking off scores of U.S. soldiers. While American tanks struggled through debris-strewn streets to dislodge defenders, German soldiers and civilians took to cellars and sewers. This strategically unimportant city cost each side some 5,000 casualties, and about 5,600 Germans were taken prisoner.

1944

October 20: American troops land on the island of Leyte in the Philippines and fulfill General MacArthur's promise to return to liberate the islands from the Japanese.

October 21: Aachen becomes the first German city to fall to the Allies, as desperately weakened German forces surrender.

October 23: Philippines president Sergio Osmeña is restored to office.

October 23–26: The Japanese navy suffers a resounding defeat as American forces dominate in the Battle of Leyte Gulf. The crowning loss for the Japanese is their super-battleship *Musashi*, which capsizes and sinks, costing the lives of more than 1,000 sailors.

October 25: SS *Reichsführer* Heinrich Himmler orders the destruction of the macabre Jewish skull collection at Berlin's so-called "Anatomical Institute." • Since it is no longer a member of the enemy Axis, Italy's diplomatic ties to the Allies are restored.

October 28: The Allies penetrate deep into German territory on General Eisenhower's orders. • U.S. major general Albert Wedemeyer replaces General Joseph Stilwell as commander in the Chinese theater. This comes 10 days after Stilwell is removed at the request of Nationalist leader Chiang Kai-shek. • The Soviets assume control of the Bulgarian armed forces, as Bulgaria capitulates to Russia. • The German army quits the small Adriatic nation of Albania. • The first of the soon-to-be-legendary *kamikaze* pilots commits suicide as he crashes his plane on the deck of the USS *Denver*.

October 30: The Auschwitz gas chambers are used for the last time, as one final transport of Jews—1,700 men, women, and children from the work camp at Theresienstadt—are murdered.

1944

November 3: The Japanese launch more than 9,000 hydrogen balloons with incendiaries attached, sending them on westerly winds to North America. Fewer than 300 of the balloons will reach their targets, but one is found and detonated in Oregon, killing a woman and five children.

November 5: German forces round up 200 Dutch citizens in the town of Heusden. The Germans barricade them inside the town hall and blow up the building, proving that they are as dangerous in retreat as they were on the offensive. • The Americans bomb Singapore.

November 7: Franklin Roosevelt wins his fourth consecutive term as U.S. president. • "Neutral" Switzerland's ties with Germany, coupled with its hostility toward communism, leaves Stalin disinclined to renew diplomatic ties. • Richard Sorge, a Soviet spy who kept Moscow apprised of Japanese war plans before his capture by the Japanese, is hanged in Tokyo.

November 8: The *Luftwaffe* loses one of its best when ace pilot Major Walter Nowotny crashes his Messerschmitt 262 over Germany.

November 10: The Japanese puppet government in Nanking, China, sees a change in leadership when Chen Kung-po succeeds a deceased Wang Ching-wei.

November 12: After many efforts to destroy the German battleship *Tirpitz*, the British finally succeed. Struck by at least two massive bombs, the great ship capsizes and goes under with most of its 1,900-man crew.

November 23: German holdings in the Alsace-Lorraine region of France are further reduced by the Allied capture of Strasbourg, the region's principal city.

Lea's graphic paintings Tom Lea III (*left*) joined *Life* magazine as an artist-correspondent in 1940. His wartime paintings included subjects as varied as politicians and battlefield scenes. His graphic images of the fighting on Peleliu Island in 1944 became famous for their realism and horror, which were unlike anything he or any other American war artist had previously depicted. In *Two-Thousand Yard Stare* (*pictured*), he portrayed, he stated, a Marine "staring stiffly at nothing," whose "mind had crumbled in battle."

The "Ace of Aces" USAAF pilot Richard Bong, pictured center beside his P-38 Lightning, was the leading American ace during the war. In the Southwest Pacific in April 1944, Bong became the first American to pass Eddie Rickenbacker's World War I score of 26. After home leave, Bong returned to the Southwest Pacific in September 1944.

U.S. protects its beachhead on Leyte The Japanese battleship *Yamato* comes under bombing attack during the Second Battle of the Philippine Sea. The super-battleship sallied out as part of Operation Sho-1, an elaborate Japanese scheme to destroy the American beachhead on Leyte, Philippines. Though a diversion successfully drew away Admiral Bull Halsey's carriers, lack of Japanese airpower doomed Sho. A handful of U.S. destroyers, destroyer escorts, and the few available aircraft from escort carriers narrowly managed to turn the Japanese naval force away from the beachhead.

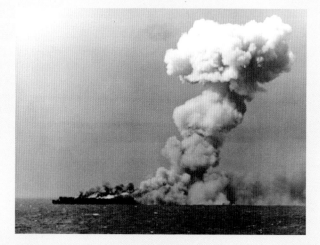

Attack on the *Princeton* Fires burn out of control on the aircraft carrier USS *Princeton* after a Japanese air attack. More than 60 land-based Japanese bombers and torpedo planes, escorted by 130 fighters, attacked U.S. naval forces covering the Leyte landings on October 24. Though these Japanese forces were decimated by U.S. fighters, one dive-bomber hit the *Princeton* with a 550-pound bomb that penetrated the flight deck. The crew abandoned ship as burning gasoline spread to parked aircraft and a munitions storage area. Damage-control parties remained to fight the conflagration, but hours later a massive explosion tore through the carrier, killing or wounding almost everyone still aboard.

1944

November 23: The Canadian Parliament approves a limited draft—a dramatic departure from what had been a strictly volunteer force. Some 16,000 additional Canadian troops will join the Allies.

November 24: Discouraged by the defeat of the Warsaw uprising and disgusted with Soviet manipulation of the Polish border, Premier in Exile Stanislaw Mikolajczyk resigns his post. • The United States attacks Tokyo with 111 B-29 long-range bombers. They operate out of forward bases on the recently occupied Mariana island of Saipan.

November 25: A German V-2 rocket levels a Woolworth department store in London. Of the more than 160 victims, many are children. • Several U.S. aircraft carriers are damaged by *kamikaze* attacks in the waters off the Philippine Islands.

November 26: As Soviet troops advance toward Auschwitz, Heinrich Himmler orders the complex of gas chambers and crematoria destroyed, along with the last of the *Sonderkommando* Jews, in an effort to hide evidence of Nazi atrocities.

November 27: A munitions dump explodes at Burton-on-Trent, England, killing 68 people and scores of animals. • Antwerp comes under heavy V-2 bomb attacks as the Allies finally open up shipping operations in the Belgian port. • The Chinese remain unable to unite for the common goal of battling Japan, and Chiang Kai-shek again refuses to share his stockpile of American weaponry with the Communists.

November 29: *Shinano*, a huge Japanese aircraft carrier commissioned earlier in the month, sinks after being torpedoed by the U.S. submarine *Archerfish*.

U.S. prevails on Leyte American troops regard the bodies of Japanese snipers on the Philippine island of Leyte. After two months of fighting, from October to December, U.S. forces secured the island as part of General MacArthur's promise to win back the Philippines. Nevertheless, Leyte was not an unqualified success. A flood of Japanese reinforcements prolonged the battle, and American casualties were higher than anticipated. But the Japanese fared worse. The naval engagements off Leyte effectively destroyed the remnants of the Japanese Navy, while the ground campaign consumed nearly 65,000 troops. In a last-gasp effort, Japanese paratroopers jumped on two U.S. airfields on Leyte on December 6. Despite creating considerable confusion, all were killed or driven off.

1944

December 3: Unchecked fighting between Greek pro- and anti-Communist factions leads to civil war. • King George VI demobilizes Britain's Home Guard.

December 8: American air forces launch a lengthy offensive against Japanese positions on the island of Iwo Jima. They will spend more than two months softening the Japanese defenses prior to the ground assault.

December 10: Representatives of the Soviet Union and France meet in Moscow and sign a 20-year treaty of friendship and aid. • The Allies build the world's longest bridge, at 1,154 feet, across Burma's Chindwin River.

December 12: Nearly 500 civilians die in a V-2 strike on Antwerp's Rex Cinema.

December 13: More *kamikaze* attacks damage U.S. Navy warships in the Sulu Sea.

December 15: The plane carrying American bandleader Glenn Miller disappears after taking off from England in foul weather.

December 16: The Battle of the Bulge begins when the Germans orchestrate a huge strike against U.S. positions in Luxembourg's Ardennes Forest. • President Roosevelt promotes General Douglas MacArthur to the rank of five-star general.

December 17: Sixty-seven American POWs lose their lives in the Malmedy massacre when a German unit randomly opens fire on a group of 170 prisoners. No motive is apparent. • The 509th Composite Group assembles at a site in western Utah for a special high-speed, high-altitude bombing mission over Japan.

December 17–18: A massive typhoon envelops the U.S. Third Fleet. More than 700 lives are lost.

Japanese desperate for food In 1944 Japan's food shortages worsened. Wild dogs roamed Tokyo streets searching for food, but sometimes became food themselves. Here, civilians farm crops and raise animals in the Olympic Stadium, built for the canceled 1940 Games. By 1941 nearly all arable land—including golf courses—had been brought under cultivation, but Japan still imported most of its soybeans and sugar. Domestic rice crops and imports helped people fend off starvation until the last year of the war. In 1945 shortages engendered by strategic bombing and the submarine blockade led to mass flight to the countryside and suffering in the cities and towns.

> **"[W]hen we reached the point of heading directly into the wind, the propellers of three or four planes, still parked on the bow, began windmilling at about 200 rpm and a few seconds later these planes were torn from their moorings and flung like chips over the side."**
>
> —Captain A. G. Olney, Jr., USS *Altamaha* (light aircraft carrier)

Typhoon in the Philippines

On December 17, 1944, U.S. Task Force 38 was 300 miles away from its destination: Luzon, Philippines. As the ships prepared to refuel at the island of Mindoro, winds began to pick up. "A moderate cross swell and

The USS *Langley* during the typhoon

a wind varying from 20 to 30 knots made fueling difficult," Admiral William Halsey recounted in his autobiography. He was told by his staff aerologist that it was only a "tropical disturbance."

As the storm intensified, Halsey suspended refueling and ordered his ships to move away from the storm. It was no longer a "tropical disturbance" but a typhoon. On December 18, it was on a collision course with the task force. Many of Halsey's destroyers were very low on fuel, causing the ships to ride treacherously high on the sea. As the center of the typhoon passed close to the

task force, hurricane-force winds buffeted massive waves against the helpless vessels. "Shortly after twelve o'clock...," an officer on the destroyer *Hull* later reported, "the wind velocity increased to an unbelievable high point which I estimated at 110 knots. The force of this wind laid the ship steadily over on her starboard side."

When the storm passed, Halsey recounted, it had "swamped three destroyers, cost the lives of 790 men, wrecked some 200 planes, and damaged twenty-eight ships." Over the next three days, every able ship and plane searched desperately for survivors. Following the disaster, the worst the U.S. Navy had suffered in a storm since 1889, new weather stations and offices were established across the Pacific.

1944

December 18: The U.S. tries to put a lid on recent Japanese gains on the Chinese mainland by directing a series of B-29 raids against Japanese positions around Hangkow.

December 19: Some 130 Belgian civilians, accused of sheltering U.S. troops, are murdered by members of the Nazi Gestapo.

December 22: Surrounded with his 101st Airborne Division in the Battle of the Bulge, Brigadier General Anthony McAuliffe receives a surrender ultimatum from the Germans, to which he delivers his immortal reply: "Nuts." In later years, he would suggest that his actual reply was a stronger four-letter word.

December 23: The American soldiers at Bastogne, Belgium, receive desperately needed supplies and offensive reinforcement.

December 24: Members of the German *Sicherheitsdienst* avenge an attack by the Belgian resistance by murdering nearly all the young men in the village of Bande. One, Leon Praile, is able to escape. • More than 800 U.S. soldiers die when the *U–486* sinks the American troop transport *Leopoldville* in the English Channel.

December 26: U.S. tanks break through the German line and end the Bastogne siege as well as the Ardennes offensive. Though they initially had been victorious locally, German forces are greatly depleted.

December 29: Hungary declares war on its former ally Germany as Soviet tanks roll in and urban warfare engulfs the city of Budapest.

December 31: Some German soldiers caught impersonating U.S. troops behind Allied lines are executed by firing squad. • The Battle of Leyte ends with the Allies losing 3,500 men of a 200,000-man force. The Japanese lose 49,000 of a force of 55,000.

Production woes doom German jet The potential of Germany's highly capable Messerschmitt Me 262 jet fighter was squandered because of slow production of the Junkers Jumo 004 jet engine that powered it. It was not because, as is commonly held, Hitler insisted that the plane be utilized as a fighter-bomber rather than as a pure fighter. The 540-mph 262 (America's P-51 Mustang could reach 437 mph) did not see combat until July 1944, too late to affect the D-Day landings or the war's larger outcome. Although some 1,400 Me 262s were delivered, fewer than 300 saw combat. During the same period, Britain fielded perhaps 20 Gloster Meteor jet fighters, and Germany experimented with the *Komet*, a difficult-to-fly Messerschmitt rocket plane capable of speeds just shy of 600 mph.

The Malmedy Massacre

On Sunday, December 17, 1944, shortly after the Germans launched their great offensive in the Ardennes, a number of American prisoners were shot by soldiers of the First SS-Panzer Regiment at Baugnez crossroads, close to the Belgian town of Malmedy. The true scale and circumstances of the Malmedy massacre remain controversial to this day. What is known is that of the 113 prisoners assembled in the field at Baugnez, 67 died there. Forty-six of them, some of whom were wounded, managed to escape the scene.

The massacre began when some of the Germans opened fire. Several survivors claim to have heard an order given. A storm of machine gun and rifle fire lasted for 15 minutes, and was followed by deliberate shots to finish off anyone still showing signs of life. These final murderous *coups de grâce* turned a possible "battle incident" into an indisputable atrocity that resonated throughout the American forces in Northwest Europe. It immediately prompted orders in some U.S. Army units to summarily shoot any SS prisoners they might capture.

GIs discovering the massacred POWs

Although those believed responsible for the massacre were later tried by a U.S. military tribunal, serious coercive and procedural irregularities by the prosecution eventually resulted in the commutation of all of the many death sentences. Those who had been imprisoned received early releases, and by 1960, all had been released.

FACING DEATH AT MALMEDY

A bullet went through the head of the man next to me. I lay tensely still, expecting the end. Could he see me breathing? Could I take a kick in the groin without wincing?…He was standing at my head. What was he doing? Time seemed to stand still. And then I heard him reloading his pistol in a deliberate manner…laughing and talking. A few odd steps before the reloading was finished and he was no longer so close to my head, then another shot a little farther away, and he had passed me up.

—U.S. Army first lieutenant Virgil T. Lary, describing the incident at Malmedy

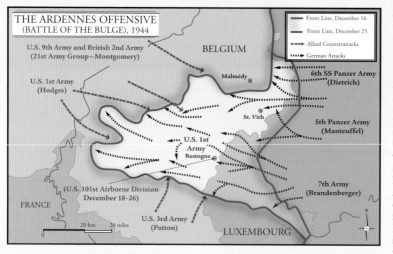

THE ARDENNES OFFENSIVE
(BATTLE OF THE BULGE), 1944

BELGIUM

U.S. 9th Army and British 2nd Army
(21st Army Group—Montgomery)

Front Line, December 16	
Front Line, December 25	
Allied Counterattacks	
German Attacks	

U.S. 1st Army
(Hodges)

Malmédy

6th SS Panzer Army
(Dietrich)

St. Vith

5th Panzer Army
(Manteuffel)

U.S. 1st
Army
Bastogne

7th Army
(Brandenberger)

(U.S. 101st Airborne Division
December 18–26)

FRANCE

20 km   20 miles

U.S. 3rd Army
(Patton)

LUXEMBOURG

Attacks and counterattacks Hitler ordered a major offensive in the West in December 1944 because he believed that it would split the Anglo-U.S. alliance, frustrate the Allied advance, and ultimately precipitate a situation similar to Dunkirk. The German strategic objective was Antwerp, Belgium, and the main attack was launched against the Americans out of the dense, snow-covered forests of the Ardennes. Elite *Waffen-SS* and armored units spearheaded the assault, initially advancing rapidly against the surprised and demoralized GIs. However, the heroic defense of Bastogne by the U.S. 101st Airborne Division, overwhelming artillery and airpower, and decisive counterstrokes mounted by Patton and Montgomery finally restored the Allied situation by the end of December.

Battle of the Bulge On December 16, 1944, Germany began a massive attack in the Ardennes region of southern Belgium. The Germans forced a "bulge" in the faltering Allied advance, plunging surprised U.S. forces into some of the fiercest fighting they would endure in Europe. According to Kenneth Koyen, an officer in the Third Army, U.S. forces did not call the engagement the Battle of the Bulge in its early days, instead referring to it as the German Breakthrough. "The end and the outcome were not yet in view," recalled Koyen, "and the desperate German assault cast a chill over the battleground."

Americans face numerous obstacles German forces took effective advantage of cloudy skies in the early stages of their surprise Ardennes offensive. Although American planes were able to take to the air when blue skies returned, that didn't automatically diminish the determination of German infantry, or the danger to American soldiers, including the GI seen here. A snowy landscape, coppices of trees that might conceal German troops and armor, loosely defined lines, the continuing cold—all of these took a toll on American troops as they regrouped to push the Germans back.

German forces depleted U.S. soldiers watch Allied and German planes battle on Christmas Day, 1944. The weather over Belgium had recently cleared, and Allied aircraft were finally able to support ground troops in a counterattack against the Germans. Hitler's belief that the Western Allies were weak and divided proved unfounded. Montgomery's British forces attacked from the north, Patton's U.S. Third Army attacked from the south, and American troops successfully defended the town of Bastogne. Beginning on January 8, the Germans retreated from the Ardennes. The Battle of the Bulge had been frightfully costly to all combatants. American casualties numbered about 81,000, and German casualties were between 60,000 and 100,000. But Germany's loss of men and materiel was irreparable.

1945

January: Germany begins to run out of fuel for its military. Tanks are abandoned where they stand.

January 1: The Soviet puppet Lublin committee assumes control of portions of Poland liberated by the Red Army. • The *Luftwaffe* launches a significant attack on Allied bases in France, Belgium, and the Netherlands, but it loses nearly half of its 800-strong air fleet.

January 2: British admiral Sir Bertram Ramsey, leader of Allied Naval forces during the Normandy invasion, dies in a plane crash after departing France for Belgium. • U.S. ships en route to Luzon from the Leyte Gulf come under vigorous attack by a fleet of Japanese *kamikaze* pilots.

January 3: Canada sends its first group of some 13,000 draftees to war in Europe, but many of them throw their rifles overboard in protest. • The U.S. Third Fleet loses 18 aircraft in raids on Okinawa, Formosa, and the Pescadores. Japan loses 12 ships and more than 100 aircraft.

January 5: Despite opposition from British and American authorities, Poland's Lublin government is recognized by the Soviet Union.

January 6: Allied attacks have whittled the number of Japanese aircraft on Luzon to 35—a reduction of about 115 in barely a month.

January 12: The Red Army stages a massive assault against Germany along the Eastern Front, sending more than a million troops to face a German force that is a fraction of that size.

January 14: The Japanese launch a counterattack against British forces at the Irrawaddy River in Burma. The Japanese will not be subdued for a month.

The bastion of Bastogne Refugees evacuate the Belgian town of Bastogne in late 1944. When German armored forces began the push that became known as the Battle of the Bulge, many Belgians fled alongside the sparsely deployed American soldiers. But Americans were also headed into the battle. The U.S. 101st Airborne Division reached Bastogne—a junction where seven main roads converged—on December 19. German tanks surrounded the town, but the 101st, elements of the 10th Armored, and supporting units held Bastogne until fighting ended in January, preventing easy movement of German tanks along those roads.

Allies bomb Nuremberg Known for Hitler's elaborate prewar rallies and later as the site of the German war-crimes trials, Nuremberg was also an important manufacturing center for the German war effort. It became a target for Allied bombing raids, and on January 2, 1945, the center of the city—with its medieval architecture—was attacked by Allied bombers. The raid was so successful that most of the town's center was destroyed in less than an hour. This photograph captures the results of the attack. More than 1,800 residents of Nuremberg were killed and thousands were left homeless.

Hitler inspects bomb damage—or does he? Though shaken and angered by Allied bomb attacks on German cities, Hitler rarely visited targeted areas. Nevertheless, London's *News Chronicle* ran this photograph in its January 31, 1945, edition, with a caption claiming that the *Führer* "is surveying ruins of a German town, the name of which is not disclosed." The paper overlooked (or ignored) the fact that Hitler stopped wearing the swastika armband as soon as the war began. The photo is almost certainly from an official visit to a prewar natural disaster or accident.

The indomitable *Hornet* Curtiss Helldivers fly over the USS *Hornet* (CV-12) in January 1945. This was the second American aircraft carrier of that name. The first (CV-8) had launched the Doolittle Raid, fought at Midway, and been sunk at the Battle of Santa Cruz in 1942. CV-12 was in continuous action for 16 months from 1943 to '45. It was attacked 59 times, but never hit. In contrast, its aircraft sank or damaged 1,269,710 tons of enemy shipping and destroyed 1,410 Japanese planes. The *Hornet* supported virtually every Pacific amphibious landing from March 1944, and contributed substantially to victory in the Battle of the Philippine Sea. In February 1945, it launched air strikes on Tokyo.

1945

January 15: Commercial shipping resumes in the English Channel for the first time in nearly five years.

January 16: Hitler moves both his residence and base of operations to the underground bunker at Berlin's Reich Chancellery.

January 17: The Red Army liberates the Polish capital of Warsaw.

January 18: Japanese stragglers at Peleliu attack U.S. ammunition dumps and the American air base.

January 19: The Germans retreat before the Red Army's advance through Poland. The Russians occupy the Polish cities of Tarnow, Łódź, and Kraków.

January 20: President Roosevelt is sworn in for his fourth term in office.

January 25: In the largest naval mining campaign of the Pacific war, the Allies seed the waters off Singapore and Indochina with nearly 370 mines.

January 26: The Soviet army liberates Auschwitz. They find nearly 3,000 inmates still in residence, with many near death.

January 27: The Japanese lose about 100 planes in U.S. counterattacks on Japanese air bases on Okinawa.

January 28: The Battle of the Bulge draws to a close as the last German soldiers are forced into retreat. • For the first time in nearly three years, supplies reach China over the Burma Road, which is newly reopened and renamed in honor of Allied general Stilwell.

January 30: With the Red Army less than 100 miles from Berlin, a defiant Hitler delivers his final radio address. • Seven thousand die when the German liner *Wilhelm Gustloff* is sunk by a Soviet submarine.

COLLAPSE OF THE THIRD REICH

FEBRUARY 1945–MAY 1945

On the afternoon of April 12, 1945, U.S. president Franklin Roosevelt collapsed and died from a cerebral hemorrhage. Vice President Harry Truman was catapulted from relative obscurity to a world stage in which the United States had to oversee the final defeat of Germany and Japan and play a key part in the reconstruction of the postwar order.

Hitler interpreted Roosevelt's death as a miracle of deliverance. Locked away in his bunker in Berlin, the German leader played out grotesque fantasies of a final victory in which his enemies became divided and hostile—or tired of the terrible cost of subduing the German people. Hitler no longer saw the reality of his battered country. The heaviest bombing of the war reduced German cities to ruins one after the other— most notoriously the city of Dresden. From February 13 to 15, 30,000 people were killed there in Allied bombing. Germany could not sustain war production. In both west and east, German forces fought on fatalistically against hopeless odds.

By February 9, American troops had breached the Siegfried Line in western Germany, and by March 5 they had reached the Rhine River at Cologne. The Germans mounted little resistance, with only 26 poorly armed divisions. Meanwhile, 214 divisions tried to hold back the Red Army in eastern Germany. By May 4, the German forces in northern Germany, the Netherlands, and Denmark surrendered to Montgomery's British Commonwealth armies. Farther south, Eisenhower swung the American advance away from the Rhine-Berlin axis toward southern Germany, where he feared the German army might make a final stand in a mountainous redoubt. Americans entered Austria in early May, by which time Axis forces in Italy had also surrendered. On April 28, Mussolini was captured by Italian partisans and killed.

Hitler survived Mussolini by just two days. Since January 1945, the Soviets had pushed relentlessly toward Berlin and Vienna. By February, a succession of rolling offensives brought the Red Army within striking distance of both capitals. In the south, Budapest was occupied by February 11 and the last Germans were driven out

Hitler's chief of operations, General Alfred Jodl (*center*), flanked by Major Wilhelm Oxenius (*left*) and Admiral Hans-Georg von Friedeburg (*right*), formally surrenders the German armed forces to the Allies at General Eisenhower's headquarters in Reims, France, on May 7. Under Soviet insistence, a second surrender ceremony was held the next day on the outskirts of Berlin.

of Hungary by early April. Farther north, Zhukov's armies reached the Oder River by February 2, but for the next month fierce pockets of German resistance held up progress toward Berlin.

The plan for the final assault was approved by Stalin in early April, and a huge semicircle of Soviet forces was launched at Hitler's capital on April 16. The final battle cost both sides exceptional casualties, but Soviet progress was remorseless. Ten days after the start of the battle, the forces of General Chuikov—defender of Stalingrad two years prior—reached the center of Berlin. When on April 30 Hitler was told that

there was no prospect of further defense, he said goodbye to his staff and commanders, retired to his bunker living room with Eva Braun—the mistress he had finally consented to marry the day before—and there poisoned and shot himself while she took poison. The bodies were incinerated in the garden of the Reich chancellery, where Soviet soldiers found charred remains a few days later.

Hitler's suicide heralded the end. On May 2, the battered remnants of the Berlin garrison surrendered. On May 7, Hitler's chief of operations, Alfred Jodl, signed the act of unconditional surrender in the early hours of the morning in Reims, France. The Soviet side wanted a more elaborate and symbolic ceremony, and a second surrender was staged in Berlin the following day. Though Victory in Europe (V-E) Day was celebrated on both sides of the Atlantic on May 8, German forces fighting a desperate last stand around Prague refused to give up until May 12.

In the Pacific, the U.S. planned its assault on Iwo Jima the previous October, when it became clear that the islands close to the Japanese homeland would make important staging posts for the eventual invasion. Both Iwo Jima and Okinawa were to be attacked and cleared as a preliminary step. On both islands, large Japanese garrisons—positioned in caves and foxholes—were ordered to resist to the last man. After a heavy bombardment, four U.S. divisions landed on Iwo Jima on February 19. Four weeks of savage fighting brought exceptionally high American losses, but almost the entire Japanese garrison, more than 20,000 men, was wiped out.

A Japanese kamikaze pilot aims his aircraft at the USS *Missouri* in the waters off Okinawa on April 11, 1945. With the war clearly lost, the Japanese resorted to increasingly desperate measures in hopes of forcing a negotiated peace. Suicide planes sank 36 ships during the Okinawa campaign, but they could not halt the Allied juggernaut.

On April 1, 1945, a similar landing was undertaken on Okinawa. After the U.S. established secure lodgements ashore, another bitter struggle followed to clear the island. The U.S. naval task force was attacked for weeks by *kamikaze* suicide planes, which sank more than 30 ships. Some 12,500 U.S. servicemen were killed, but so were 110,000 Japanese. Resistance on Okinawa did not end until June 21. The intense combat indicated just how difficult a final battle for the home islands of Japan might prove to be.

Before the capture of Iwo Jima, Stalin, Churchill, and Roosevelt met in conference together for the last time. In the Crimean city of Yalta, from February 4 to 11, Stalin repeated his earlier agreement that the Soviet Union would enter the war against Japan once Germany was defeated. In exchange, he was promised the Kurile Islands and the return of the Japanese half of Sakhalin Island. Agreement was also reached on creating a new Polish state.

Roosevelt, in poor health, was also determined to lay the foundation for a postwar world order in which the Soviet Union could participate. The result was a conference in San Francisco, California, that began on April 25, 1945. Participants laid the foundations for the United Nations organization, whose founding charter was signed on June 26. By that time, Roosevelt—whose vision the organization largely reflected—was dead.

Among the Western Allies, well more than a million people died during the war. The Soviet Union lost an estimated 27 million, Poland six million, and Germany more than five million. "What a terrible war," Stalin told Zhukov. "How many lives of our people it has carried away. There are probably very few families left who have not lost someone near to them...."

The Yalta Conference Roosevelt, Churchill, and Stalin (the Big Three) met for the second and last time from February 4 to 11, 1945, at Yalta on the Crimean Peninsula. Although Roosevelt was exhausted, Stalin refused to travel any farther west than Yalta. In negotiations for the fate of Germany and Eastern Europe, Stalin had the advantage since most of that area was already in Soviet hands. He was, therefore, able to violate the promises he made about free elections in Poland and democratic governments in the liberated states of Central and Southeastern Europe. The Soviet leader confirmed his prior promise to enter the war against Japan. Stalin also reduced his demand for all 16 Soviet republics to be represented in the United Nations to two: the Ukraine and Belorussia.

Allies firebomb Dresden The beautiful German city of Dresden was known as the "Florence of the Elbe" before it suffered a series of bombings in 1945. The heaviest of these were conducted by British and American aircraft from February 13 to 15. These bombings caused firestorms that destroyed much of the city and killed approximately 30,000 people. Outdoor temperatures reached as high as 2700°F, making it impossible for people to escape from their doomed homes. The military efficacy of the bombings has been questioned. Dresden was poorly defended from air attack at times, and its industries were mainly on its outskirts.

1945

February 13–15: The Allies unleash a devastating attack on Dresden, Germany, killing more than 30,000 in a bombing raid that triggers intense firestorms.

February 16: Two battalions of U.S. forces invade the Philippine island of Corregidor by air and sea. They encounter fierce Japanese resistance. • Aircraft carriers attached to the U.S. Navy's Fifth Fleet, along with dozens of support ships, launch a series of air raids over Tokyo.

February 17: Some 170 U.S. Navy frogmen lose their lives in an ill-fated effort to thwart Japanese beach defenses on Iwo Jima.

February 18: General Ivan Chernyakhovsky, 39, one of the youngest Red Army generals to command a front during World War II, dies of wounds received in combat.

February 19: One of the bloodiest battles of the Pacific war ensues when 30,000 U.S. Marines storm the Japanese-held island of Iwo Jima.

February 20: Red Army troops advance on Berlin, Germany's capital and the heart of the Third Reich. • Allied troops breach the Siegfried Line in Germany and reach the banks of the Rhine River. • Twenty-three American aircraft are lost when some 1,500 bombers and fighters attack infrastructure targets in Nuremberg, Germany.

February 21: The Americans recapture the Philippine province of Bataan, site of the infamous Bataan death march three years earlier.

February 23: The USS *Henry Bacon* becomes the last Allied merchant ship to go down at the hands of the *Luftwaffe* when it is sunk in the Arctic Sea by German bombers. • The U.S. Marines capture Iwo Jima's Mount Suribachi and raise a foreign flag on Japanese soil.

Japanese kill Manila civilians The burned corpse of a Filipino civilian murdered by Japanese troops lies in a Manila street, his hands still tied behind his back. Trapped by U.S. forces and facing certain death, Japanese naval personnel in Manila ran amok, butchering and raping thousands of helpless civilians. "I saw the bodies of priests, women, children and babies that had been bayoneted for sport...by a soldiery gone mad with blood lust in defeat," recalled Filipino editor Carlos Romulo. An estimated 100,000 civilians perished in what became known as the "Manila Massacre."

Marines land on Iwo Jima U.S. Marines hug a sandy terrace under enemy mortar fire after landing on Iwo Jima on February 19, 1945. Americans hoped to seize the island, located only 660 miles south of Tokyo, to eliminate a source of interference with B-29 raids from Saipan. They also wanted to provide a refuge for crippled bombers on their way home from Japan. The Marines found that the three-day preliminary naval bombardment had done little damage to Iwo Jima's 21,000 defenders, who had literally moved underground into a maze of tunnels and shelters. Japanese gunners waited patiently until the U.S. beachhead was congested with successive landing waves. They then opened fire, inflicting severe casualties.

Japanese troops embedded in rock A U.S. assault team warily clears a cave on Iwo Jima. Though dominated by 556-foot Mount Suribachi, the island's greatest defensive potential lay along a plateau two and a half miles to the north. General Kuribayashi Tadamichi located his best forces there among a nightmarish jumble of upheaved rock, gorges, caves, and ridges. The Japanese took full advantage of Iwo Jima's porous volcanic rock to burrow underground beyond the reach of U.S. heavy guns. Above ground, blockhouses with five-foot concrete walls and a multitude of pillboxes awaited U.S. Marines. These American forces had no alternative but to assault them one by one with flamethrowers and demolitions.

Raising the flag Private First Class Jim Michels keeps watch as members of Company E, 28th Marines, raise the first flag on top of Mount Suribachi at about 10:30 a.m. on February 23, 1945. The 54" x 28" flag was hoisted aloft on a piece of discarded pipe after a Marine patrol, led by Lieutenant Harold Schrier, had scaled the height and engaged in a brief firefight with Japanese soldiers at the summit. Later that day, another patrol brought a larger, more visible flag up the mountain. The raising of the larger flag was photographed by Joe Rosenthal and became one of the most celebrated images of World War II.

1945

February 24: Ahmed Maher Pasha, prime minister of Egypt, is assassinated on the floor of parliament, moments after reading a declaration of war against Japan and Germany.

February 26: In a daytime air raid, the USAAF drops 500,000 incendiary bombs on Berlin. British RAF units take over the attack after darkness falls. • U.S. forces capture Corregidor, leaving 5,000 Japanese troops dead and suffering 1,000 casualties.

March 1945: In a last-ditch effort to regain an upper hand in the air war, Germany forms its own suicide units, manned by some 300 volunteers. • With the exception of a few stragglers, the U.S. Navy has eliminated the enemy from shipping lanes throughout the central Pacific.

March 3: The Philippine capital of Manila is declared clear of Japanese forces.

March 4: The Finnish government in Helsinki declares war on Germany.

March 5: Continuing their advance into the German homeland, Allied troops march on Cologne. • Desperate for troops, the German army begins conscription of boys as young as 16.

March 6: Germany's Sixth Panzer Army launches Operation Spring Awakening against Soviet forces in Hungary in an effort to recapture the area between the Danube River and Lake Balaton. • In a move that leaves the Western Allies concerned about Communist expansion in postwar Europe, King Michael appoints a new, strongly pro-Communist Romanian government. • With Iwo Jima largely secure, the U.S. Air Force begins to use the island as a forward base.

March 7: Allied forces cross the Rhine River at Remagen and advance into central Germany, as German soldiers in the north capitulate in droves.

Americans cross the Rhine On March 7, 1945, American Lieutenant Karl Timmerman led his company of the 27th Armored Infantry Battalion to the west end of the Ludendorff Bridge (*pictured*) near Remagen, Germany. Since this was the last bridge still spanning the Rhine, Timmerman halted and looked closely for explosives. An explosion did occur as Timmerman and his men advanced across, but, as the smoke settled, he saw that the bridge still stood. More than 8,000 Americans crossed within 24 hours, establishing the first bridgehead across the Rhine. When Hitler learned that the bridge had not been destroyed, he had four of the officers in charge of destroying it executed.

1945

March 7: The Jewish Brigade, under the command of Brigadier General Ernest Benjamin, launches operations in Italy. • Josip Broz Tito consolidates the government of newly liberated Yugoslavia under his authority. • The Chinese 37th Division captures Lashio, Burma, the southwest terminus of the Burma Road.

March 8: Office of Strategic Services chief Allen Dulles opens cease-fire negotiations with SS commander Karl Wolff for a surrender of German forces in Italy. • More than 100 civilians die when a German V-2 rocket destroys London's Smithfield Market.

March 9–10: The deadliest air raid of the Pacific war claims the lives of 80,000 to 100,000 Japanese civilians when the U.S. attacks Tokyo with incendiary bombs.

March 10: Following the Allied breach of the Rhine, Hitler appoints Field Marshal Kesselring to replace Rundstedt as commander of German armies in the West. • Transylvania, the mountainous region in central Europe that has been occupied by Germany since early in the war, is restored to Romania. • President Roosevelt tells a Spanish delegation that the United States will be unable to supply aid to Spain as long as Franco remains in power. • The Japanese disarm and eject Vichy authorities and establish the "Empire of Annam" in French Indochina.

March 11: An RAF raid on Essen, Germany, halts production at the Krupp Works munitions plant.

March 13: The U.S. House of Representatives reauthorizes the Lend-Lease Act for the last time.

March 14: The RAF drops the 22,000-pound "Grand Slam," the largest bomb of the war to date, on Germany's Bielefeld railway viaduct.

1945

March 14–15: Thousands die in an American bombing raid on Japan's southern port city of Osaka.

March 16–17: American bombers attack Kobe, on the Japanese island of Honshu, inflicting several thousand casualties.

March 18: Nearly 30 Allied planes are lost in large-scale bombing runs over the German cities of Frankfurt and Berlin.

March 19: Hitler issues the "Nero Decree," a scorched-earth directive calling for the destruction of all German infrastructure presumed in danger of falling to the Allies. • The *Sarawak Maru*, the final surviving ship of a 21-vessel Japanese convoy, is sunk, illustrating Allied strength and Japanese isolation in Asian waters. • Japanese *kamikaze* attacks on U.S. Task Force 58 damage American aircraft carriers *Essex*, *Wolf*, *Enterprise*, and *Franklin*, killing 832 on the *Franklin* alone.

March 20: Hitler appears in public for the last time. • The fiercely defended Burmese city of Mandalay is captured by Allied forces of the British 19th Indian Division.

March 21: More than 100 Danish civilians die when they become "collateral damage" in a British raid against Copenhagen's Gestapo headquarters. • Japanese piloted bombs make their debut against U.S. forces in the waters off Japan's home islands.

March 23: Charles de Gaulle announces that France will grant limited independence to Indochina at the conclusion of the war. • Allied forces from Britain, Canada, and the United States under General Bernard Montgomery launch Operation Plunder. They will cross the northern Rhine while protected by heavy air and artillery support.

Americans land on Okinawa GIs of the U.S. 77th Infantry Division use spliced ladders to bridge a gulch during the fighting on Okinawa. Intending to seize a base for the invasion of Japan, the Americans landed on Okinawa on April 1, 1945. It was the largest invasion of the Pacific war. The Navy fired more than 100,000 shells in a weeklong bombardment of the landing beaches. This expenditure was largely wasted, since Japanese general Ushijima Mitsuru had decided to fight from prepared positions inland. The initial landings by four U.S. divisions were virtually unopposed, but progress stalled when U.S. forces encountered the main defenses across the southern end of the island.

1945

March 23: Task Force 58 launches air raids on the Japanese island of Okinawa in preparation for an eventual American landing.

March 24: The war in northern Burma comes to an end as the Chinese 50th Division meets the Chinese New First Army near Hsipaw, Burma.

March 26: The remainder of the Japanese force on Iwo Jima stages one final, suicidal attack against the U.S. forces that occupy the strategically critical island.

March 27: Soviet officials convene a meeting with anti-Communist Polish leaders under false pretenses. They will incarcerate the Poles and eliminate opposition to communism by Poland's government-in-exile. • Britain suffers an attack by the terrifying German V-2 rockets for the last time. • The U.S. begins a program of mining Japanese waters in an effort to completely blockade the home islands.

March 29: American troops occupy the German heartland city of Frankfurt am Main.

April 1945: The first helicopter rescue is achieved when a Sikorsky YR-4 is used to rescue Captain James Green, a U.S. Air Force pilot who crashed in the Burmese jungle.

April 1: More than 300,000 German soldiers are entrapped as the U.S. Army closes ranks around the economically critical Ruhr region. • Nazi propaganda chief Joseph Goebbels launches Radio *Werwolf* in an effort to bolster German resistance to Allied forces in portions of Germany occupied by Allies. • In an effort to ensure that all Japanese are available to assist the cause of victory, all schools in the nation are closed. • Some 60,000 U.S. troops land on the island of Okinawa, launching one of the bloodiest battles of the Pacific war.

Few African Americans honored On April 5, 1945, Second Lieutenant Vernon Baker's company was pinned down while attacking a German position near Viareggio, Italy. Baker crawled forward and destroyed four machine gun nests, killing nine Germans. For this action, he was awarded the Congressional Medal of Honor. Since he was African American, however, it took the military 52 years to award it. More than 1.2 million African Americans served in the war, but few received battlefield decorations and none were awarded the Medal of Honor until January 13, 1997, when seven African Americans received it from President Bill Clinton. The 77-year-old Baker was the only one still living.

"Boys, if you ever pray, pray for me now."

—HARRY TRUMAN, ONE DAY AFTER BEING SWORN IN AS PRESIDENT, APRIL 13, 1945

Harry Truman

When Harry Truman ascended to the presidency in the spring of 1945, *Time* magazine decried his inexperience in high-level politics. Others worried that he would be too cautious and conservative in his decision-making. *Time* and others underestimated the new president, as Truman would soon make one of the most audacious decisions of the war.

Calling himself an "ordinary man," Truman hailed from Lamar, Missouri. He served in World War I, prospered as a farmer, and opened a haberdashery in Kansas City. As a Democrat, he was elected judge of a county court in 1922 and U.S. senator in 1934. President Franklin Roosevelt and party leaders chose Truman as the 1944 vice presidential candidate largely because he was "safe"—not controversial.

Truman was sworn in as president on April 12, 1945, following the death of Roosevelt, only 83 days after filling the office of vice president.

Roosevelt had not taken his new vice president into his confidence, so one of Truman's first acts was to meet with the deceased president's advisers to catch up on matters of national security. Truman did not learn of the existence of the atomic bomb, or of Soviet espionage into the project, until the day he was sworn in.

After Japan did not adhere to the Allies' July 26 demand for unconditional surrender, this "ordinary man" had to make one of the most monumental decisions in world history. Following discussions with Secretary of War Henry Stimson and Army Chief of Staff General George Marshall, Truman agreed to drop an atomic bomb on a Japanese city in order to shock its leadership into surrender. No one doubted that the atomic bomb would kill a massive number of Japanese people. Truman justified its use by saying that the alternative to the atomic bomb—an Allied invasion—would result in far more deaths on both sides.

Inouye's heroics On April 21, 1945, during combat near San Terenzo, Italy, U.S. Army second lieutenant Daniel Inouye was shot in the abdomen. He continued to lead his platoon while bleeding. After his right arm was shattered, he threw a grenade at the Germans with his left hand. Inouye earned the Distinguished Service Cross but spent 20 months in the hospital, where his right arm was removed. A review of the military records of the 442nd Regimental Combat Team, a Japanese American unit, 50 years later identified 20 members who were blocked, due to prejudice, from receiving the Congressional Medal of Honor. U.S. senator Inouye of Hawaii was among them. This infraction was rectified on June 21, 2000, when he and 19 others from the 442nd were awarded the medal.

1945

April 3: The Red Army lays siege to the Slovak city of Bratislava in an effort to drive out German forces. The Soviets will liberate the city the following day. • Washington announces that General MacArthur and Admiral Nimitz will command land and sea forces, respectively, for the Allied invasion of Japan.

April 4: American troops liberate the Nazi concentration camp at Ohrdruf, Germany. Upon witnessing the carnage at the camp, a disgusted General Patton assembles local townspeople for a viewing.

April 5: Soviet foreign minister Molotov puts the Japanese on notice that the USSR does not intend to renew the 1941 nonaggression pact between the two nations. • The Japanese high command orders its entire Second Fleet to make a run against U.S. forces off Okinawa.

April 6: Yugoslavian forces under the government of Josip Broz Tito take control of the Bosnian capital of Sarajevo. • A fierce air and naval battle erupts off Okinawa. Japanese *kamikaze* pilots rain from the sky.

April 7: For the first time, the RAF launches bombing raids on Berlin from Allied bases in mainland Europe. • For the first time since the Allied capture of Iwo Jima, the island is successfully utilized as a base for operations against the Japanese home islands. • American planes engage the super-battleship *Yamato*, causing it to capsize in the East China Sea. Nearly 2,500 Japanese sailors die.

April 9: The German fortress at Königsberg falls to the Soviets. • Some 300 die when a bomb-laden Liberty ship explodes in the harbor at Bari, Italy. • The final offensive on the Italian front is launched by a multinational troop contingent that includes soldiers from Africa, Asia, Europe, and the Americas.

1945

April 9: Former *Abwehr* chief Admiral Wilhelm Canaris is executed on the gallows at Germany's Flossenburg concentration camp.

April 10: American soldiers of the Ninth Army capture the central German city of Hanover.

April 11: Red Army troops of the Ukrainian army group penetrate the center of the Austrian capital of Vienna. It will fall to the Allies on the 13th. • The Russians liberate the notorious Buchenwald concentration camp. • American forces reach the southern German region of Bavaria, the birthplace of Hitler's Nazi Reich. • Japanese *kamikaze* pilots continue their barrage unabated off Okinawa, hitting the U.S. ships *Missouri* and *Enterprise*.

April 12: President Roosevelt dies suddenly after suffering a stroke at his Warm Springs, Georgia, vacation home. Vice President Harry Truman is sworn in as president.

April 13: The South American nation of Chile joins the Allies and declares war on Japan.

April 14: The Allies march through the center of encircled German troops in the Ruhr Pocket, taking prisoners and splitting the German ranks. • The Allies launch Operation Teardrop in an effort to locate German U-boats in the North Atlantic rumored to be carrying V-2 rockets to be used against New York City.

April 14–15: Japanese imperial loyalists crush an attempted coup by hard-line military officers who, convinced that Emperor Hirohito was on the brink of surrender, had decided to seize control.

April 15: The Bergen-Belsen concentration camp, with a survivor population of 40,000, is liberated by the British Army.

Civilians forced to bury camp victims On April 21, 1945, American troops of the 102nd Division ordered the males of the German town of Garde-legen to carry spades and white wooden crosses to a burned barn on the outskirts of their town. They were ordered to disinter and rebury the bodies of 1,016 prisoners who had been burned or shot by the Germans eight days earlier. Throughout occupied Germany, the Allies forced German civilians to confront the atrocities that took place in concentration camps short distances from their homes. Here, two women are forced to bury slave workers executed by German troops.

The Ruhr

A major portion of Germany's coal, steel, and iron—all vital to the nation's war effort—was produced in the Ruhr, a region in western Germany. These industries were centered in Bochum, Dortmund, and Essen. Krupp of Essen was Germany's principal armaments manufacturer.

The Allies knew the importance of the Ruhr, so the area was subjected to intensive raids from the earliest days of the Allied strategic bombing offensive. Five years of bombing took a heavy toll, and by spring 1945 much of the Ruhr's industrial production ceased completely for protracted periods. Moreover, the destruction of canals and railroads meant that anything that was produced could not be out-loaded.

U.S. troops in the Ruhr Valley, April 1945

On February 22, 1945, in preparation for an Allied ground envelopment of the 320,000 German troops still manning their defensive positions in the Ruhr, the Allied air forces destroyed most of the area's remaining rail network. Then on March 11–12, the RAF dropped almost 1,000 tons of bombs on Essen and Dortmund. The RAF and USAAF also destroyed all the remaining road and rail bridges that provided access to the region. Before winter was over, the Third Reich's industrial heartland, its *Wehrmacht* defenders, and some four million civilians were effectively isolated within the Ruhr Pocket.

On March 25, the Second British Army, Ninth U.S. Army, and First Canadian Army of Field Marshal Montgomery's 21st Army Group struck north and east of the Ruhr. In addition, General Bradley's 12th U.S. Army Group advanced eastward from the south, spearheaded by General Hodges' First U.S. Army and General Patton's Third U.S. Army. The Allied advance was rapid, and—despite a concerted German attempt to break out—soldiers of the First and Ninth U.S. armies linked up near Lippstadt on April 1. They thereby closed the Ruhr Pocket and neutralized the thousands of German troops trapped inside it.

1945

April 16: Hitler announces that he expects his officers to fight to the death. He orders summary execution for any officer who orders a retreat. • The German transport ship *Goya* is torpedoed. It goes down in the Baltic Sea with 6,200 Germans who had just been rescued from the Hela Peninsula. • The Allied air force announces that future operations over Germany will focus on cleanup rather than strategic targets, effectively ending the air war.

April 18: German field marshal Walter Model leads his remaining 225,000 troops, encircled in Germany's Ruhr, in mass surrender to the Allies. • Pulitzer Prize–winning Scripps-Howard columnist Ernie Pyle is felled by a Japanese sniper's bullet while reporting on the Battle of Okinawa.

April 20: The Allies capture Stuttgart and Nuremberg. They raise the U.S. flag over Nuremberg Stadium, the site of the Nazis' iconic political rallies.

April 23: Street-to-street fighting erupts in the German capital of Berlin as the Soviets storm the city. • *Reichsführer* Heinrich Himmler offers the Allies a conditional surrender, stipulating that he will not capitulate to a Soviet official. Allied officials will reject the offer.

April 24: Furious over Göring's play for power in the Reich's final days, Hitler orders the arrest of his former right-hand man.

April 25: Berlin is fully encircled by Belorussian and Ukrainian army groups of the Red Army. • Northern Italy continues to fall to the Allies. Verona and Parma are liberated, and citizens of Milan and Genoa rise up against their Nazi occupiers.

April 26: Marshal Philippe Pétain, former leader of Vichy France, is arrested and charged with collaborating with the Nazis.

Hitler Youth forced to fight Allies German soldier Hans-Georg Henke, age 15, cries after being captured by the U.S. Ninth Army in April 1945. On April 20, Hitler presented several 12-year-olds the Iron Cross for bravery in combat. After the ceremony, the boys returned to the front lines, joining youths and old men in battle against Soviets in the streets of Berlin. Three days after Hitler's presentation, Hitler Youth were chosen to defend bridges south of Berlin to be used by reinforcements that would never come. More than 5,000 boys fought the Soviets there, and when the fighting ended five days later, 4,500 Hitler Youth were dead or wounded.

DESPERATION IN BERLIN

We left the cellar at longer and longer intervals and often we could not tell whether it was night or day. The Russians drew nearer; they advanced through the underground railway tunnels, armed with flame-throwers; their advance snipers had taken up positions quite near us; and their shots ricocheted off the houses opposite. Exhausted German soldiers would stumble in and beg for water—they were practically children. I remember one with a pale, quivering face who said, "We shall do it all right; we'll make our way to the north west yet." But his eyes belied his words and he looked at me despairingly. What he wanted to say was, "Hide me, give me shelter. I've had enough of it." I should have liked to help him; but neither of us dared to speak. Each might have shot the other as a "defeatist."

—BERLIN RESIDENT CLAUS FUHRMANN, DESCRIBING THE HOURS BEFORE THE SOVIET TAKEOVER OF THE CITY

Hitler's last birthday April 20, 1945, was Hitler's 56th birthday. The celebration in his underground headquarters, the *Führerbunker*, in the Reich Chancellery Park was very subdued. The Soviet Army was advancing toward Berlin, and Hitler knew that the end of his Third Reich was near. Later that day, Hitler left the bunker to decorate 20 Hitler Youth, most 12 to 15 years old, for bravery in combat, as seen in this picture. He then returned to the bunker in which he had lived since January 16, 1945. Protected by 16 feet of concrete and six feet of earth, Hitler's sanctuary protected him but did not mask the sounds of Soviet shells falling closer each day.

The death of Mussolini On April 25, 1945, Mussolini's puppet government in northern Italy dissolved, as Italian partisans and American forces ended German control of the region. Two days later, Mussolini and his mistress, Clara Petacci, were captured in the Italian village of Dongo while trying to flee to Switzerland. On the 28th, Mussolini, Petacci, and 15 aides were executed at *Giulino di Mezzegra*. The bodies were brought to the *Piazzale Loreto* in Milan on April 29. Six of them, including Mussolini and Petacci, were hung by the feet while a crowd of Italians spit on and beat the remains.

The fall of Berlin For 12 days, beginning on April 20, Stalin's troops fought through the streets of Berlin, one neighborhood at a time. Hitler ordered his Ninth and 12th armies to cut through the Soviet line and defend the city. But the Ninth was encircled and eventually decimated, and the 12th lacked the manpower or arms to attack the Soviets after holding up the Americans. The defense of Berlin was left to a disorganized band of soldiers as well as old men and boys of the Hitler Youth. They fought hard, inflicting 300,000 casualties on the Soviets.

1945

April 27: Hitler sends one last message to his ally, Benito Mussolini. Defiant to the end, he asserts that "Bolshevism and the armies of Jewry...join their malignant forces...to precipitate chaos in our continent."

April 28: Italian partisans execute Benito Mussolini and his mistress, Clara Petacci.

April 29: Hitler and Eva Braun exchange wedding vows in Hitler's underground Berlin bunker. • General Vietinghoff, the German commander of Axis forces in Italy, signs documents surrendering to the Allies. • A U-boat wolf pack attacks Allied convoy RA-66 in the Arctic, in what will be the last convoy attack of the war.

April 30: The newly wed Hitlers commit suicide in the Berlin bunker. Joseph and Magda Goebbels follow suit, murdering their six children before taking their own lives. • Soviet forces capture the *Reichstag*. • The Dachau concentration camp is liberated as the Allies capture the Bavarian capital of Munich.

May 1: Admiral Karl Dönitz, Hitler's handpicked successor, establishes a government in Flensburg to control Germany following Hitler's suicide.

May 2: Some 490,000 German soldiers in Italy lay down their weapons, honoring the terms of the unconditional surrender signed by Vietinghoff three days earlier. • The British 26th Indian Division meets no Japanese resistance during an amphibious invasion of Rangoon, Burma.

May 3: Red Army units link up throughout Berlin as German resistance ends, completing the capture of the capital of the Third Reich. • Hamburg, Germany, and Innsbruck, Austria, fall to the Allies.

Germany's "secret leader" Martin Bormann, head of the Nazi *Parteikanzlei* (Chancellery), completely controlled personal access to the *Führer*. By manipulating Hitler, Bormann also affected Nazi Party directives, promotions, appointments, and finances. Present in the bunker during Hitler's final days, Bormann was a witness to the wedding of Hitler and Eva Braun. After that, he disappeared. Evidence indicates that he perished in Berlin while attempting to escape through heavy gunfire. After the war, Bormann was tried at Nuremberg *in absentia*. He was convicted and sentenced to death.

Americans skeptical of Hitler suicide This cover of *Time*, illustrated by Boris Artzybasheff, shows Hitler's face with a blood-red X over it. It appeared on the issue dated May 7, 1945, a week after the German leader's suicide. When word reached America that Hitler had taken his own life, the report was met with skepticism. In fact, the FBI conducted an extensive, 11-year investigation into whether the German leader faked his death. His suicide was confirmed in the 1960s by Russian journalist Lev Bezymenski. He reported that Soviets had performed an autopsy on corpses found buried in a shallow grave that were identified as belonging to Hitler, his wife, and their two dogs.

1945

May 3: RAF planes attack and sink three German ships—the *Cap Arcona*, *Thielbek*, and *Deutschland*. Unknown to the RAF, these ships—under the direction of the Red Cross—are carrying rescued prisoners (mostly Jews) from German concentration camps. Some 8,000 lose their lives.

May 4: German troops surrender en masse throughout northern Germany and the Netherlands.

May 5: German and Allied officials meet in Reims, France, to reach agreement on the terms of Germany's capitulation. • The German army lays down its weapons throughout Bavaria. • American troops performing mop-up operations near Berchtesgaden capture Hans Frank, occupied Poland's Nazi governor general, who had established his headquarters in the city of Kraków. • U.S. forces liberate French and Austrian officials—including premiers Reynaud, Daladier, Blum, and Schuschnigg—from captivity in Austria. • Czech partisans rise up against the German occupation force in Prague. • A Japanese balloon bomb kills a woman and five children in Oregon, becoming the only such bomb of the war to induce casualties.

May 6: Admiral Lord Louis Mountbatten, supreme Allied commander of the Southeast Asia theater, announces that the Allied campaign in Burma has come to an end.

May 7: German general Alfred Jodl signs the formal surrender documents in Reims, France, as Germany surrenders unconditionally to the Allies. • The Red Army captures Breslau, Germany, after laying siege to the German garrison for 82 days. • *U-2336* sinks two merchant ships in the North Atlantic—the last U-boat "kills" of the war.

The liberation of Dachau A flatbed truck hauls away bodies of prisoners who died at Dachau. Located near Munich, Germany, the Dachau concentration camp had been built in 1933 to confine political opponents of the Nazi movement, and in November 1938 11,000 Jewish prisoners were sent there. Dachau was used as a model for other concentration camps in Germany and Eastern Europe. In spring 1943, a crematorium with four ovens was put into use at the camp. Upon liberating Dachau on April 30, Americans discovered more than 30,000 prisoners and hundreds of unburied corpses. In its 12 years, more than 30,000 of Dachau's 200,000 prisoners died.

U.S. troops execute Dachau guards When Dachau was liberated on April 30, 1945, an unknown number of American GIs lined 16 SS camp guards against a coal yard wall in the adjacent SS training camp and executed them (*pictured*). Additional executions took place at Dachau's rail yard, at a guard tower, and at Würm creek. In all, 37 to 39 SS personnel were dispatched that day. These actions were "unauthorized" and did not reflect U.S. Army policy toward captured SS.

1945

May 8: Victory in Europe (V-E) Day is declared as German troops continue to surrender to Allies throughout Europe. • Hermann Göring surrenders to Allied troops. He will become, along with Admiral Dönitz, the highest-ranking Nazi to face trial at Nuremberg.

May 9: Norwegian collaborator and infamous turncoat Vidkun Quisling turns himself in to the authorities in Oslo. • The Allies assume control of the German heavy cruiser *Prinz Eugen* in the port of Copenhagen, Denmark.

May 10: The U.S. high command announces that more than three million American troops stationed in Europe will soon be on their way home or to the Pacific Theater.

May 11: Australian troops capture Wewak from the Japanese, giving control of all of New Guinea's ports to the Allies.

May 12: Washington temporarily suspends Lend-Lease aid to the Soviet Union. • American Marines suffer heavy casualties as Japanese troops defend their positions on Okinawa's Sugar Loaf Hill.

May 14: Austrian self-determination returns to Vienna for the first time since the *Anschluss*. • The Allies discover a fortune in gold, currency, and looted art hidden by the Nazis in an Austrian salt mine. • USAAF B-29 bombers drop some 2,500 incendiary devices on the Japanese city of Nagoya.

Mid-May: The 1.2 million soldiers in German Army Group Center disband. Most will end up in U.S. or Soviet custody.

May 16: The Japanese cruiser *Haguro* goes down in the Malacca Strait after coming under attack by a small force of British destroyers.

Göring surrenders Brigadier General Robert Stack, assistant commander of the U.S. 36th Infantry Division, was handed an envelope on May 7, 1945, addressed to General Eisenhower. It was from Hermann Göring (*center*), who agreed to surrender if Eisenhower would work with him to reorganize Germany. Göring's request was refused, and he surrendered to the 36th Division the next day. Göring had incensed Hitler on April 23 by requesting that the *Führer*, who was trapped in a bunker in Berlin, name him as Hitler's successor. Accusing Göring of treason, Hitler ordered his arrest and considered ordering his execution.

The German surrender Field Marshal Wilhelm Keitel signs the ratified surrender terms for the German military on May 8, 1945. The terms included the unconditional surrender of all German armed forces, cessation of active operations, and surrender of all weapons and equipment to local Allied commanders. Though the document neglected to mention the civilian government, an Allied Control Council was subsequently formed with authority over all military and civilian agencies.

British celebrate V-E Day On May 8, 1945, the Allies celebrated Victory in Europe (V-E) Day. Here, Mrs. Pat Burgess of Palmers Green in North London waves a newspaper announcing Germany's surrender. She was one of more than a million Londoners who took to the streets to celebrate. They listened to an address by King George VI, cheered at exploding fireworks, and burned effigies of Hitler. In his speech that day, Winston Churchill somberly reminded the British that their rejoicing must be brief. "Japan, with all her treachery and greed, remains unsubdued," he said.

The American celebration Just as Londoners had done in Piccadilly Circus, New Yorkers packed Times Square on May 8, 1945, to celebrate V-E Day. By the end of the European phase of the war, the United States found itself a major player on the world stage, already assured leadership status in the soon-to-be-founded United Nations. However, America's V-E Day celebrations were dampened by the April 12 death of President Franklin Roosevelt, who had done so much to assure an Allied victory and the creation of the UN.

Kamikazes strike the *Bunker Hill* Wrecked aircraft litter the USS *Bunker Hill*'s flight deck after the carrier was struck by two *kamikazes* on May 11, 1945, off Okinawa. The first enemy plane careened through parked aircraft on the flight deck, igniting numerous fires while its 550-pound bomb exploded below decks. The second *kamikaze* hit near the base of the ship's aft deck. Fires were brought under control within five hours, but casualties totaled 346 dead and 246 wounded. The damage put the veteran carrier out of the war. It eventually returned to duty in September with the "Magic Carpet" fleet, transporting servicemen back to the States for discharge.

1945

May 17: U.S. forces capture Manila's Ipo Dam following a three-day bombing campaign in which more than 100,000 gallons of napalm were dropped on Japanese positions.

May 18: An intense, 10-day battle on Okinawa ends when the U.S. Marines capture the hotly contested Sugar Loaf Hill.

May 19: Nazi functionary Dr. Alfred Rosenberg is captured. Rosenberg had promoted the belief in Aryan racial superiority and the need for German *Lebensraum* (living space).

May 21: A division between Britain's Labour and Conservative parties leads Churchill to call for general elections for the first time in a decade.

May 23: *Reichsführer* Heinrich Himmler commits suicide while in British custody. • Julius Streicher, the fanatical anti-Semitic publisher of the Nazi periodical *Der Stürmer*, is arrested in Bavaria. • Eisenhower orders the arrest of leaders of the German military and of the new Flensburg government headed by Admiral Dönitz. • The U.S. military leadership determines that Operation Olympic, the invasion of the Japanese mainland, will commence November 1.

May 27: Up to 200,000 Japanese troops are stranded when the Chinese reoccupy Nanning, cutting the Japanese supply route from Southeast Asia. • USAAF planes deliver the Chinese Sixth Army from Burma to China, marking the first airborne transport of an army in world history. • Japanese authorities close the crippled Japanese port of Tokyo.

May 28: British radio personality William Joyce ("Lord Haw-Haw") is captured by the Allies. • Shipping rules for wartime are abolished everywhere outside the Pacific. Merchant traffic is allowed to use navigation lights, and abandon convoys.

Surrender leaflets This is one of millions of leaflets dropped among Japanese soldiers and civilians to encourage surrender. The *I Cease Resistance* phrasing was developed after it was discovered that Japanese soldiers were alienated by any mention of actual surrender. Leaflets were produced and printed by the Office of War Information and by the Far Eastern Liaison Office and Psychological Warfare Branch in the South West Pacific Area command. Early efforts brought few surrenders, but results improved dramatically in 1945, both because of deteriorating Japanese morale and a growing willingness among Allied troops to take live prisoners.

Himmler's final days On April 28, 1945, Hitler learned that his trusted lieutenant, Heinrich Himmler, had tried to negotiate the surrender of the German army to the Allies. Incensed, Hitler ordered Himmler's arrest. Following Hitler's suicide, the *Führer*'s successor, Grand Admiral Karl Dönitz, denounced Himmler. Hunted by Allied agents, Himmler disguised himself as a sergeant major and attempted to flee to Bavaria. Although he shaved his mustache and wore a patch over his left eye, he was arrested and eventually identified. To escape his trial and inevitable execution, he killed himself by swallowing a cyanide capsule on May 23, 1945.

Cologne takes a beating The Allied bombing of Cologne, Germany, began in March 1942. During the war, the city was attacked by air numerous times, primarily because it was a military, economic, and manufacturing center along the Rhine River. The most destructive of the raids occurred on the night of May 30–31, 1942, when more than 1,000 planes of the Royal Air Force dropped about 1,500 tons of explosives on the city in only 75 minutes. By war's end, more than 20,000 Cologne civilians had been killed or wounded and most of the city was destroyed, leaving tens of thousands of civilians homeless.

THE DEFEAT OF JAPAN

JUNE 1945–SEPTEMBER 1945

After the replacement of Tojo Hideki as prime minister in July 1944 by General Koiso Kuniaki, the Japanese continued to adhere to their basic strategy. That was to fight so hard and inflict such heavy casualties on the Americans that the latter would be willing to settle for a peace in which Japan could retain some of its gains, would not be occupied or disarmed, and would not have its military or civilian leaders tried as war criminals. The Japanese government made an effort to persuade the Soviet Union to either mediate some sort of compromise or, alternatively, reverse alliances and join Japan in fighting the Western powers. A new prime minister, Admiral Suzuki Kantaro, saw these efforts fail; he did not grasp that this was because Stalin had decided to fight Japan, not his current allies.

By the summer of 1945, Japan's situation had become desperate. Allied aircraft and submarines had decimated its already inadequate merchant fleet. Oil and other raw materials could not be delivered by sea. The big reason for this was U.S. airpower. A year earlier, the American bomber force

was built up on the conquered islands of the Marianas. From those islands, especially Tinian and Saipan, long-range B-29 bombers began to pound the home islands in the fall of 1944 and the winter of 1944–45. Under a new commander, Major General Curtis LeMay, the Americans shifted much of their effort from high-level aimed bombing with explosives to low-level area bombing with incendiaries.

The raid on Tokyo on March 9, 1945, was the first large incendiary raid. Some 16 square miles of the city were burned, more than 80,000 people were killed, and a million Japanese civilians were left homeless. Similar if somewhat smaller raids were mounted against other large Japanese cities in the following months. In addition, aircraft carriers brought additional planes to raid coastal cities, and land-based planes dropped mines in the main shipping lanes.

While havoc reigned on the home islands, the Japanese land forces in China and those forces still holding islands and parts of islands in the South and Southwest Pacific found themselves without many of the supplies they needed. The Americans and Australians launched one invasion after the other in the East Indies, and the British prepared to follow up on their reconquest of Burma with a landing on the coast of Malaya in order to retake Singapore.

The planning for an invasion of the Japanese home islands went forward; on June 18 President Truman gave his tentative approval of the landing on Kyushu (Operation Olympic). Both the final go-ahead for this assault, scheduled for November 1, and the subsequent landing on Tokyo Bay (Operation Coronet) scheduled for March 1, 1946, would have to come later. The bloody fighting that was still going on at Okinawa and elsewhere suggested that invasion of the home islands would result in huge casualties. The Pentagon ordered hundreds of thousands of Purple Hearts for wounded soldiers, and there was discussion of the possible need to draft nurses.

The collapse of Chinese military resistance in the summer of 1944 made it all the more imperative that Soviet forces attack the Japanese on the mainland of Asia and thereby prevent them from reinforcing the home islands. President Truman was greatly relieved when Stalin reiterated his promise to invade Manchuria three months after the defeat of Germany. By the time Stalin made his promise at the July 16–August 2 meeting of the three powers at Potsdam, Germany, large numbers of Red Army units and commanders were already on their way to the Soviet East Asian provinces.

At the meeting, Truman told Stalin that a powerful new weapon was now ready. Having been briefed on Soviet espionage discoveries about the atomic bomb project, the president thought Stalin might know what he was talking about. Regardless, he urged Truman to use the powerful weapon promptly. Just before the meeting, Truman had been informed that the first A-bomb test conducted in New Mexico had been successful. The project, initiated by Roosevelt years earlier, was now beginning to produce the first bombs.

At the conclusion of the Potsdam meeting, the Allies issued a special "Declaration" calling on Japan to surrender, but the threat was ignored. Therefore, Truman ordered that an atomic bomb be dropped on Hiroshima on August 6. The results were devastating. Casualties were close to 80,000 dead.

In discussion with Secretary of War Henry Stimson and Army Chief of Staff George Marshall, Truman had decided that if the first bomb did not shock the Japanese into surrender, a second one would be dropped on another city. But if that did not persuade the Japanese to surrender, the bombs that later would become available would be saved for use in support of Operation Olympic. Since the

Major General Curtis LeMay (*second from left*), commanding general of the 21st Bomber Command, receives a firsthand report of a Superfortress raid against Nagoya, Japan, on March 26, 1945. LeMay's fire-bombing campaign laid waste to Japan's cities. All the while, Japanese military forces far from home suffered one defeat after another.

bomb on Hiroshima did not prompt Japan to surrender, the second one was dropped on Nagasaki on August 9.

Anxious discussion took place inside the Japanese government, especially after Tokyo learned that the Soviet Union was joining Japan's enemies and invading Manchuria. Even after the second bomb was dropped, half of the Japanese leadership wanted to continue the war, hoping that the casualties that they expected to inflict on the Americans during landings at Kyushu would produce a change in American objectives. It was in the face of an evenly split group of leaders that Emperor Hirohito insisted that surrender was the only possible course. A coup attempt by those who wanted to continue fighting failed narrowly. The stage was set for a formal surrender, which was signed on the battleship *Missouri* on September 2.

Japan surrendered peacefully, and was not divided into zones of occupation the way Germany had been. Although western Honshu was under a British Commonwealth Occupation Force (BCOF), the home islands as a whole retained a Japanese administrative system that was under the supervision of an American occupation force and supreme commander (General Douglas MacArthur).

The Soviet Union, in addition to seizing the Kurile Islands, also took control of small islands off the coast of the northern home island of Hokkaido and removed the Japanese inhabitants. While Japan thus escaped the decades of partition that became Germany's fate, the Soviet action precluded the signing of a peace treaty between Russia and Japan.

1945

June 1: As many as 700 of 40,000 Cossack troops who fought alongside the Nazis die when they resist British efforts to forcibly repatriate them to the Soviet Union. • Some 27 American P-51 Mustang fighters are lost to foul weather en route to an assault on Osaka, Japan.

June 5: Brazil, which had long been at war with Germany, declares war on Japan. • Nearly 500 U.S. B-29 bombers drop 3,000 tons of incendiaries on the Japanese city of Kobe. • A powerful typhoon strikes Okinawa, badly damaging more than 30 U.S. warships.

June 7: Norway's King Haakon returns to the throne of his liberated nation. • All German civilians living in the Western Allies' occupation zones are made to watch films of the concentration camps at Buchenwald and Bergen-Belsen. • Osaka suffers heavy damage as 400 American B-29 bombers rain terror on the Japanese city.

June 9: The RAF Vampire jet, boasting a maximum speed of more than 500 mph, is unveiled in Britain.

June 11: Czech police and civilians continue the process of driving ethnic Germans from the Czech Sudetenland into occupied Germany.

June 12: With a U.S. Marine victory on Okinawa's Oroku Peninsula a virtual certainty, Japanese troops on Okinawa commit suicide en masse.

June 13: The U.S. 24th Corps attacks Japanese-held caves on Okinawa with flamethrowers.

June 14: U.S. military leadership in the Pacific Theater receives orders from the Joint Chiefs of Staff to prepare for the invasion and occupation of Japan. • Former Nazi foreign minister Joachim von Ribbentrop is captured in Hamburg.

The "Beast" and "Bitch" of Belsen Irma Grese and Josef Kramer (*both pictured*) were two of many German concentration camp commanders and guards who faced postwar prosecution as war criminals. Kramer, commandant of the Bergen-Belsen camp, was called the "Beast of Belsen" by the inmates. He placed few controls over the activities of his guards, including Irma Grese, the most notorious of the female guards at all the camps. Grese had been transferred to Auschwitz at age 19. She was then sent in March 1945 to Bergen-Belsen, where she was known as "Bitch of Belsen" for torturing and murdering inmates. Kramer and Grese were tried with more than 40 other guards from the camp. Both were found guilty and were hanged for their war crimes on December 13, 1945.

Operation Downfall

Planning for Operation Downfall, the invasion of Japan, began in earnest in early 1945 when strategists decided that a naval blockade alone probably would not bring about a timely Japanese surrender. Downfall called for two huge amphibious assaults, each dwarfing the Normandy landings of 1944. The first, code-named Olympic, would take place on November 1, 1945, when 14 divisions would land on three beaches on Kyushu, the southernmost of the Japanese home islands. Seizure of southern Kyushu was expected to take 90 days and would involve more than 427,000 Allied troops.

If the Japanese government failed to capitulate, phase two of Downfall, code-named Coronet, would take place on March 1, 1946. Coronet planners contemplated an assault over the Kanto Plain before Tokyo with as many as 23 divisions. Unlike Olympic, which drew on organizations already in the Pacific, Coronet would include a number of divisions redeployed from the European Theater.

Almost exclusively, Operation Downfall would be an American undertaking. Initially, planners counted on Russian forces to tie down potential Japanese reinforcements in Manchuria. Some British Commonwealth and French forces would be involved in Downfall, but their numbers would be small.

Planners, of course, worried about potential U.S. casualties. The Japanese had identified Kyushu as a likely invasion point and were pouring troops into the area. After the war, U.S. officials said American losses in Downfall might have totaled between 500,000 and one million men. Others felt such numbers were exaggerated. General Douglas MacArthur, who would have commanded the ground assault, estimated casualties for Olympic at about 56,000 dead, wounded, and missing over a period of 60 days. With Japan functioning with depleted resources, Coronet might have seen even fewer U.S. losses.

The atomic bombs ensured that those figures would remain historical speculation. Still, it was a near thing. Two American divisions from Europe, the 86th and 97th, were already arriving in the Pacific when the war ended, and Olympic was only three months away.

Bombs devastate Osaka Desolation stretches as far as the eye can see after repeated B-29 incendiary raids on Osaka, which was Japan's second largest industrial city and the site of a military arsenal. The first incendiary raid on Osaka was conducted by 300 B-29s on the night of March 13, 1945. Within three hours, more than eight square miles of the city was in flames. The heat turbulence was so great that one B-29, *Thunderin' Loretta*, was flipped over on its back. On June 7, Osaka was hit by 400 B-29s. This was followed by another attack a week later. By then, there was little left to destroy.

1945

June 17: Japanese Admiral Ota Minoru commits ritual suicide after U.S. troops breach Japan's final defense on Okinawa.

June 18: The USAAF launches a devastating series of air raids that target the civilian populations of major Japanese cities. • U.S. 10th Army commander General Simon Bolivar Buckner is felled by shrapnel while inspecting the Okinawan front line.

June 19: Manhattan honors General Eisenhower with a ticker tape parade upon his return to the United States following victory in Europe.

June 21: U.S. troops capture Aparri, the last Japanese port on the Philippine island of Luzon. However, substantial Japanese forces will continue the fight on Luzon until the August surrender.

June 22: The bloodiest battle of the Pacific war ends as American troops secure Okinawa following their hard-won victory over the Japanese.

June 24: General Zhukov rides a white horse into Red Square (while troops defile captured Nazi flags) as the Soviet Union celebrates victory over Germany.

June 26: Fifty nations sign the United Nations Charter in San Francisco.

June 27: Czechoslovakian Nazi puppet Emil Hacha, former president of the Bohemia-Moravia Protectorate, dies in a prison hospital before he can be tried for treason.

June 27: A *kamikaze* strike on the USS *Bunker Hill* claims the lives of 373 American sailors.

July 3: The Western Allies occupy the sectors of Berlin allocated to the Americans, British, and French by prior agreement with the Soviet Union.

Heavy casualties on Okinawa A U.S. Marine takes aim with his submachine gun during an assault near Wana Ridge on Okinawa. Despite heavy casualties, the American divisions continued to batter the enemy defenses, transforming the terrain into a moonscape. Japanese resistance continued as General Ushijima Mitsuru's best units were gradually annihilated. Shuri fell in late May, and by mid-June the Japanese 32nd Army began to collapse. Ushijima committed suicide on June 22, and Japan lost 110,000 men in the battle. American dead totaled 12,281, making Okinawa the most costly Allied operation of the Pacific war—which did not bode well for the upcoming invasion of Japan.

Australians overtake Balikpapan Australian troops go ashore at Balikpapan on the southeast coast of Borneo in the last major amphibious assault of the Pacific war. The Seventh Australian Division landed in July 1945 to seize Balikpapan's port and oil fields. Outnumbered and outgunned, the Japanese offered stubborn resistance, but were eventually forced to retreat into the hills. Balikpapan cost the Australians 229 killed and 634 wounded. Japanese casualties totaled about 2,000. Conducted six weeks before Japan's surrender, the operation was later criticized as a waste of lives, although no one at the time could have realized that the war would end so abruptly.

1945

July 5: General MacArthur announces that forces under his command have succeeded in liberating the Philippines from Japanese rule. • John Curtin, Australia's wartime prime minister, dies of heart disease at age 60.

July 8: In what will prove to be the worst massacre at a POW camp in American history, guard Clarence Bertucci strafes a Utah tent city full of sleeping German prisoners with machine gun fire, killing eight. • RAF sergeant Simon Eden, son of British foreign secretary Anthony Eden, is listed as missing in action in Burma.

July 10: Tokyo's production and military facilities come under intense attack.

July 12: Britain honors Soviet general Zhukov and the Red Army in a ceremony at Berlin's Brandenburg Gate in occupied Germany.

July 13: Former Axis partner Italy declares war on Japan.

July 14: General Eisenhower officially dissolves the Supreme Headquarters Allied Expeditionary Force.

July 15: After more than 2,000 nights of mandatory blackouts, Britain turns on the lights.

July 16: Truman, Churchill, and Stalin meet near Berlin at the Potsdam Conference, at which they will issue a new public demand for Japan's surrender. • As Truman begins the summit at Potsdam, he receives word of the first successful detonation of an atomic bomb, at New Mexico's Alamogordo testing grounds.

July 19: In the largest B-29 bomb raid to date, 600 of the heavy bombers drop 4,000 tons of munitions on Japanese cities, including Choshi, Fukui, Hitachi, and Okazaki.

UNRRA administers DP camps The war was far from over in 1943. However, the leaders of 44 nations began to plan for rehabilitating the nations freed from Axis control and caring for the millions of displaced persons. On November 9, 1943, the United Nations Relief and Rehabilitation Administration (UNRRA) was formed to provide much-needed relief. After the war, the UNRRA administered hundreds of displaced-persons camps, primarily in Italy, Austria, and Germany. Here in July 1945, UNRRA volunteers give bread to survivors of a German concentration camp.

Ex-*Wehrmacht* officer heads intelligence group Soon after the war in Europe ended, Major General Reinhard Gehlen, an intelligence officer in the German army, surrendered to the U.S. Army Counter Intelligence Corps. He negotiated his release and that of his colleagues from American POW camps in exchange for volumes of intelligence that his department, Foreign Forces—East, had collected on the activities of the Soviet Union (but which proved mostly erroneous). Within a year, Gehlen became the head of a West German intelligence group that eventually would grow to more than 4,000 agents. He remained the leader of this group until he retired in 1968.

Prostitution in Berlin To prevent black market activity, looting, and prostitution, Allied commanders made a futile attempt to prohibit soldiers from fraternizing with civilians in occupied Germany. It soon became apparent that violations of this order were unenforceable. Within six months of the fall of Berlin, more than 500,000 women turned to prostitution, many to provide for themselves and their families. One German official observed that even "nice girls of good families, good education and fine background have discovered their bodies afford the only real living." Incidents of venereal disease in Berlin more than doubled in the last six months of 1945.

The Krupp empire In 1957 *Time* magazine stated that German manufacturer Alfried Krupp was "the wealthiest man in Europe—and perhaps in the world." Krupp rebuilt his industrial empire in less than six years after his release from prison, to which he had been sentenced in 1945 to 12 years as a war criminal. In his trial, it had been determined that his factories used slave laborers from concentration camps. Thousands of these laborers died due to poor rations, over-work, and deliberate killing. Krupp was released from prison early, and his property was returned, when Allied leaders decided that the steel produced by his factories was important for the stability of West Germany and the free world.

The first atomic explosion On July 16, 1945, a plutonium-core nuclear bomb was raised to the top of a 65-foot-high steel tower in the New Mexican desert about 30 miles southeast of Socorro. The Trinity test began when the bomb, called "the gadget," was detonated on July 16 at 5:30 a.m. The scientists, watching 10 miles from the tower, had disagreed on what would happen following the detonation—from nothing to the end of the world. Instead it caused an explosion that was about the equivalent of 19 kilotons of TNT. The flash it created brightened the surrounding mountains and emitted a mushroom cloud about eight miles high.

1945

July 23: The trial of Nazi collaborator Marshal Philippe Pétain begins at Paris' *Palais de Justice.*

July 24: The USAAF raids the densely populated Japanese cities of Osaka and Nagoya with some 600 B-29 bombers.

July 26: Truman, Attlee, and Stalin issue a statement from Potsdam warning the Japanese that they face "utter destruction" if they do not surrender unconditionally. Tokyo will reject the ultimatum within the week. • The USS *Indianapolis* delivers critical atomic bomb components to the bombing base at Tinian. • The Labour Party takes power in Britain, forcing out Conservative Winston Churchill. He will be replaced at Potsdam by the new prime minister, Clement Attlee, on the 27th.

July 27: The USAAF drops some 600,000 leaflets over 11 Japanese cities, warning civilians of probable air raids.

July 28: More than a dozen people die when a B-25 bomber pilot becomes disoriented in heavy fog and crashes into New York's Empire State Building. • Japan's *kamikaze* pilots sink their last Allied ship, as the USS *Callaghan* goes down off Okinawa. • More than 13,000 Japanese troops die, either from hostile fire or drowning, in an attempt to retreat over Burma's Sittang River.

July 29–30: The USS *Indianapolis* goes down after being struck by two torpedoes fired from a Japanese submarine. A series of operational errors will delay rescue for days, by which time three-quarters of the crew will perish, many from shark attacks.

July 30: The Japanese government instructs its civilian population to collect acorns to stave off starvation.

The Occupation of Korea

Although Japan invaded and annexed Korea in 1910, it wasn't until 1937 that Japan launched a campaign to assimilate Koreans into the Japanese culture. The occupiers forbade the use of the Korean language and the practice of Christianity, and they demanded that all names be converted to Japanese.

Not only did Japan confiscate cattle, crops, and other material resources during the course of the Pacific war, but they also forced about 2.5 million Korean civilians into labor camps. Nearly one million young Korean men were conscripted into the Japanese army and sent to work at mines, factories, and military bases stretching across the Pacific. Thousands of Korean women were forced into sexual slavery as "comfort women" for Japanese soldiers.

At the urging of U.S. president Harry Truman, the Soviet Union declared war on Japan on August 8, 1945. Included in the declaration of war was the Soviet promise of support for the independence of Korea. Its troops, however, entered the northern districts of the country

Residents of Seoul, Korea, greeting American troops

only days later. The instrument of surrender that Japan signed on September 2, 1945, called for Japanese troops north of the 38th parallel in Korea to surrender to the USSR, while the troops to the south were to surrender to the Americans. Korea was no longer in the grip of Japan, but the nation became two, split north and south, Communist and free. The Korean peninsula would quickly become a locus of grave international friction.

Hiroshima and Nagasaki

The selection of potential atomic bomb targets began even before the Trinity test bomb was detonated near Alamogordo, New Mexico, on July 16, 1945. The Target Committee at Los Alamos recommended Hiroshima as a likely target as early as May. By late July, the list of potential targets included four cities: Hiroshima, Kokura, Kyoto, and Niigata. Kyoto was later dropped from the list due to its significance as a cultural center. Nagasaki took Kyoto's place.

A-bomb blast above Hiroshima

Hiroshima remained the primary target, followed by Kokura and Nagasaki. Each city had military facilities of some type. Hiroshima was a headquarters and logistics base; Kokura had a large munitions plant; Nagasaki had various arms factories.

Of equal importance, these sprawling urban areas did not require precision bomb drops and would vividly demonstrate the destructiveness of the new weapons. Civilian casualties were not an issue. This was total war, and civilian populations were considered a legitimate target in the effort to break Japan's will to fight.

At 8:15 a.m. on August 6, 1945, the B-29 Superfortress *Enola Gay* dropped a U-235 bomb nicknamed "Little Boy" on the primary target, Hiroshima. The resulting blast instantly killed upwards of 80,000 people and damaged or destroyed 90 percent of the city's buildings.

Three days later, the B-29 *Bock's Car*, carrying the plutonium bomb "Fat Man," aborted over its primary target, Kokura, due to heavy cloud cover. *Bock's Car* proceeded to Nagasaki, its secondary target, and dropped the second atomic bomb of the war shortly after 11 a.m. About 25,000 people were instantly killed. On August 15, Japan capitulated.

The morality of the bombings has been passionately debated. Critics maintain that Japan was already near surrender; that the bombs were intended primarily as a warning to the Russians; and that racism was a motivating factor. Proponents argue that the bombings saved hundreds of thousands of American lives—and, in the long term, perhaps millions of Japanese as well—by forcing a speedy surrender.

"[H]e saw there were about twenty men, and they were all in exactly the same nightmarish state: their faces were wholly burned, their eyesockets were hollow, the fluid from their melted eyes had run down their cheeks."

—JOURNALIST JOHN HERSEY, RECOUNTING WHAT FATHER WILHELM KLEINSORGE (A GERMAN PRIEST) HAD SEEN IN HIROSHIMA

The Hiroshima blast Hiroshima is devastated following the atomic bomb attack by *Enola Gay* on August 6, 1945. The bomb detonated at 8:16 a.m., 1,900 feet above Shima Hospital. The fireball was so intense, it melted granite. The concussion obliterated virtually every building within two miles. A column of smoke and debris as high as Mount Everest rose into the sky. Upwards of 80,000 people were killed outright. Thousands would die later, many from radiation sickness. Nevertheless, the bombing probably saved lives elsewhere in Japan. Had the bomb not encouraged an end to the war, millions of Japanese might have died of starvation, of disease, in fire-bombing raids, and in efforts to resist a U.S. ground invasion of the home islands.

ATOMIC FIRE

Beyond the zone of utter death in which nothing remained alive, houses collapsed in a whirl of beams, bricks and girders. Up to about three miles from the center of the explosion lightly built houses were flattened as though they had been built of cardboard. Those who were inside were either killed or wounded. Those who managed to extricate themselves by some miracle found themselves surrounded by a ring of fire....

About half an hour after the explosion, whilst the sky all around Hiroshima was still cloudless, a fine rain began to fall on the town and went on for about five minutes. It was caused by the sudden rise of over-heated air to a great height, where it condensed and fell back as rain. Then a violent wind rose and the fires extended with terrible rapidity, because most Japanese houses are built only of timber and straw.

By the evening the fire began to die down and then it went out. There was nothing left to burn, Hiroshima had ceased to exist.

—JAPANESE JOURNALIST, AS TOLD TO MARCEL JUNOD OF THE RED CROSS

The Nagasaki bomb A workman stands next to "Fat Man," the atomic bomb dropped on Nagasaki on August 9, 1945. Unlike "Little Boy," the uranium bomb used against Hiroshima, Fat Man was an implosion-type weapon that employed plutonium. About 11 feet long and five feet in diameter, it was twice as wide as Little Boy. The new design resulted from the greater availability of plutonium and the fact that the implosion method was less susceptible to accidental detonation than the simple "gun type" ignition used with Little Boy. The new design also yielded a greater blast.

The second A-bomb attack A mushroom cloud boils skyward over the industrial city of Nagasaki following the detonation of a plutonium bomb on August 9. The B-29 *Bock's Car*, piloted by Major Charles Sweeney, aborted an attack on Kokura due to heavy cloud cover and proceeded to Nagasaki, the secondary target. Finding a break in the clouds, he carried out the bombing shortly after 11 a.m. Heated controversy arose later over the necessity for the second bomb attack, but the mission was carried out because of the lack of reaction from the Japanese government following the Hiroshima bombing.

1945

July 31: Former Vichy prime minister Pierre Laval surrenders in Austria.

August 2: Some 6,600 tons of bombs, a wartime high, are dropped overnight on several Japanese cities. The city of Toyama is almost totally destroyed.

August 3: The Allies emerge victorious from the Battle of the Breakthrough, bringing an end to all Japanese resistance in Burma. • The Allies tighten the noose around Japan as U.S. bombers complete their mining of Japan's major ports.

August 6: The United States drops an atomic bomb on Hiroshima, Japan, killing approximately 80,000 civilians. • A crash during an experimental jet test-flight claims the life of Major Richard Bong, the most successful American WWII flying ace (40 kills).

August 8: President Truman delivers a radio address in which he threatens to unleash more nuclear devastation on Japan. • The Soviet Union declares war against Japan.

August 9: With President Truman's signature, the United States becomes the first country to ratify the United Nations Charter. • Approximately 25,000 die as the U.S. drops a second atomic bomb, this one on Nagasaki, Japan.

August 11: The Japanese offer of surrender, delivered on August 10 and conditional on the continued sovereignty of Emperor Hirohito, is rejected by U.S. secretary of state James Byrnes.

August 12: Emperor Hirohito orders a divided Japanese government to surrender.

August 14: Washington orders the suspension of hostilities in Asia and the resumption of automobile production on the home front.

Results of the Nagasaki attack Pictured is ground zero in Nagasaki before and after the bombing. Though the city had good bomb shelters, many Japanese had become blasé about air raids and ignored the warning sirens on August 9. Due in part to the hilly topography, damage was confined to an area about 2.3 miles by 1.9 miles. Fire was limited by waterways. Some medical services survived, and even train service continued. The number of deaths was lower than at Hiroshima, with the Japanese government assessing the figure at 25,000. Ironically, Emperor Hirohito was at that very moment trying to decide how to end the war.

Japanese "bear the unbearable" A Japanese prisoner of war on Guam cries as he listens to Emperor Hirohito's radio broadcast announcing Japan's surrender. Hearing the voice of their "living god" for the first time, the populace strained to make out his message through the formal language and poor reception. "The war situation has developed not necessarily to Japan's advantage," observed the Emperor. The Japanese people "must now bear the unbearable and endure the unendurable." Millions wept. Some military officers committed suicide, while others talked of continued resistance. But for many Japanese, beneath the grief and shock was also a sense of relief. The war was over.

"Tokyo was like a giant wake. It was like walking into a cemetery. The people wouldn't even look at us."

—NICK CARIDAS, U.S. ARMY

Tokyo in ruins Tokyo lies in ruins after Japan's surrender. By war's end, B-29 raids had transformed more than half of the city into a wasteland. With rice severely rationed, civilians were advised to supplement their diets with acorns and sawdust. In March, the cabbage ration was one leaf per person every three days. Hundreds of thousands were still homeless. Cooking and heating fuel had been in short supply for months. Malnutrition, malaria, and typhoid were widespread. The bombings did produce one surplus item: plenty of debris to use for kindling.

POWs are freed and fed American women prepare food after being freed from Japanese captivity in Manila, Philippines, in 1945. For most freed prisoners, liberation meant adequate food for the first time in years. Spam, cocoa, cigarettes, gum, and clothing were airdropped on prison camps throughout Asia, often accompanied by leaflets that warned: "Do not overeat." Within six weeks, most POWs were on their way home, although many would be plagued by health and psychological problems for the rest of their lives. Suicide, alcoholism, and depression were common.

Allies reeducate Germany's students Rebuilding the German education system was one of the highest priorities for the Allies. In those sections of Germany and Berlin controlled by the U.S., Britain, and France, the emphasis was placed on reeducating youth—who had been raised for years on Fascist doctrines—in the fundamentals of democracy. In the Soviet sectors, Marxist and Leninist principles were taught. The first step in the denazification process was to replace any teacher who was unwilling or unable to give up his or her Fascist beliefs. Before this new educational process could begin, however, students were required to turn in their Nazi-oriented textbooks (*pictured*).

Japan's surrender delegation Led by Foreign Minister Shigemitsu Mamoru (*with cane*) and Army Chief of Staff Umezu Yoshijiro (*to his left*), the Japanese delegation arrived aboard the USS *Missouri* in Tokyo Bay on September 2, 1945, to sign the instrument of surrender. Though the formal terms called for unconditional surrender, it had been inferred that the emperor would retain nominal authority. Umezu was present under duress; he agreed to participate only after a personal appeal by the emperor. Shigemitsu, who felt the war must end, viewed his assignment as "a painful but profitable task." Unsure of protocol, the 11-member delegation had been advised to put on a *shiran kao* (nonchalant face) during the proceedings. Civilians should remove their hats and bow, they were told. Military personnel should salute.

Japanese surprised by GIs' kindness A Japanese civilian watches curiously as elements of the U.S. 33rd Infantry Division come ashore during the occupation of Japan. Wild rumors prior to the American occupation told of rapes and looting. Women and valuables were hidden, and some factories issued poison capsules to female workers. Despite Japanese fears, American troops were generally well behaved, and the occupation proceeded smoothly. "We had images of glaring demons with horns sprouting from their heads," recalled Naokata Sasaki, a young student at the time. "We were disappointed, of course. No horns at all." To his surprise, the Americans seemed quite friendly and even gave the children chocolate.

The surrender ceremonies General Douglas MacArthur stands at the broadcast microphone as General Umezu signs the instrument of surrender on behalf of the Japanese Imperial Headquarters. Foreign Minister Shigemitsu signed on behalf of the emperor. MacArthur signed on behalf of the Allied powers, while Admiral Chester Nimitz signed for the United States. Those in attendance included representatives of all the Allied powers, as well as such military officers as Admiral William Halsey and Lieutenant General Jonathan Wainwright. The ceremony, broadcast worldwide, lasted only 23 minutes, ending at 9:25 a.m. Minutes later, hundreds of Navy fighters and Army B-29s roared overhead in a prearranged show of American military might.

MacArthur takes charge in Japan This widely circulated photograph of General Douglas MacArthur and Emperor Hirohito, taken on September 27, 1945, shocked the Japanese public, as it left little doubt as to who was now in charge of Japan. MacArthur successfully resisted efforts to put the defeated emperor on trial as a war criminal. He believed Hirohito would be of greater value as a symbol of continuity, as one who would discourage resistance to the occupation, and as an instrument to transform Japan into a democracy with a minimum of social upheaval. The emperor cooperated. He renounced his "divinity" and left MacArthur as the most powerful man in Japan.

AFTERMATH OF THE WAR

The end of the war opened the way for the building of a new world order. It was a very different order from the one Germany, Italy, and Japan had envisioned when they divided the world into spheres of influence in the Tripartite Pact of September 1940.

In the first place, the war proved to be a victory for European communism, which only a few years before—as German forces bore down on Moscow—had seemed close to defeat. Yet it was also a victory for Western liberal capitalism, as the Western Allies set out to secure free economies and parliamentary politics in Western Europe after years of economic crisis and political authoritarianism.

One of the few issues on which the wartime Allies could agree was the International Tribunal, which put German leaders on trial at Nuremberg for crimes against peace and for crimes against humanity. The trial opened in November 1945. In October 1946, all but three of the 22 defendants were found guilty. The attempt to create a new framework of international law was compromised throughout by the knowledge that Stalin's Soviet Union was just as guilty of aggressive war and

systematic violation of human rights. Nevertheless, the trials did promote a desire for a new international morality. In 1948 the United Nations agreed on a convention outlawing genocide. A year later, a new Geneva Convention established clear rules for the conduct of war. And in 1950, the European Convention on Human Rights was established to protect human rights and fundamental freedoms.

On almost every other issue, the Soviets and the Western powers strongly disagreed. The future of Germany could not be settled, since neither side was prepared to see a reunited German state dominated by one of the two ideologies. In January 1947, the American and British zones of occupation were merged into Bizonia. Two years later, with the addition of the southern French zone, a separate West German state was created based on a democratic, federal constitution. Stalin blockaded Berlin in 1948, which was situated in the Soviet zone but was jointly administered by the four occupying powers. Then, when the blockade proved ineffective (due to the Western Allies' airlift of supplies into the city), Stalin created a rival German Democratic Republic in the

President Harry Truman signs the North Atlantic Treaty, which marked the beginning of NATO and the end of any lingering hopes that the Soviets and the West could collaborate constructively in the postwar world. Positions would only harden as each side suspiciously eyed the other over the so-called "iron curtain."

accepted the division of the world into "two camps." In 1947, U.S. secretary of state George Marshall convened a conference in Paris to draw up plans for financial aid to the struggling economies of Europe. The Soviet delegation responded by walking out when it became clear that aid would be forthcoming only if the Soviet Union agreed to international scrutiny of its economic policy.

Over the next two years, Communist regimes were confirmed in all the states of Eastern Europe occupied by the Red Army. Political pluralism was ended in those states, and Stalinist economies and police systems were imposed. In Yugoslavia, Josip Broz Tito succeeded in establishing the only Communist state independent of Moscow. A savage civil war in Greece ended in 1949 with the defeat of the Communist insurgents. In Austria, a treaty allowed the creation of a nonaligned parliamentary state after 10 years of division into occupation zones.

In eastern Asia, the end of the war brought a long period of turmoil. In the European colonies occupied by Japan,

Soviet zone, run by a Communist-dominated regime. No formal treaty ending the war could be signed under these circumstances, and Germany remained partitioned.

The rest of the European continent was split between a capitalist west and a Communist east, divided by what Winston Churchill famously called an "iron curtain." When President Harry Truman announced in 1947 that the Western world would defend the right of free peoples everywhere who were "resisting subjugation," Stalin reluctantly liberation movements were established—some strongly Communist in outlook. In Indochina, Indonesia, and Malaya, wars were fought against the colonial powers as well as between rival factions. The messy aftermath of war precipitated the final crisis of the old European imperialism; by the early 1950s, most of Southeast Asia was independent. In Burma and India, Britain could not maintain its presence. India was divided into two states in 1947, India (Hindu) and Pakistan (Muslim), and Burma was granted independence a year later.

Japan was not restored to full sovereignty until after the San Francisco Treaty was signed on September 8, 1951. The emperor was retained, but the military was emasculated and a parliamentary regime had been installed. Japanese prewar possessions were divided up. Manchuria was restored to China in 1946 (though only after the Soviet Union had removed more than half the industrial equipment left behind by the Japanese). Taiwan was returned to Chinese control. Korea was occupied jointly by the Soviet Union and the United States, and two independent states—one Communist, one democratic—were established there in 1948.

The most unstable area remained China, where the prewar conflict between Chiang Kai-shek's Nationalists and the Chinese Communists led by Mao Zedong was resumed on a large scale in 1945. After four years of warfare, the Nationalist forces were defeated and Chiang withdrew to the island of Taiwan. The People's Republic of China was declared in 1949, and a long program of rural reform and industrialization was set in motion. The victory of Chinese communism encouraged Stalin to allow the Communist regime in North Korea to embark on war against the South in the belief that America would avoid another military conflict.

The Korean War began on June 25, 1950, when the troops of Kim Il Sung crossed the 38th parallel, the agreed-upon border between the two states. By this stage, the international order had begun to solidify into two heavily armed camps. In 1949 the Soviet Union tested its first atomic bomb. That same year, the U.S. helped organize a defensive pact, the North Atlantic Treaty Organization (NATO), to link the major Western states together for possible armed action against the Communist threat. By 1951 Chinese forces were engaged in the Korean conflict, exacerbating concerns that another world war—this time with nuclear weapons—might become a reality. The optimism of 1945 had, in only half a decade, given way to renewed fears that international anarchy and violence might be the normal condition of the modern world.